The Large Corporation and
Contemporary Classes

FOR MY MENTORS, Albert Zeitlin and Morris Goldberg–from whom I learned so much, listening to them argue ALEHEM HASHALOM

The Large Corporation and Contemporary Classes

MAURICE ZEITLIN

Polity Press

First published 1989 by Polity Press
in association with Basil Blackwell

Editorial office:
Polity Press, Dales Brewery, Gwydir Street,
Cambridge CB1 2LJ, UK

Marketing and production:
Basil Blackwell Ltd
108 Cowley Road, Oxford OX4 1JF, UK

ISBN 0 7456 0605 9

British Library Cataloguing in Publication Data
A CIP catalogue record for this book is available from the
British Library.

Typeset in 10 on 12 pt Palatino
by Photo-graphics, Honiton, Devon
Printed in Great Britain by T. J. Press (Padstow) Ltd.

Contents

Tables

Preface

Joseph Schumpeter remarks, in the preface to the English translation of his *Theory of Economic Development*, that 'Books, like children, become independent beings when once they leave their parents' home. They lead their own lives, while the authors lead their own also. It will not do to interfere with those who become strangers to the house.' If the same applies to one's articles, it is not, I think, interfering with them too much to bring selected ones together in one place, where – no longer isolated from each other – their reunion might, at least, stimulate a modicum of intellectual synthesis. Read in tandem to each other, moreover, the scope of their author's sensibilities and the underlying logic of inquiry and guiding intellectual thread uniting them might more fully be revealed. Otherwise, following Schumpeter's example, I have tried not to further 'interfere' with the articles reprinted in this volume. After all, they also have been – some for over 20 years now – leading their own lives. Several have been widely cited and influential; some, including a couple of my favorites, have (so far as I can tell) unjustly been given little attention. But all of them, except for one, appear here (apart from minor editorial changes) as they first left their authors' home.

The exception is the 'popular' (i.e. nonacademic) article, 'Who Owns America? The Same Old Gang' (which won Project Censored's award as one of the Ten Best stories of 1978). I have added new material to it, enclosed in brackets, in order to provide the reader with the most reliable up-to-date information on the inequalities that now weigh even more heavily on the American people than when I first wrote that article a decade ago. I have also added notes, enclosed in brackets, to a few other articles, mainly for purposes of clarification. Finally, I have added an appendix note to 'Corporate Ownership and Control.' Omitted from the original article for want of space, this note disputes Baran and Sweezy's claim that 'communities of interest' are no longer relevant to understanding the American economy and that the 'basic unit of capital' is now the 'giant corporation.'

I have chosen not to write a lengthy introduction to this volume. I wanted to spare readers an apologia of excuses and explanations for this or that infelicity, or a recitation of what they should pay special attention to (though I have not entirely resisted the latter urge).

This volume draws together some salient strands of my work on classes and class relations. But it also leaves out, as it must, some critical recent strands, about which I say a few words below. Part I constitutes something of a book in itself; its first four chapters, in combination, provide a sketch of a theory and the start of a coherent empirical analysis of several separable but closely related questions about the large corporation and the inner structure of the capitalist class in the United States. Part II focuses mainly on the working class, dealing with such issues as the impact of class and poverty on the death rates of US soldiers in Vietnam, the comparative unionization of the decisive segments of the American working class, and the sources of political radicalism among workers and peasants in Cuba and Chile. Part III examines the origins and consequences of revolution and radical change in Cuba and Chile, and the potential for democratic economic reform in the United States.

The studies of the capitalist class in part I were done while I was also at work (with Richard E. Ratcliff) on the study of another dominant class in a Western capitalist democracy, *Landlords & Capitalists: The Dominant Class of Chile*. The penetration of the inner relations of both these dominant classes has been deepened, I think, by the parallel analyses carried out on each. The work on Chile's landlords and capitalists was written on the premise that its basic concepts and propositions, as well as its concrete procedures of investigation, would also apply, allowing for the necessity of historical specification, to the discovery and analysis of the innermost structural secrets of the dominant classes of 'advanced' capitalist societies. It is a work, then, of immediate relevance to readers who want to go more deeply into the theoretical and empirical questions raised in the studies in part I.

These studies unavoidably treat the internal relations of the American capitalist class as if they had been frozen in that moment in time to which our data apply. But every real social class is also a historical class, not merely a social category or analytical abstraction; and the shape of its inner structure and its specific historical experience are indissoluble. Again, this is a critical issue – the historical implications of the constituent inner relations of a dominant class – which I have tried to address elsewhere, in a study of the internal contradictions and internecine conflicts within Chile's dominant class, *The Civil Wars in Chile (or the bourgeois revolutions that never were)*.

Many of the studies in parts II and III, though they are not *per se* historical studies, implicitly address *the* primordial historical question: how men and women make their own history, though not just as they please. A latent theme here is the so-called relative autonomy of politics. By this I mean the independent effects of political phenomena in the shaping (and transformation) of basic social relations and political forces – of course, within the limits imposed and the options made possible by the 'objective conditions.' This question is ignored by – indeed it cannot be posed within – the prevailing paradigm in political sociology. The latter focuses instead on the 'social bases' or 'social correlates' of the aggregated individual political attitudes (or 'political behavior') of various social categories; and it simply assumes that they are somehow (which is never specified) translated into relative political power. As a result, what is not asked is how the existing political demarcations and balance of political forces have been produced historically, through concrete political struggles.

An *author* working within this prevailing paradigm could raise this question. But the *paradigm* itself, the method of analysis, simply would not allow it to be answered adequately, if at all. When, for instance, I interviewed workers in Cuba in the midst of the revolution, a quarter of a century ago, I knew that survey research limited what I could ask, and answer, about the origins of 'revolutionary politics.' Analyses of political attitudes based on survey data, I wrote at the time, ignore such determinants of 'decisive political importance' as 'the whole gamut of qualities that *competing political organizations and movements present to the workers* . . . [and] condition their success.'

I tried to overcome this limitation of survey data by focusing on the historical impact of previous social eruptions and political struggles in Cuba, as seen through the prism of the 'political generations' they formed within the working class (chapter 8). Similarly, my ecological analysis of the voting patterns of Chile's peasants (chapter 9) does not focus merely on the so-called 'objective conditions' in which their consciousness emerges. Rather, I focus on how the radical political culture of the miners tended to diffuse to, and politicize, the neighboring segments of the peasantry. The Left parties, understanding this, also made special efforts to reach the peasants in the 'mining satellites.' 'The politicization of the peasantry,' as I wrote, 'is thus the result both of a "natural process" and of conscious effort.'

But, emphatically, none of this implies that I hold to some sort of 'voluntaristic theory' of politics or social change – as should be evident from my report and analysis of the struggles unfolding in the first months of Chile's socialist government (chapter 11), and my attempt to explain the unparalleled rapidity and thoroughness of the Cuban revolution (chapter 10). In the latter analysis, for instance, I try to answer for the Cuban revolutionaries the type of question that everyone engaged in a realistic political struggle, let alone a struggle aiming to put through a social revolution, ignores at their (and their allies') peril: 'What were the constraints and the options that were given to the leaders of the Cuban revolution by the prerevolutionary social structure? What did they have to put up with, what was the social material they had to work with in order to make this revolution?'

The studies in this volume (even, to the extent possible, in an advocacy piece or two) aim at answering the questions they pose in accordance with the accepted scientific canons of reasoning and evidence in sociology. But the analytical problems they address are scarcely the product of 'normal science.' For they were not meant merely to replicate, in a standard way, the solution of a set of selected, acceptable sociological problems. The questions addressed in most of them could not have been asked or answers to them sought, in the way I sought them, if I had simply accepted the then conventional conception of what a sociological problem is (antiseptic, apolitical, 'value neutral'), and how it should be posed and solved (ahistorically). Rather, I have tried through my work to respond to, to *engage* – implicitly or explicitly – some of the momentous questions of our time, on class domination and class conflict, on reform and revolution. Only such questions, which touch the essential and whose answers reveal dangerous truths, are worth asking and worth trying to answer.

Maurice Zeitlin

Acknowledgments

The 'chapters' of this book were all previously published as articles. I am grateful to Jane Bitar, Margaret Brownlie, and Nancy Rhan, of the University of California at Los Angeles, who skilfully 'word-processed' the manuscript of this book from the reprints of these articles. For permission to include these articles in this collection, I wish to thank the editors and publishers of the journals and books in which the articles originally appeared. I am especially indebted to Howard Kimeldorf, Kenneth G. Lutterman, Samuel Norich, James Petras, James W. Russell, and Michael Soref for allowing me to include our coauthored articles in this volume. I also want to thank Christine A. Sharrock (Omega Scientific) for copyediting the manuscript with special care and intelligence and Dahlia Austridunn for diligent assistance in the compilation of the index.

By chapter numbers, the articles in this volume were originally published as follows:

1 'Corporate Ownership and Control: The Large Corporation and the Capitalist Class.' *American Journal of Sociology* 79, No. 5 (March 1974): 1073–119. (University of Chicago Press.)

2 'On Class Theory of the Large Corporation.' *American Journal of Sociology* 81, No. 4 (January 1976): 894–903. (University of Chicago Press.)

3 Maurice Zeitlin and Samuel Norich, 'Management Control, Exploitation, and Profit Maximization in the Large Corporation: An Empirical Confrontation of Managerialism and Class Theory.' *Research in Political Economy* 2 (1978): 33–62. (JAI Press 1979.)

4 Michael Soref and Maurice Zeitlin, 'Finance Capital and the Internal Structure of the Capitalist Class in the United States.' Pages 56–84 in *Intercorporate Relations: The Structural Analysis of Business*, edited by Mark Mizruchi and Michael Schwartz. Cambridge, England, and New York: Cambridge University Press, 1988.

5 'Who Owns America? The Same Old Gang.' *The Progressive* 42,

No. 6 (June 1978): 14–19. (The Progressive, Inc.)

6 Maurice Zeitlin, Kenneth G. Lutterman, and James W. Russell, 'Death in Vietnam: Class, Poverty, and the Risks of War.' *Politics and Society* 3, No. 3 (Spring 1973): 313–28. (Butterworth Publishers.)

7 Maurice Zeitlin and Howard Kimeldorf, 'How Mighty a Force? The Internal Differentiation and Relative Organization of the American Working Class.' Pages 1–64 in *How Mighty a Force? Studies of Workers' Consciousness and Organization in the United States*, edited by Maurice Zeitlin. Los Angeles: Institute of Industrial Relations, University of California, 1983. (Permission of the Regents of the University of California.)

8 'Political Generations in the Cuban Working Class.' *American Journal of Sociology* 71, No. 5 (March 1966): 493–508. (University of Chicago Press.)

9 James Petras and Maurice Zeitlin, 'Miners and Agrarian Radicalism.' *American Sociological Review* 32, No. 4 (August 1967): 578–86. (American Sociological Association.)

10 'Cuba – Revolution Without a Blueprint.' *Transaction* 6, No. 6 (April 1969): 38–42; 61. (Transaction Publishers.)

11 'Chilean Revolution: The Bullet or the Ballot.' *Ramparts Magazine* 9 (April 1971): 20–8. (Noah's Ark, Inc.)

12 'Democratic Investment.' *Democracy* 2, No. 2 (April 1982): 69–79. (The Common Good Foundation.)

Part I

The Capitalist Class in the United States

1

Corporate ownership and control: the large corporation and the capitalist class

The originating question of this study is, how has the ascendance of the large corporation as the decisive unit of production affected the class structures and political economies of the United States, Great Britain, and other 'highly concentrated capitalist' countries?[1] In particular, our concern is with the alleged 'separation of ownership and control' of the large corporation and the presumed impact of this separation on the internal structures, if not actual social existence, of the 'dominant' or 'upper' classes in these countries. This study does not provide any answers to this difficult issue; rather it questions the evidence for the accepted ones, which underlie what Ralf Dahrendorf (1959), a leading proponent of the prevailing view, has called the 'astonishing degree of consensus among sociologists on the implications of joint-stock companies . . . for the wider structure of society' (p. 42). This consensus extends, it should be emphasized, to other social science disciplines. E. S. Mason, though himself dissatisfied with economic theories derived from the prevalent view, wrote recently: 'Almost everyone now agrees that in the large corporation, the owner is, in general, a passive recipient; that, typically, control is in the hands of management; and that management normally selects its own

I have benefited from critical comments on an earlier draft of this article by many colleagues of diverse and often opposing theoretical persuasions, all of whom are absolved of any responsibility for what follows. Thanks are due Michael Aiken, Robert Alford, Daniel Bell, G. W. Domhoff, Lynda Ann Ewen, Robert Larner, Ferdinand Lundberg, Harry Magdoff, Robert K. Merton, Barrington Moore, Jr., Harvey Molotch, Willard F. Mueller, James O'Connor, Victor Perlo, and Paul M. Sweezy. The comments of several anonymous referees for the *American Journal of Sociology* were also useful. I am particularly grateful to the editors of *American Journal of Sociology*, especially to Charles Bidwell and Florence Levinsohn, for their careful reading and cogent criticisms.

replacements' (1967, p. 4). Peter Drucker (1971), himself an early managerial theorist, writes that ideas concerning the separation of ownership and control represent 'the most conventional and most widely accepted theses regarding American economic structure' as expressed in 'the prevailing and generally accepted doctrine of "managerialism"' (pp. 50–1). For Robert A. Dahl (1970), the facts are 'resounding'; indeed, it is 'incontrovertible' that ownership and control have been 'split apart.' In his view, 'the question that was not asked during the great debate over socialism versus capitalism has now been answered: ownership has been split off *de facto* from internal control' (p. 125).

The question is whether this 'astonishing consensus' derives from the findings of appropriate social research or from an unwitting acceptance of what Robert K. Merton (1959) has termed 'the socially plausible, in which appearances persuade though they may deceive.'

Thus, this article poses a type of question which, however simple, 'is often undervalued in sociology' – a question which 'calls,' in Merton's words, 'for discovering a particular body of social fact. It might at first seem needless to say that before social facts can be 'explained,' it is advisable to ensure that they actually are facts. Yet, in science as in everyday life, explanations are sometimes provided for things that never were. . . . In sociology as in other disciplines, pseudofacts have a way of inducing pseudoproblems, which cannot be solved because matters are not as they purport to be' (1959, pp. xiii-xv). Such pseudofacts may, of course, also serve to deflect attention from critical aspects of social structure, determinant social relations, and basic social processes. They may inspire not merely 'explanations' but 'inferences' and 'theories' as well, which further confuse and obscure social reality. The methodological premise of this article, then, as well as its irreducibly minimal rationale, is the 'obvious and compelling truth that "if the facts used as a basis for reasoning are ill-established or erroneous, everything will crumble or be falsified; and it is thus that errors in scientific theories most often originate in errors of fact."'[2]

The prevailing view is that the diffusion of ownership in the large corporation among numerous stock owners has resulted in the separation of ownership and control, and, by severing the connection between the family and private property in the means of production, has torn up the roots of the old class structure and political economy of capitalism. A new class of functionaries of capital, or a congeries of economic 'elites,' in control of the new forms of productive property, appear: nonowning corporate managers displace their capitalist predecessors. 'The capitalist class,' as Pitirim Sorokin (1953, p. 90) puts it, is 'transformed into the managerial class.' In Talcott Parsons's view, 'The basic phenomenon seems to have been the shift in control of enterprise from the property interests of founding families to managerial and technical personnel who as such have not had a comparable vested interest in ownership' (1953, pp. 122–3).

In the view of these writers, a class theory of contemporary industrial society, based on the relationship between the owners of capital and formally free wage workers, 'loses its analytical value as soon as legal ownership and factual control are separated' (Dahrendorf 1959, p. 136). This class theory is therefore inapplicable to the United States, England, and other 'advanced' societies in which ownership and control have been severed; it cannot explain nor serve as a fruitful source of hypotheses concerning the division of the social product, class conflict, social domination, political processes, or historical change in these societies. Thus, Parsons and Smelser refer to the separation of ownership and control as 'one particular change in the American economic structure which has been virtually completed within the last half century' – a 'structural change in business organization [that] has been associated with changes in the stratification of the society.' The families that once 'controlled through ownership most of the big businesses . . . by and large failed to consolidate their positions as the *dominant* class in the society' (1957, p. 254, italics added).

This 'shift in control of enterprise from the property interests of founding families to managerial and technical personnel,' according to Parsons, is the 'critical fact' underlying his interpretation that 'the "family elite" elements of the class structure (the Warnerian "upper uppers") hold a secondary rather than a primary position in the overall stratification system.' The shift in control, 'high progressive taxation,' and other 'changes in the structure of the economy, have "lopped off" the previous top stratum,' leaving instead 'a broad and diffuse one with several loosely integrated components. Undoubtedly its main focus is now on occupational status and occupational earnings. Seen in historical as well as comparative perspective this is a notable *fact*, for the entrepreneurial fortunes of the period of economic development of the nineteenth century, especially after the Civil War, notably failed to produce a set of ruling families on a national scale who as family entities on a Japanese or even a French pattern have tended to keep control of the basic corporate entities in the economy.' Thus, in Parsons's view, a '"ruling class" does not have a paramount position in American society' (1953, pp. 123, 119, italics added).

Similarly, Daniel Bell (1958, pp. 246–9) has argued that a 'silent revolution' has subverted the former 'relations between power and class position in modern society.' In his view, 'The singular fact is that in the last seventy-five years the established relations between the systems of property and family . . . have broken down,' resulting in 'the breakup of "family capitalism," which has been *the social cement of the bourgeois class system*' (italics added). If, in general, 'property, sanctioned by law and reinforced by the coercive power of the State' means power, and if a class system is maintained by the 'fusion' of the institutions of the family and private property, economic development in the United States has 'effected a radical separation of property and family.' Consequently, in his view, if 'family capitalism meant social and political, as well as economic, dominance,' that is no longer the situation in the United States. 'The chief consequence, politically, is the breakup of the "ruling class"' – 'a power-holding group which has both an established community of interest and a continuity of interest' no longer exists in the United States.

The profound implications of the acceptance of the separation of ownership and control as a 'notable fact' are, according to Parsons, that the previous relations between classes have been replaced by an occupational system based on individual achievement, in which 'status groups' are ordered hierarchically in accordance with their functional importance. Further, as Dahrendorf has put it (1959, pp. 275–6), the basic social conflict is no longer between capital and labor because 'in post-capitalist society the ruling and the subjected classes of industry and of the political society are no longer identical; . . . there are, in other words, in principle [sic], two independent conflict fronts. . . . This holds increasingly as within industry the separation of ownership and control increases and as the more universal capitalists are replaced by managers.' The political economy of capitalism and the class interests which it once served have been replaced by a sort of capitalism without capitalists (Berle 1954) – if not post-capitalist society – shorn of the contradictions and class conflicts that once rent the social fabric of 'classical capitalism.' The basis of social domination in such societies, as these theorists would have it, is no longer class ownership of the means of production, and such a class clearly does not 'rule' in any sense, economically, socially, or politically. 'The decisive power in modern industrial society,' in John Kenneth Galbraith's (1971, p. xix) representative formulation, 'is exercised not by capital but by organization, not by the capitalist but by the industrial bureaucrat.'

Assuredly, the answer to this 'theory' – particularly the propositions concerning the separation of ownership and control – rests on 'empirical' grounds (Bell 1958, p. 246). However, logic, concepts, and methodology are certainly intertwined and inseparable aspects of the same intellectual process of discovering the 'facts.'

One common source of conceptual and analytic confusion in the writings on the issue of ownership and control derives from a teleology of bureaucratic imperatives. Bureaucratization is implicitly assumed to be an inexorable historical process, so that even the propertied classes and their power have fallen before its advance. Parsons and Smelser have written, for example, that the 'kinship–property combination typical of classical capitalism was *destined*, unless social differentiation stopped altogether, to proceed toward "bureaucratization," towards differentiation between economy and polity, and between ownership and control' (1957, p. 289, italics added).

The tendency toward the bureaucratization of enterprise, and of management in particular, is taken as an index of the appropriation of the powers of the propertied class by the managers. This confuses (a) the existence of an extensive administrative apparatus in the large corporation, in which the proportion of management positions held by members of the proprietary family may be negligible, and (b) the locus of control over this apparatus. Dahrendorf, for instance, noting that the managers of large enterprises generally have neither inherited nor founded them, concludes from this that these new managers, 'utterly different than their capitalist predecessors,' have taken control for themselves. In place of the 'classical' or 'full capitalist,' there stands the bureaucratic manager and 'organization man' (1959, pp. 42, 46). From the observation, that in the large corporation, functions that (allegedly) were fulfilled in the past by a single owner-manager are now institutionalized and split up among differing roles in the bureaucratic administrative organization, it is concluded that bureaucratic *management* (if such it is) means bureaucratic *control*. But there is nothing in bureaucratic management itself that indicates the bureaucracy's relationship to extrabureaucratic centers of control at the apex of or outside the bureaucracy proper, such as large shareowners or bankers, to whom it may be responsible.

Max Weber conceptualized this relationship clearly, referring to the 'appropriation of *control* over the persons exercising managerial *authority* by the interests of *ownership*.' If 'the immediate appropriation of managerial functions' is no longer in the hands of the owners, this does not mean the separation of *control* from ownership, but rather 'the separation of the managerial *function*' from ownership. 'By virtue of their ownership,' Weber saw, 'control over managerial positions may rest in the hands of property interests outside the organization as such' (1965, pp. 248–9, italics added).

It is precisely this relationship between propertied interests and the bureaucracy, and between 'capitalists' and 'managers,' that has received at best inadequate and usually no attention among those who report that they have seen a 'corporate revolution' silently abolish private ownership in the means of production. Thus, Daniel Bell (1961, p. 44) can write that 'private productive property, especially in the United States, is largely a fiction,' and Dahrendorf can claim: 'Capital – and thereby capitalism – has dissolved and given way in the economic sphere, to a plurality of partly agreed, partly competing, and partly simply different groups' (1959, p. 47).

Two issues, then, have to be separated: (a) whether the large corporations continue to be controlled by ownership interests, despite their management by functionaries who may themselves be propertyless; (b) whether the undisputed rise of managerial functions means the rise of the functionaries themselves. Do they constitute a separate and cohesive stratum, with identifiable interests, ideas, and policies, which are opposed to those of the extant owning families? Are the consequences of their actions, whatever their intentions, to bring into being social relationships which undermine capitalism? How, with their 'rise,' is 'the incidence of economic power' changed? (Bendix 1952, p. 119).

These are not merely analytically distinguishable issues. A number of social scientists, 'plain marxists' preeminent among them,[3] are quite ready to concede that the split between ownership and control is a reality in most large corporations. But they reject the implication that this renders inapplicable to the United States and other developed capitalist countries a theory of historical/social change which roots classes in the concrete economic order and historically given system of property relations, and which focuses, in particular, on the relationship between the direct producers and the owners of the means of production. In their view, whatever the situation within the corporation as the predominant legal unit of ownership of large-scale productive property, the 'owners' and 'managers' of the large corporations, taken as a whole, constitute different strata or segments – when they are not merely agents – of the same more or less unified social class. They reject the notion, as Reinhard Bendix has observed (1952, p. 119), 'that people in the productive system constitute a separate social group because they serve similar functions and that they are powerful because they are indispensable.'

Rather, the corporations are units in a class-controlled apparatus of appropriation; and the whole gamut of functionaries and owners of capital participate in varying degrees, and as members of the same social class, in its direction (cf. Baran and Sweezy 1966, ch. 2; Miliband 1969, ch. 2; Nichols 1969, pp. 140–1; Playford 1972, pp. 116–18). This class theory, as we discuss below in detail, demands research concerning the ensemble of social relations, concrete interests, and overriding commitments of the officers, directors, and principal shareowners of the whole set of large corporations. Rather than limiting analysis to the relationship between the 'management' and principal shareowners of a given corporation, the analysis must focus on the multiplicity of their interconnections with other 'managements' and principal share-owners in other large corporations, as well as with the owners of other forms of large-scale income-bearing property.[4]

Were research to show that the putative separation of ownership and control within the large corporation is a 'pseudofact' and that identifiable families and other cohesive ownership interests continue to control them, this might surprise certain 'plain marxists,' but it would still be consistent with their general class theory of contemporary capitalism.[5] Most important, were 'managers' and 'owners' to be found to occupy a common 'class situation' (Weber 1968, p. 927), the theory that ownership and control of the large corporations reside in the same social class would be confirmed. In contrast, either set of findings would tend to invalidate the basic assumptions, propositions, and inferences of managerial theory. In any event, each alleged implication requires careful analysis and empirical testing on its own.

Managers and Capitalists: The Historical Controversy

The theory of managerial capitalism has hoary antecedents. Not only did Marx himself make rather confusing Hegelian comments about the emergence of the corporation, but the theory of a society in which the capitalist class is gradually replaced by an administrative stratum no longer devoted to the interests of property was being enunciated even while the epoch of 'finance capital' and the large corporation was dawning in late nineteenth- and twentieth-century Germany. Eduard Bernstein and Konrad Schmidt, Social Democratic theoreticians of what came to be known as 'revisionism,' argued that the property form of the corporation presaged and was part of a gradual alteration in the essence of capitalism. The splitting up of property into shares brought with it 'armies of shareholders' representing a new 'power over the economic life of society.' 'The shareholder,' wrote Bernstein (1961, p. 54), 'takes the graded place in the social scale which the captains of industry used to occupy before the concentration of businesses.' The capitalist class, said Schmidt, was undergoing a process of 'expropriation by stages.' While the 'decomposition of capital' was leading to the gradual extension of the rights of 'sovereignty' over property to society as a whole, the capitalist was being transformed 'from a proprietor to a simple administrator.'[6]

This was substantially the thesis of a work which appeared three decades later in 1932 in the United States and which has been the most enduring source of the theory of managerial capitalism: *The Modern Corporation and Private Property*, by Adolph Berle, Jr., and Gardiner C. Means. 'The dissolution of the atom of property,' they wrote (1967, p. 8), 'destroys the very foundation on which the economic order of the past three centuries has rested.' They reported that 65 percent of the 200 largest corporations appear to be 'controlled either by the management or by a legal device involving a small proportion of ownership' (p. 110). The latter category, 'control through a legal device,' such as pyramiding, is clearly a form of ownership control, as Larner (1970, p. 132) points out, 'since it is based on stock ownership and not on a strategic position in management. The legal device simply reduces the share of stock ownership required for control.'

Berle and Means classified 44 percent of the top 200 corporations as actually under management control. They claimed, however, to have 'reasonably definite and reliable information' on at most two-thirds of the companies (Berle and Means 1967, p. 84). Indeed, they cited, in a detailed and extended table covering 20 pages of their book (pp. 86–105), the source of their information on each corporation and, most important, noted those corporations about whose locus of control they were merely surmising. Thus, they listed 73 corporations under the heading 'majority of stock *believed* to be widely distributed and working control held either by a large minority interest or by the management' (italics added). Of these, 29 were considered 'presumably' under the control of a minority interest, while 44 were 'presumably' under management control. Indeed, of a total of 88½ [sic] corporations that they classified under management control,[7] they provided no information on 44, which they could only consider 'presumably' management controlled. Among industrials, they classified fully 39 of 43 management-controlled corporations as only 'presumably' under management control. Thus, they had information which permitted them to classify as definitely under management control only 22 percent of the 200 largest corporations, and of the 106 industrials, only 3.8 percent! Yet numerous scholars over the years have cited the work by Berle and Means (when giving citations at all) as the main or only source of their own assertions that ownership and control were split apart in the large corporations. In part, this may be explained by the fact that Berle and Means presented their summary table and conclusions (pp. 109–10) without any mention of their earlier qualifications concerning the adequacy and validity of their information. If we take the information contained in parts J and K of their table 12 on pages 103–5, a correct summary of their findings, with the necessary qualifications made explicit, would be as shown in table 1.1. In 1945, R. A. Gordon published a study, based in part on a secondary analysis of the Temporary National Economic Committee (TNEC) data, which came to conclusions much like those of Berle and Means. Gordon wrote that 'the real revolution [in property rights] has already largely taken place; the great majority of stockholders have been deprived of control of their property through the diffusion of ownership and the growth in the power of management' (1966, p. 350).

Quite recently, Robert J. Larner (1970, p. 21) duplicated the Berle–Means methods in his own study of the 500 largest nonfinancial corporations in the United States and concluded that the 'managerial revolution' in process in 1929 was now 'close to complete.'

Table 1.1 *Type of control of the 200 largest corporations, 1929, according to Berle and Means*

Type of control	RR		PU		Ind.		Totals	
	N	%	N	%	N	%	N	%
Private ownership	2	4.8	2	3.8	8	7.5	12	6.0
Majority ownership	1	2.4	3	5.8	6	5.7	10	5.0
Minority control								
'Presumed'	0	0	5	9.6	24	22.6	29	14.5
Others	4½	10.7	2½	4.8	10½	9.9	17½	8.7
Legal device	7½	17.8	19	36.5	14½	13.7	41	20.5
Management control								
'Presumed'	0	0	5	9.6	39	36.8	44	22.0
Others	26	61.9	14½	27.9	4	3.8	44½	22.3
In receivership	1	2.4	1	1.9	0	0	2	1.0
Total	42	100	52	100	106	100	200	100

RR, railroads; PU, public utilities; Ind., industrials; minority control was assumed to be present when a single individual or cohesive group was found to own at least 20 percent of the corporation's stock; 'presumed' refers to Berle and Means's classification of firms believed to be widely distributed and presumably under a specified type of control.

Corporations in which the largest individual stockholder or members of a single family or a group of business associates were found not to own 10 percent or more of the voting stock were classified by Larner as under 'management control.' By this criterion, he classified 84 percent of the top 200 and 70 of the next 300 largest nonfinancial corporations in 1963 in the United States as 'management controlled.'[8] John Kenneth Galbraith (1967, p. 90), who had relied on the studies of Berle and Means and Gordon to advance his own interpretation of the loss of stockholder control in the 'new industrial state' not merely to management but to the new 'technocracy,' found that Larner's findings, some of which appeared as Galbraith's book was going to press, 'explicitly confirmed' his view of the process.

In contrast to these studies and others following more or less the same methods of analysis and classification are several studies by analysts taking a quite different approach. These researchers have argued that without an investigation of the specific situation in a given corporation, and of the interconnections between the principal shareholders, officers, and directors, and other corporations, the actual control group is unlikely to be identified.

Thus, at virtually the same time that the Berle and Means work appeared, other works by Anna Rochester (1936) and Ferdinand Lundberg (1946) concluded, as Lundberg put it, that 'a very small group of families,' through their ownership interests and control of the major banks, were still in control of the 'industrial system.' Analyzing the same corporations that Berle and Means claimed were under management control, Lundberg found that 'in most cases [the largest stockholding] families had themselves installed the management control or were among the directors,' while several others were 'authoritatively regarded in Wall Street as actually under the rule of J. P. Morgan and Company.' 'Exclusion of stockholders from control, within the context as revealed by Berle–Means,' Lundberg concluded (1946, pp. 506–8), 'does not mean that large stockholders are excluded from a decisive voice in the management. It means, only, that small stockholders have been [excluded].' The National Resources Committee (NRC) also conducted a study of the control of the largest US corporations during the same period. Unlike either Berle and Means or Gordon, the NRC study included not only the 200 largest nonfinancial corporations but also the 50 largest banks, which permitted its author (Paul M. Sweezy) to discover centers of 'outside' control or abiding influence which were missed by the former studies. The NRC study also took account of corporation histories and information on the careers of key officers and directors, as well as of information on primary interlocks between corporations. Almost half of the top 200 corporations and 16 of the banks were found to belong to eight different 'interest groups' binding their constituent corporations together under a significant element of common control by wealthy families and/or financial associates and investment bankers (NRC 1939, pp. 100–3; 306–17; Sweezy 1953).

Of 43 industrial corporations which Berle and Means categorized under 'management control,' 36 appeared on the lists of top corporations studied by the TNEC (Goldsmith and Parmelee 1940) and NRC in the late 1930s. Victor Perlo compared their findings concerning these particular corporations and found that of these 36, the TNEC located 'definite centers of control' for 15 and the NRC for 11; in addition, Perlo's research (1957, p. 49) revealed that another seven were under the control of identifiable ownership interests, leaving only three industrial corporations on the original Berle and Means list for which other investigators did not locate definite control centers.

Differences in the findings of recent studies also indicate the wisdom of considering the empirical question as open: Don Villarejo studied the locus of control in 250 of the largest industrial corporations (though not other types of nonfinancial corporations) on the 1960 *Fortune* list. He concluded that, of the 232 corporations on which he obtained usable data, 'at least 126 corporations,' or 54 percent, and perhaps as many as 141, or 61 percent, were controlled by ownership interests, i.e. he found 'the existence of concentrated ownership to the extent of securing potential working control of the corporation in question' (1961–2, p. 68). His findings were criticized by Larner (1970, p. 22) 'as open to challenge because he aggregated the stockholdings of directors, investment companies and insurance companies in each corporation without providing specific evidence, such as family or business relationships, to suggest a community of interests or to indicate the likelihood of either intragroup of intergroup cooperation.' This criticism of Villarejo's work may or may not be correct, but it is remarkable that Larner should make it, since it is at least as applicable – if not more so – not only to Berle and Means's original study, which Larner chose to emulate procedurally, but also to Larner's own findings. Larner certainly does not present systematic evidence of the kind he requires of Villarejo, yet he concluded that most large corporations were under 'management control.' It is relevant, therefore, that an investigation by *Fortune*, using essentially the same definitions and procedures as Larner, and taking 10 percent as the minimum necessary for proprietary control, found in 1967 that 147 corporations of the top 500 were controlled through ownership interests, or over half again as many as Larner's 95 (Sheehan 1967).

Problems of Method and Measurement

Further brief review of recent contradictory findings concerning the control of the largest corporations in the United States highlights the most significant problem faced by investigators of this subject: the data needed for adequate measurement are, in the first place, often inaccessible. As Joseph Kahl (1957, p. 10) points out, power, 'because it is potential, . . . is usually impossible to see. Furthermore, where it exists it tends to be deliberately hidden; those who sit among the mighty do not invite sociologists to watch them make their decisions about how to control the behavior of others.' Two separate problems of 'inaccessibility of the data,' the relative importance of which cannot be settled a priori, require investigation so that we can assess the limitations to our understanding: first, there is no official list of the largest corporations, ranked by assets, sales, or profits. Investigators must have access to the sources of information that will allow them to compile such a list or even make reasonable guesses. Studies in recent years have relied largely on the *Fortune 500* listing of the 500 top firms by sales as their primary source of which corporations to investigate. Thus, even the Patman Committee on Banking and Currency of the House of Representatives used the *Fortune* list in its analysis of interlocking relationships between large commercial banks and the largest corporations (Patman Report 1968, p. 91).

In 1966, *Fortune* plainly disclosed that over the years since it had been publishing its list it had been omitting 'privately owned or closely held companies that do not publish certified statements of their financial results.' It now named 26 companies which it believed 'had sufficient sales in 1965 to qualify for the 500 list' (Sheehan 1966). (Because of a high ratio of sales to assets, some of these firms might not rank among the top 500 if we knew their assets.) Obviously, any adequate generalization about the ability of families to maintain control through ownership, indeed private ownership, of very large firms would have to take account of such previously ignored privately owned firms. Were these added to the 'list,' there would be not merely five privately owned firms, as found by Larner, but 31, over six times as many as were previously counted among the 500 largest. Whether other such large privately owned firms have still escaped notice is an important question to which there is no present reliable answer.

Perhaps of greater importance as a source of inaccessibility of the relevant information is the fact that new methods of control, some of which rely on secrecy, have been devised by the principal shareowning families. The extent (though not the fact) of this secrecy is, once again, unknown. The problem, put most simply, is to discover who are the actual 'beneficial owners' of the shareholdings held by the 'shareholders of record.' Shareholdings may appear in the name of voting trusts, foundations, holding companies, and other related operating corporations in which the given family has a dominant interest. 'Use of nominees [brokers, dealers, bank trust departments], also known in the securities trade as "street names" or "straws" [usually nonfinancial firms listed as record shareholders but whose control is not publicly known] to hide beneficial ownership of stock is a common corporate practice today,' as Senator Lee Metcalf recently noted (1971). Corporations 'habitually list nominees rather than beneficial owners,' whatever the supposed formal reporting requirements (Metcalf and Reinemer 1971). In this way, the presence of principal proprietary families may be hidden or rendered scarcely noticeable among the corporate reports of stock ownership filed with the Securities and Exchange Commission (SEC), which are required by law to list the stockholdings of each director of the corporation and of the beneficial owners of 10 percent or more of the outstanding amount of its stock.

Even the presence of large bank holdings may be hidden in this way – not to speak of the proprietary controlling interests of the bank itself. Thus, in addition to the discrepancy between *Fortune*'s findings and Larner's, the Patman Committee's unprecedented studies (1968, pp. 13–15) suggest that three dozen corporations classified as 'management controlled' by Larner are really under the control of very large banks. Larner has rejected the Patman Committee's conclusions on the grounds that the banks do not hold at least 10 percent of the voting stock in most of the corporations named by the committee. There are six, however, in which more than 10 percent of the common stock is held by a single bank, and another in which 9.5 percent is held by a single bank. To Larner's 95 corporations controlled through ownership interests, then, we may add the 17 privately owned firms that the *Fortune* lists have excluded,[9] the 52 discovered by *Fortune* among the 500 to be under proprietary control through at least 10 percent minority holdings by an individual or family, and at least the six found by the Patman Committee to be under 'bank minority control' by 10 percent or more stock ownership. This is a total of 170 firms, or 34 percent of the 500 largest nonfinancial firms which are controlled through ownership interests. Further, Larner (1970, p. 132) correctly argues, as we noted earlier, that 'control through a legal device' such as pyramiding, contrary to Berle and Means's view, is 'more realistically seen . . . as a form of ownership control.' He found 26 corporations in this category. Larner also classified two corporations as under 'unknown' control; he believes, however, that 'it is likely' that these are, in fact, privately owned. Adding these 28, we have a total of 198, or 39.6 percent of the top 500 firms controlled through a minimum of 10 percent ownership interest – a figure more than double Larner's original 95, or 19 percent.

I want to emphasize that I have so far used the criterion of 10 percent as the minimum proportion of the outstanding stock which an individual or cohesive group must have to exert minority control through ownership. This is the standard employed by Larner and other recent authorities (e.g.Sheehan 1967; Monsen *et al.* 1968, 1969; Hindley 1970; Vernon 1970), in place of the original 20 percent cutoff point used by Berle and Means, on the assumption that stock is now even more widely dispersed and that a block of 10 percent should therefore assure working control. However, on the basis of its investigations, the Patman Committee concluded that effective control could be assured with even less than a 5 percent holding, 'especially in very large corporations whose stock is widely held' (1968, p. 91). If this assumption is correct, then another 14 corporations in which the Patman investigators found a single bank holding more than 5 percent but less than 10 percent of the voting stock would also clearly belong under proprietary rather than management control – bringing the total so far to 211, or 42.2 percent of the top 500 firms controlled by identifiable ownership interests.[10]

Moreover, these findings do not consider 'any of the various coalitions that may indeed assure working control for small groups in many companies' (Sheehan 1967). (For example, in another six corporations which Larner classified under 'management control,' the Patman investigators found a group of two or three banks holding 10 percent or more of the corporation's common stock between them.) Indeed, the official sources of information ordinarily relied on in such investigations are highly unlikely to permit discovery of such coalitions. These coalitions surely cannot be revealed by a residual definitional mode of analysis which merely classifies by exclusion, i.e. corporations are classified as management controlled when no specified minimum proportion of shares is *known* to be in the hands of a single individual or cohesive group. Genuine disclosure would require an investigation into the recent history of the corporation, and, perhaps, 'inside information' which is not immediately accessible. At the least, information on critical phases of the founding, promotion, and expansion (or mergers) of the corporation – and the place in the present structure of control of individuals and families that played important roles during these phases – is needed to identify the implications of given shareholdings (Sweezy 1953, p. 160). Not since the NRC investigation of 'interest groups in the American economy' has such a study been done in the United States.

Most recently, however, a very important study attempted – paradoxically – to systematically mine the publicly available 'inside information' on the controlling interests in America's largest industrial corporations. Our own reference to *Fortune* and the *New York Times* (Sheehan 1966, 1967; Murphy 1967; Jensen 1971) has already indicated their possible value as sources of publicly available inside information. Thus, Philip Burch 'searched carefully' through *Fortune, Time, Business Week, Forbes* and the business section of the *New York Times* over the period dating roughly from 1950 to 1971 in order to collect the information these business media contained on any of the 300 biggest manufacturing and mining corporations (plus the next biggest 200 less intensively) as well as the top 50 merchandising and transportation companies. He supplemented this information by *Moody's* manuals and *Standard and Poor's Corporation Records*, as well as SEC reports, though he found these of less use. 'The results of this research and analysis,' according to Burch, 'show a marked difference in stock ownership totals as contrasted with those arrived at through examination' of the SEC's Official Summary of Securities Transactions and Holdings. He found 'disparities of very sizeable proportions' and is 'of the firm opinion that the higher figures [using his business sources] are the more accurate ones' (1972, pp. 25–7). He did a 'company-by-company analysis of the control status of most [300] of America's large corporations . . . as of the mid 1960's'; classified the corporations, ranked by *Fortune's* figures on sales, into three categories, 'probably management control,' 'possible family control,' and 'probably family control'; and he found that only among the top 50 industrial corporations did his category of 'probably management control' bulk largest, with 58 percent of them falling in that category. Of the total top 300, he found that 40 percent are probably under management control, 45 percent are probably under family control, and 15 percent are possibly under family control. Burch considers these 'conservative figures.' In his view, 'they represent the most reliable findings that can be assembled on this difficult and important subject without resort to governmental subpoena and investigatory powers.' In particular, his estimates of family control are low because his study took no account of 'vast blocks of corporate stock held by the big institutional investors, particularly the top 50 commercial banks and trust companies' (1972, pp. 29, 70, 17).

Burch's findings obviously contradict the received view that the largest corporations are virtually all under management control – and which Larner purportedly showed in his own recent study. One question, then, aside from Burch's use of business sources not utilized systematically before, is by what criteria Burch classified the corporations under probable family control. Two conditions had to be met: (a) 'that approximately 4 percent–5 percent or more of the voting stock was held by a family, group of families, or some affluent individual' according to one or more of his sources; and (b) that he found representation 'on the part of a family on the board of directors of a company, generally over an extended period of time' (Burch 1972, pp. 29–30). Whether this is a more or less reliable and valid indicator of proprietary control than using 10 percent as the required minimum (drawn predominantly from official sources based on company self-reporting whose reliability has been shown to be questionable) cannot easily be ascertained – precisely because we have no independent criteria by which to measure 'control' other than by the variety of hints, clues, and more or less solid information obtainable on the real proprietary interests in a given corporation.

The Concept of Control

In short, how 'control' is conceptualized is a critical question – apart from the problem of obtaining reliable and valid information. Following Berle and Means, 'control' has generally been defined to refer to the 'actual *power* to select the board of directors (or its majority),' although control may also 'be exercised not through the selection of directors, but through *dictation to the management*, as where a bank determines the policy of a corporation seriously indebted to it' (Berle and Means 1967, p. 66, italics added). Thus, control refers to the '*power of determining the broad policies* guiding a corporation and not to . . . the actual influence on the day to day affairs of an enterprise' (Goldsmith and Parmelee 1940, pp. 99–100, italics added). Control is not business management, or what Gordon (1966, p. 150) has termed 'business leadership.'

This would seem to be clear conceptually. In practice, however,

Berle and Means and their followers have simply assumed away the analytical issues by their operational definitions. They have merely assumed, not demonstrated, that once a cohesive ownership interest having at least a minimum specified proportion of the stock disappears (whether 20 percent as in the original Berle and Means work or the current 10 percent criterion), the corporation slips imperceptibly and inevitably under 'management control.' At this point, presumably, the top officers, given the wide dispersion of stock among small shareowners and the officers' control of the proxy machinery, become capable of nominating and electing a compliant and subservient board of directors, of perpetuating themselves in office, and of abrogating, thereby, the control of proprietary interests (Gordon 1966, pp. 121–2; Larner 1970, p. 3; *Business Week*, May 22, 1971, p. 54). 'In the mature corporation,' as Galbraith sums it up, 'the stockholders are without power; the Board of Directors is normally the passive instrument of the management' (1967, pp. 59, 90–5).

But, as I have emphasized repeatedly, it is necessary to study both the concrete situation within the corporation and the constellation of intercorporate relationships in which it is involved before it becomes possible to discover the locus of control. Indeed, the Berle and Means method of investigation, the definitions and procedures utilized, do not, in fact, even begin to accord with the actual content of their own concept of control. For this reason, it seems advisable to conceptualize corporate control in such a way as to link it inextricably with a method that is not reducible to a single criterion, such as a minimum percentage of stock held by a single minority bloc, but which requires instead a variety of interrelated yet independent indicators. The modalities of corporate control utilized by specific individuals and/or families and/or groups of associates differ considerably, vary in complexity, and are not easily categorized. The concept of control must therefore compel attention to essential relationships. No less than the generic sociological concept of power, the concept of control, as Berle and Means (1967, p. 66) themselves put it, is elusive, 'for power can rarely be sharply segregated or clearly defined.'

How the real locus of control, formal authority (bureaucratic executive posts), and legal rights (shareownership) are actually connected is problematic. If control refers to the capacity – either by selecting the directors or dictating to them – to determine the broad policies of a corporation, then it refers to a social *relationship*, not an attribute. Control (or power) is essentially relative and relational: how much power, with respect to whom? (cf. Etzioni 1968, pp. 314–15; Wrong 1968, p. 679). I, therefore, conceptualize control as follows: when the concrete structure of ownership and of intercorporate relationships makes it probable that an identifiable group (e.g. of proprietary interests) can realize their corporate objectives over time, despite resistance, then, according to this concept, they have 'control' of the corporation (cf. Weber 1968, p. 926). Thus, to estimate the probability that a given individual or group of associates controls a corporation, we must know who the rivals or potential rivals for control are and what assets they can bring to the struggle.

This has two important implications for the study of corporate control. It means that a specific minority percentage of ownership in itself can tell us little about what potential for control it represents. This only can be revealed by a case study of the pattern of ownership within the given corporation. But it also means that confining our attention to the single corporation may, in fact, limit our ability to see the pattern of power relationships of which this corporation is merely one element; and it may restrict our understanding of the potential for control represented by a specific block of shares in a particular corporation. An individual or group's capacity for control increases correspondingly, depending upon the number of many other large corporations (including banks and other financial institutions) in which it has a dominant, if not controlling, position. The very same quantitative proportion of stock may have a qualitatively different significance, depending on the system of intercorporate relationships in which the corporation is implicated.

Of course, I am referring here to 'structural' analysis of potential control rather than to 'behavioral' analysis of who wins in actual 'struggles for control.' Even analyzing such struggles, however, can rarely provide an understanding of corporate control without the type of analysis advocated here. Otherwise, it is not possible to know who the contending powers really are – what may look like a 'proxy fight' between 'management' and certain shareowners may actually be a struggle between contending proprietary interests. The latter type of research, therefore, also requires the former, if it is to provide valid and reliable findings.

The question remains, what are the 'broad corporate policies or objectives' over which control is exercised? I have found no usable definition of them in my studies of the writings on this question.

Nor do I think that corporate policies and objectives are amenable
to definition apart from a specific theory of the objective necessities
of corporate conduct and the imperatives of the political economy.
But attempting to outline such a theory here would take us rather
far afield from the focus of this study. The theory would have to
cover such essential questions as the following: what relationships
must the corporations in an oligopolistic – and global – economy
establish with each other? with the state? with foreign governments?
with the workers? with sources of raw materials and markets? What
common problems, created by their very interaction, must they
confront? Only after these questions are answered can we properly
ask whether the individuals who actually decide among proposed
long-range strategies and decide on the 'broad policies and
objectives' of the corporations are merely members of 'management.'

We know, for instance, that the largest corporations in the United
States are now typically 'multinational' or 'transnational' in the
sense that the 'sheer size of their foreign commitment,' as *Fortune*
puts it (Rose 1968, p. 101), and the 'extent of their involvements is
such that, to some degree, these companies now regard the world
rather than the nation state as their natural and logical operating
area.' Is it the 'managements' of these corporations that determine
their broad policies? Or do the individuals, families, and other
principal proprietary interests with the greatest material stake in
these corporations impose their conceptions of the issues and
demand that their objectives are pursued in order to maintain the
'world . . . as their natural and logical operating area'?

Here, clearly, we verge, once again, on the class questions raised
at the outset of this article. To take a more limited issue, however:
many of the multinational corporations face increasing risk of
nationalization of their foreign properties. 'Management' may plan
for such contingencies, exercise their 'discretion,' and decide on the
tactics to be adopted. When their planning goes awry or proves
ineffective, however, must the management answer to their corporation's principal shareowners and other proprietary interests (such
as banks) or not? Having left management in charge of the everyday
operations of the corporations abroad, with little or no interference,
do the principal proprietary interests have the power to interfere
when deemed necessary? Without an analysis of concrete situations
and the specific control structure of the corporations involved, we
cannot answer such questions – though occasionally particular
events momentarily illuminate the actual relationships involved

(even if they may still remain largely in the shadows).

Thus, for example, the Chilean properties of Kennecott Copper Corporation and Anaconda Company were recently (1971) nationalized in Chile. These two corporations, which owned the major copper mines of Chile, had adopted different long-range strategies to deal with the rising probability of nationalization. We cannot explore the details here, but suffice it to say that Kennecott's strategy was reportedly aimed at ensuring, as Robert Haldeman, executive vice-president of Kennecott's Chilean operations explained, 'that nobody expropriates Kennecott without upsetting customers, creditors, and governments on three continents' (Moran 1973, pp. 279–80). Kennecott was able to 'expand very profitably in the late 1960's with no new risk to itself and to leave, after the nationalization in 1971, with compensation greater than the net worth of its holdings had been in 1964. In contrast, Anaconda, which had not spread its risk or protected itself through a strategy of building transnational alliances, lost its old holdings, lost the new capital it committed during the Frei regime [preceding Allende's socialist government], and was nationalized in 1971 without any hope of compensation' (Moran 1973, pp. 280–1).[11]

Now, according to Berle and Means (1967, p. 104) and Larner (1970, pp. 74–9), both Kennecott and Anaconda have long been under 'management control.' In Kennecott's case, there is relatively persuasive evidence that it is, in fact, probably controlled by the Guggenheim family and associated interests rather than by 'management.'[12] Whether this is so or not, Kennecott's 'successful tactics' in Chile did not test the reality of its alleged control by management. But Anaconda's 'management' was submitted to a rather clear test of the extent to which it had control. Within two months after the Chilean government 'intervened' in Anaconda's properties and a month after it took over Anaconda Sales Corporation's control of copper sales, it was announced in the *New York Times* (May 14, 1971, p. 55) that Mr John B. Place, a director of Anaconda, and a vice-chairman of the Chase Manhattan Bank (one of its four top officers, along with David Rockefeller, chairman, and the president and another vice-chairman), was to become the new chief executive officer of the Anaconda Company. (Other Anaconda directors who were bankers included James D. Farley, an executive vice-president of First National City Bank, and Robert V. Roosa, a partner in Brown Brothers, Harriman and Company.) As the *New York Times* reporter (Walker 1971) explained, Mr Place had no mining expertise ('it is assumed he would not know a head frame from a drag line'), and though he had been an Anaconda director since 1969 he 'lives in the East and has never attended the annual [stockholders] meeting held regularly in Butte, Montana,' where Anaconda's most important American copper mines are located. In the wake of this Chase Manhattan officer's installation as Anaconda's chief executive officer, 'at least 50 percent of the corporate staff,' including John G. Hall, Anaconda's former president, 'were fired. Chairman [C. Jay] Parkinson took early retirement' (*Business Week*, February 19, 1972, p. 55). The decimation of Anaconda's allegedly controlling management illustrates the general proposition that those who really have control can decide when, where, and with respect to what issues and corporate policies they will intervene to exercise their power.

Profit Maximization?

Fortunately, some issues to which the question of control is relevant are somewhat more amenable to systematic, even quantitative, analysis than the ones just posed. Chief among these, which has occupied considerable theoretical, but little empirical, attention, is the proposition concerning 'managerial discretion' (see and compare Kaysen 1957, 1965; Simon 1957; Baumol 1959; Marris 1963, 1964; Williamson 1963, 1970; Gordon 1966; Galbraith 1967). It posits different motives and conduct for managers than owners, and, thereby, differences in the profit orientations of owner-controlled versus management-controlled corporations. 'The development of the large corporation,' as Gordon puts it, 'has obviously affected the goals of business decision-making. . . . It clearly leads to greater emphasis on the non-profit goals of interest groups other than the stockholders,' such as the management. The executives 'do not receive the profits which may result from taking a chance, while their position in the firm may be jeopardized in the event of serious loss' (1966, pp. xii, 324).

Dahrendorf has stated the sociological proposition succinctly. In his view, the separation of ownership and control 'produces two sets of roles the incumbents of which increasingly move apart in their outlooks on and attitudes toward society in general and toward the enterprise in particular. . . . Never has the imputation of a profit motive been further from the real motives of men than it is for modern bureaucratic managers. Economically, managers are interested in such things as rentability, efficiency and productivity' (1959, p. 46). This is an oft-asserted but rarely investigated proposition, on which Larner has recently provided systematic negative evidence. Drawing on his study of the separation of ownership and control, he found the following: using multiple-regression analysis and taking into account assets, industrial concentration, Federal Reserve Board indices of economy-wide growth and fluctuation of profit rates, and equity–asset ratios, Larner found that the rate of profit earned by 'management'- and 'owner'-controlled firms was about the same; both were equally profit oriented. Second, the evidence on fluctuations in profit rates suggested no support for the view that allegedly nonowning managements avoid risk taking more than owners do. Third, Larner found that the corporation's dollar profit and rate of return on equity were the major determinants of the level of 'executive compensation.' Compensation of executives, he concluded, has been 'effectively harnessed' to the stockholders' interests in profits. In Larner's words, 'Although control is separated from ownership in most of America's largest corporations, the effects on the profit orientations of firms, and on stockholders' welfare have been minor. The magnitude of the effects,' he concludes (1970, p. 66), 'appears to be too small to justify the considerable attention they have received in the literature of the past thirty-eight years.'[13]

Larner's findings contradict managerial theory, but are consistent both with neoclassical and neo-Marxian reasoning concerning corporate conduct: even where management is really in control, it is compelled to engage in a 'systematic temporal search for highest practicable profits' (Earley 1957, p. 333). The conduct of the large corporation, in this view, whether under management control or ownership control, is mainly determined by the market structure – the nature of competition, products produced, and the constraints of the capital (and labor) markets (Peterson 1965, pp. 9–14; O'Connor 1971, p. 145). Growth, sales, technical efficiency, and a strong competitive position are simultaneously inseparable managerial goals and the determinants of high corporate profits – which, in turn, are the prerequisites of high managerial income and status (Earley 1956, 1957; Baran and Sweezy 1966, pp. 33–4; Sheehan 1967, p. 242; Alchian 1968, p. 186). Management need not spend much of its time contemplating profits as such (Peterson 1965, p. 9), so long as its decisions on pricing and sales and on the planning and organization of production must be measured against and not imperil corporate profitability. 'This,' argues Shorey Peterson (1965, p. 9), 'is the essence of profit-seeking and of capitalist behavior in employing resources.' Significant deviation from profit-maximizing behavior also would lead to the lowering of the market price of the corporation's stock and make it an attractive and vulnerable target for takeover – and the displacement of the incumbent management (Manne 1965; *Business Week*, May 22, 1971, p. 55).

Further, some economists have suggested that professional management, especially the use of 'scientific budgetary planning' and the emphasis on the 'time-value of money' (Earley 1956; Earley and Carleton 1962; Tanzer 1969, pp. 32–4), *strengthens*, rather than weakens, the drive toward profit maximization. Whether or not managers are actuated by the 'profit motive,' as a subjective value commitment, the effort at 'profit maximization' is an objective requirement, because profits constitute both the only unambiguous criterion of successful managerial performance and an irreducible necessity for corporate survival (Peterson 1965; Tanzer 1969, pp. 30–2). In the words of Robin Williams, Jr., 'the separation of ownership and control shows that the "profit motive" is not a motive at all . . .; it is not a psychological state but a social condition' (1959, p. 184).

This reasoning is persuasive and consistent with the findings that purportedly management-controlled and owner-controlled corporations are similarly profit oriented, and that profits and stock market values determine executive compensation. But once again the difficulty is that since independent investigations concerning the control of the large corporations, including the two most recent and exhaustive studies by Larner and Burch, have come to very different conclusions, how do we know if the 'independent variable' has even been adequately measured? In reality, the allegedly management-controlled corporations may – appearances aside – be subject to control by minority ownership interests and/or 'outside' centers of control.

Entangling Kinship Relations and Spheres of Influence

The problem is further complicated if a number of seemingly independent corporations are actually under common control. Few today consider the concept of the 'interest group' or 'financial group' or 'family sphere of influence' relevant to the workings of the large corporations. Indeed, Paul M. Sweezy (Baran and Sweezy 1966, pp. 17–20) has discarded the concept also, as noted earlier, although he was the principal author of the investigation for the NRC (1939) which provided one of the two most authoritative studies (the other by the TNEC) of the question to date (Goldsmith and Parmelee 1940, chap. 7). We know, however, that the very object of such groups, as was relatively well documented in the past, 'is to combine the constituent companies into a system in such a way as to maximize the profits of the entire system irrespective of the profits of each separate unit,' as Gardiner Means himself long ago pointed out (Bonbright and Means 1932, pp. 45–6). Much as in the multinational corporation's relations with its affiliates and subsidiaries, the constituent corporations in a group can adjust intercorporate dealings in such a way as to raise or diminish the profit rates of the different ostensibly independent corporations (cf. Rose 1968, p. 101; Tanzer 1969, pp. 14ff.). Under such circumstances, studies attempting to compare the conduct of corporations, several of which may in fact be involved in different groups to which their policies are subordinated, cannot provide valid or reliable results (see, for instance, Knowles 1973). We cannot be certain what is being measured.

In the United States today, the Mellons and DuPonts are among the most publicized instances of enduring 'family spheres of influence.' The TNEC found the Mellon 'family . . . to have considerable shareholdings in 17 of the 200 corporations, 7 of which they controlled directly or indirectly' (Goldsmith and Parmelee 1940, p. 123). Today, according to *Fortune* (Murphy 1967; see also Jensen 1971) the Mellons, utilizing 'various connections, and through a complicated structure of family and charitable trusts and foundations' and other 'eleemosynary arrangements,' have known controlling interests in at least four of the 500 largest nonfinancial corporations (Gulf Oil, Alcoa, Koppers Company, and Carborundum Company), as well as the First Boston Corporation, the General Reinsurance Corporation, and the Mellon National Bank and Trust Company (the fifteenth largest US bank by deposits (Patman Report 1968, p. 79)). In turn (according to the Patman Report (1968, p. 14)), Mellon National Bank holds 6.9 percent of the common stock in Jones and Laughlin Steel, another of the top 500.[14] It seems as reasonable to hypothesize that the Mellons are only instances of a less visible but prevalent situation among principal proprietary families as to assume they are 'deviant cases' or historical vestiges (cf. Gordon 1966, pp. 158–9).

Moreover, family 'spheres of influence' radiate out among several large corporations; so when such a family owns a small proportion of the stock in a given corporation, that stockholding carries different implications and potential for control than it would if it were owned by an individual or other family without a 'sphere of influence,' i.e. without other major resources and interconnected institutions to buttress the owner's position. Many related individuals can participate in the ownership of a block of shares, utilizing a complex holding pattern to keep the family's control concentrated, despite the diffusion of share ownership among its members. If control can be exercised through entangling interests in several interrelated corporations, then kinship analysis is indispensable to an under-standing of the control structure in any single corporation. Indeed, the kinship relations among the top officers, directors, and principal shareholders of the large corporations (and banks), though usually ignored, may well form the underpinning of the control structure.[15]

Bank Control?

The banks are major institutional bases of economic power and corporate control that managerialists, from Berle and Means to John Kenneth Galbraith, have either ignored or considered unimportant. Offering no substantial evidence to support his assertion, Gordon recently re-stated (in a new preface to his original study of the situation as of the 1930s) the accepted view that 'large-scale industry is much less dependent on the banking community than it was a half-century ago, and such power as bankers have is less likely to be translated into corporate control than was true then.' Noting the extensive interlocking between the largest banks and corporations, he simply claims that this is a 'far cry from what was once meant by "financial control"' (1966, pp. ix–x). What implications such interlocking might have, Gordon fails to suggest. Galbraith's 'commonplace observation' is that 'the social magnetism of the banker' is 'dwindling,' and that the largest corporations are emancipated from reliance on bankers and outside sources of financing because they now have a source of their own capital, derived from their earnings, and 'wholly under [their] own control' (1967, pp. 68, 92).

Contrary to Galbraith's commonplace observations, however, uncommon but systematic research on the question does not seem to indicate decreased corporate dependence on external funds. For all US firms whose assets exceed $5 million, John Lintner reports that 'the dependence on outside liabilities for financing is about the same regardless of the size of the firm' and that the 'relative shifts in the reliance on internal or external funds . . . have been remarkably stable over a full half century' (1967, pp. 179, 184). The Federal Reserve Bank of San Francisco reports a sharp increase in the past decade in reliance on external funds for financing, and if the bank's data are reanalyzed to exclude depreciation allowances – on the premise that only profits can be used to finance net investments to increase the firm's capital stock – the reported trend is even more clearly toward dependence on external financing. Most important, the largest corporations are found to be least self-financing (cited in Fitch and Oppenheimer 1970, no. 1, pp. 68ff.).

If, contrary to managerialist assumptions, the large corporations must continue to rely on the capital market no less than in the past, this is of critical importance: since the distribution of banking assets and deposits is highly skewed, this means that 'reliance on external financing' is, in fact, dependence on a small number of very large financial corporations. As of 1964, the top 100 commercial banks in the United States held 46 percent of all the deposits of the 13,775 commercial banks in the country. The 14 largest alone, representing one-tenth of 1 percent of all commercial banks, held 24 percent of all commercial bank deposits (Patman Report 1966, p. 8704). Thus, analysis of the connections between the large banks and corporations is essential to our understanding of the locus of corporate control. Where it might otherwise appear as if, lacking a visible controlling ownership interest, a corporation is under 'management control,' it may, on the contrary, be under the control of one or more banks and other financial institutions. Even in corporations in which a substantial minority (or even a majority) of the stock is held by an identifiable ownership interest, this may not assure control: if the corporation has a long-term debt to a given bank or insurance company, has that institution's representatives on its board, and must receive prior approval of significant financial and investment decisions, then control of that corporation may be exerted from the 'outside'; and this may be accentuated if several related financial institutions have a similar interest in that corporation. (The dismissal under the 'prodding' of its bankers of Anaconda's chief executive officer and other top officers – discussed earlier – when their performance in Chile turned out to be inferior to Kennecott's, and which had led, in any case, to the company's deteriorating business situation, seems to be a case in point (see *Business Week*, February 19, 1972, pp. 54–5)).

Whatever the dwindling 'social magnetism' of bankers divined by Galbraith, this may be a questionable indicator of their economic power. Indeed, the Patman Committee, which gathered unprecedented information on the stockownership of large commercial banks, believes the power of the banks is growing. The committee found a '. . . pattern of control whereby large blocks of stock in the largest nonfinancial corporations in the country are becoming controlled by some of the largest financial corporations in the country.' This, the Patman Committee concludes, 'is shifting economic power back to a small group, repeating in somewhat different manner the pattern of the trusts of the late nineteenth and early twentieth centuries.' This 'emerging situation' appears to the committee to be one involving increasing 'bank minority control.' The committee found that the largest banks surveyed in 10 major cities, not including the West Coast, hold 5 percent or more of the common stock in 147 (29 percent) of the 500 largest industrial corporations. At least 5 percent of the common stock of 17 of the 50 largest merchandising companies and the same number of transportation companies is held by one or more of the 49 banks. These 49 banks are also represented on the boards of directors of 286 of the top 500 industrial corporations. The same pattern appears among the 50 largest merchandising, utilities, transportation, and insurance companies (Patman Report 1968, p. 13). Whether or not, and to what extent, such fusion of financial and industrial capital indicates 'financial' or 'bank' control is an open question. It cannot be ignored, however, if we want to understand its implications. Thus, Peter C. Dooley (1969, p. 318) found that precisely those corporations – the largest ones – which the managerialists claim to be most independent of the banks are, in fact, most closely interlocked with large banks and other financial corporations. Among the 200 largest nonfinancial corporations ranked by assets, the bigger the nonfinancial corporation, the more interlocks it has with the 50 largest financial corporations (32 banks and 18 insurance companies).

This suggests that thinking of the largest corporations, banks, and insurance companies as independent organizations may obscure the actual coalescence of financial and industrial capital that has occurred. On the one hand, as noted above, large banks and insurance companies frequently are themselves principal shareholders in the large corporations. On the other, the very same individuals and families may be principal shareowners in large banks and large corporations, even when these do not have institutional holdings in one another. Aside from the Mellons, with controlling interests in at least four of the 500 largest nonfinancial corporations and in an investment bank, insurance company, and the fifteenth largest commercial bank, whom we noted above, other well-known industrialist families in the United States may be cited who also have dominant and/or controlling interests in the largest banks. Outstanding examples are both main branches of the Rockefeller family trunk, as well as other principal owning families, in the Standard Oil corporations. The Rockefellers and associates reportedly (*Time*, September 7, 1962; Abels 1965, p. 358) hold over 5 percent of the stock in the Chase Manhattan Bank (ranking second by deposits of all banks as of 1963),[16] whose chairman of the board is David Rockefeller; the Stillman-Rockefellers and associates are said to be dominant in the First National City Bank (ranking third as of 1963) (*Fortune*, September 1965, p. 138). The Fisher and Mott families, among the principal shareowning families in General Motors, reportedly hold over 5 percent of the stock of the National Bank of Detroit (US Congress 1963, pp. 227, 416), the country's sixteenth largest bank as of 1963. The Henry Ford family owns 4 percent of the thirtieth ranking Manufacturer's National which, in turn, owns 7 percent of Ford Motor Company common stock (Patman Report 1968, p. 664). The M. A. Hanna family that controls at least two of the 500 largest industrial corporations, National Steel and Consolidation Coal (Larner 1970, p. 120; Burch 1972, p. 58), has a dominant minority interest of at least 3 percent in the thirty-fourth ranking National City Bank of Cleveland (US Congress 1963, p. 165), which, in turn, holds 11 percent of the stock of Hanna Mining Company.

These are, of course, merely instances, as I said, of prominent owning families whose interests overlap banking and industry. They illustrate the general theoretical issue, however, of the extent to which it is valid to speak at all of 'bank control' of 'industry' – as does the Patman Report, for instance, or other recent writers (Fitch and Oppenheimer 1970). Rather, these families' interests transcend the banks and corporations in which they have principal or controlling interests; and the banks may merely be units in, and instrumentalities of, the whole system of propertied interests controlled by these major capitalist families.

Indeed, there may well be a distinctive segment of the corporate world that represents the fusion of financial and industrial capital. As early as 1910, Rudolf Hilferding ([1910] 1947, chs. 7, 14, 23) first called attention to what he termed 'finance capital' and 'finance capitalists' (cf. also Lenin [1917] 1967, vol. 1, ch. 3; Schumpeter [1919] 1955a, pp. 80–1; Sweezy 1956, pp. 261, 266). Hilferding argued that 'thanks to their personal ownership of capital or as representatives of the concentrated power of other people's capital (bank directors), a circle of men sit upon the governing boards of many corporations. So, a sort of personal union arises both among the different corporations themselves and between them and the banks; this circumstance must be of the greatest importance for the policy of these institutions, because of the community of interests it establishes among them' (Hilferding [1910] 1947, p. 141).

Do such 'finance capitalists' or men who sit simultaneously on the boards of big banks or other financial institutions and large nonfinancial corporations have a special role in coordinating these corporations' interests? Do they differ socially, for example, from other outside directors who interlock the largest nonfinancial corporations among themselves, as well as interlocking with other nonfinancial firms? These are critical questions, which no single indicator can suffice to answer. We would need information concerning the finance capitalists' own propertied interests, their relative wealth, and their kinship relations, before being able to ascertain whether they represent a special social type in contrast to other officers and directors of the largest corporations and banks. We do have some information, however, on one relevant issue, namely, whether they are more likely to sit on a number of large nonfinancial corporation boards than other 'outside directors' (i.e. non-officer directors) who are not bankers. My analysis of raw data presented elsewhere (Smith and Desfosses 1972) on interlocking directorates among the top 500 industrial corporations, ranked by sales, as of 1968, reveals that commercial and investment bankers are disproportionately over-represented among the occupants of multiple corporate directorships (table 1.2). Bankers constitute 21 percent of all outside directors in the 500 largest industrials, but well over twice that proportion among the outside directors with seats on three or more corporate boards. Indeed, the proportion of

Table 1.2 *Principal employer of outside directors of the 500 largest industrial corporations in the United States in 1968 (percent)*

Type of principal employer	Number of seats occupied						
	1	2	3	4	5	6 plus	Total
Other top 500 firm	13.9	25.9	15.7	12.9	18.2	0	15.4
Law firm	14.1	10.3	3.4	3.2	9.1	0	13.0
Bank	18.5	25.8	41.6	45.1	45.5	80.0	20.9
Commercial	10.8	14.5	19.1	29.0	36.4	40.0	12.0
Investment	7.7	11.3	22.5	16.1	9.1	40.0	8.9
Consulting firm	6.3	6.0	1.1	6.5	0	0	6.0
Other[a]	47.3	32.0	38.2	32.3	27.2	20.0	44.7
Total %	100	100	100	100	100	100	100
Total *N*	1,932	282	89	31	11	5	2,350

[a] Types of employers which did not employ more than 5 percent of the total number of outside directors in the 500 largest industrials, including utilities; merchandising, insurance, real estate, railroad firms, as well as educational institutions, foundations, government agencies, plus 'unlisted companies'.
Sources: calculated from raw data given in Smith and Desfosses (1972, table 4, p. 65), on the composition of the outside directorships of the 500 largest industrials listed in *Fortune*, May 15, 1969, ranked by 1968 sales. Principal employer was obtained from information in the proxy statements of the 460 corporations and from *Standard and Poor's Register of Corporations, Directors, and Executives*, 1970, for 35 corporations. Smith and Desfosses did not obtain information on five corporations.

bankers who are outside directors rises directly with the number of corporate posts held. And among the select few (*N* = 16) outside directors having five or more posts, 56 percent are bankers; of the five outside directors with six or seven posts, four are bankers. Viewing the same relationships differently (table 1.3), commercial and investment bankers stand out in marked contrast to other outside directors in the top 500 corporations: a far higher proportion of them have multiple corporation posts than do outside directors from other top 500 corporations, law firms, consulting firms, or other types of companies and institutions. Outside directors from other top 500 corporations are second only to the bankers in the proportion having multiple directorships. But well over twice the proportion of bankers occupy multiple posts: 11 percent of the commercial bankers and 15 percent of the investment bankers have seats on

Table 1.3 *Number of the 500 largest US industrial corporations on whose boards outside directors are represented, by type of principal employer, 1968 (percent)*

Type of principal employer	Number of seats occupied				
	1	2	3	4 plus	(N)
Other top 500 firm	74	20	4	2	(361)
Law firm	89	9	1	1	(306)
Bank					
Commercial	75	15	6	5	(283)
Investment	71	15	10	4	(208)
Consulting firm	86	12	1	1	(141)
Other[a]	87	9	3	1	(1,051)
All outside directors	82	12	4	2	(2,350)

[a] See table 1.2
Sources: see table 1.2

three or more top 500 corporate boards compared with 6 percent of the directors from other top 500 firms.

Who Controls the Banks?

Who the controlling interests are in the largest banks is not publicly known. The US Congress House Select Committee report on chain banking (1963) and the Patman Reports (1964, 1966, 1967) for the first time provided an authoritative glance – however limited – inside. The 1963 and 1964 reports list the 20 largest shareholdings of record (and the percentage of stock held) in each of the 200 largest commercial bank members of the Federal Reserve System in recent years. The 1966 Patman Report focuses on commercial banks' holdings of their own shares and also lists the total market values (though without calculating the percentages) of the outstanding stock held by all financial institutions in the 300 largest commercial banks in 1966; and the 1967 Patman Report also focuses on holdings in the banks by other financial institutions, particularly the major commercial banks in 10 metropolitan areas. The lists of the reported 'beneficial owners' of the banks' shares obtained by the Patman

Committee have not been released. With only the shareholdings of record available so far, the same difficulties arise here as has already been discussed earlier in detail. Any attempt to reveal the actual ownership interests by identifying recognizable surnames alone, without knowledge of kinship relations, nominees, etc., cannot provide reliable and valid evidence. A study of this type, based on the 1963 Select Committee report, utilizing the 10 percent minimum to define an ownership-controlled bank, comes to the predictable conclusion that 'management control had become the dominant form of control among the large member banks by 1962,' accounting for 75 percent of the banks (Vernon 1970, p. 654).

In contrast, Burch utilizes other business sources of information cited earlier, as well as the 1963 Select Committee report; he investigated representation on boards of directors, and consulted several family histories. Like Vernon, however, he did not attempt any systematic investigation of kinship ties, so, once again, his are absolutely minimum estimates of the control of big banks by ownership interests. Studying only the 50 largest, he found that 30 percent probably are under family control, another 22 percent possibly under family control, and 48 percent probably under management control (Burch 1972, pp. 89–96). Because Vernon provides categories of banks by total bank assets, rather than by rank, no direct comparison is possible from their published reports. But one suggestive comparison can be made: of the 27 banks having $1 billion in assets or more, Vernon classifies only two under 'owner control,' with the possible addition of another three in which he identified an interest greater than 5 percent but less than 10 percent (1970, p. 655). Of the 27 top banks listed by Burch, however, he classifies eight as *probably* under family control and four more as *possibly* under family control. Once again the disparities in results by two different methods are striking. Other close students of the banks (aside from the Patman investigators (1968, p. 91) already cited) object to the ownership level of 10 percent as 'arbitrary.' Thus, Eisenbeis and McCall (1972, p. 876), financial economists at the Federal Deposit Insurance Corporation, argue that '"minority control" can be achieved . . . through ownership of a much smaller proportion of stock than the arbitrary 10 percent levels.'

In any event, the theoretical significance of such an alleged split between ownership and control in large banks is not suggested by Vernon; nor, to my knowledge, has any managerial theorist yet to suggest that the banks might somehow or other become non-profit-maximizing institutions if they were no longer under the control of identifiable principal owners. Furthermore, neither Vernon nor Burch take account in their studies of the extent to which the banks are interlocked among themselves or, most important, hold substantial amounts of stock in each other. The Patman Committee (1966) did a survey of bank ownership, whose results have only been partially reported. It found that 57 percent of the 210 largest commercial banks hold more than 5 percent of their *own* shares and 29 percent hold more than 10 percent of their *own* shares. The banks (and other types of corporations) buy their own stock – sometimes termed 'defensive buying' on Wall Street – to keep their shares out of the 'unfriendly hands' of potential rivals for control.[17]

If other financial institutions (including commercial banks, mutual savings banks, and insurance companies) in which the same owning families appear among the principal shareholders, or which have long-standing business associations and common interests (including interlocks between banks and insurance companies), also hold a given bank's stock, this further decreases the amount of stock that the principal individual and familial shareholders must own to control it. In nearly a third (30 percent) of the 275 large banks surveyed by the Patman Committee, more than 10 percent of their shares could be voted exclusively by other financial institutions. In nearly half (47 percent), more than 5 percent of their shares are similarly held (Patman Report 1966, p. 832). In addition, the extent and pattern of interlocking bank stockownership by the same principal shareowners is not known. Very preliminary data received by the Patman Committee found several 'situations where the beneficial owners of large blocks of commercial bank stock are in fact holdings by a few families who have management connections with competitor banks in the same geographic area.' In the United States, commercial banks may not legally interlock with each other; but officers and directors (and their families) of one bank can own principal shareholdings in other banks – as the preliminary data of the Patman Committee also revealed (Patman Report 1966, pp. 878–9).

Conclusion

Our review of discrepant findings on the alleged separation of ownership and control in the large corporation in the United States,[18] and of the problems entailed in obtaining reliable and valid evidence on the actual ownership interests involved in a given corporation, should make it clear that the absence of control by proprietary interests in the largest corporations is by no means an 'unquestionable,' 'incontrovertible,' 'singular,' or 'critical' social 'fact.' Nor ought we any longer to have confidence in such assurances as the following by Robert A. Dahl: 'Every *literate* person now *rightly takes for granted* what Berle and Means *established* four decades ago in their famous study, *The Modern Corporation and Private Property*' (1970, p. 125, italics added). On the contrary, I believe that the 'separation of ownership and control' may well be one of those rather critical, widely accepted, pseudofacts with which all sciences occasionally have found themselves burdened and bedeviled.[19]

News of the demise of capitalist classes, particularly in the United States, is, I suspect, somewhat premature. In place of such unsupported generalizations, extrapolated from an insufficiently examined American experience or deduced from abstract ahistorical theoretical premises, detailed empirical studies are necessary.

The methods and procedures, and the basic concepts and units of analysis, in such research will have to be quite different from those which have been most commonly employed until now. The new research must focus at the outset on the complex structural relationships in which the single corporation is itself involved: the particular pattern of holdings and their evolution within the corporation and the connections between it and other corporations; the forms of 'personal union' or interlocking among corporate directorates and between the officers and directors and principal owning families; the connections with banks, both as 'financial institutions' and as the agents of specified propertied interests, including those who control the banks themselves; the network of intercorporate and principal common shareholdings. In a word, it will be necessary to explore in detail not only the institutional but the *class* relations in which large corporations are situated.

For these purposes, the concept of class has to be reclaimed from the disuse and misuse into which it has fallen. Classes, as Dahrendorf (1959, p. 76) rightly states, 'are clearly not layers in a hierarchical system of strata differentiated by gradual distinctions. Rather, "the analysis of social class is concerned with an assessment of the chances that common economic conditions and common experiences of a group will lead to organized action." ... Class is always a category for purposes of the analysis of the dynamics of social conflict and its structural roots, and as such it has to be separated strictly from stratum as a category for describing hierarchical systems at a given point in time.'[20] If, as I think Daniel Bell argues correctly, a class system is maintained through the fusion of the family as an institution and extant property relations, and 'capitalism . . . is a social system, wherein power has been transmitted through the family,' then we must make that an important focus of our empirical investigations (1958, pp. 246–7). Indeed, we should pursue Bell's own analytical starting point and original (though subsequently ignored) sociological emphasis on the relationship between 'the peculiar cohesiveness of dominant economic classes' and 'the linkage of the family and property system' (1961, pp. 39–40). In turn, it will also be necessary to focus, to use Parsons's term, on the 'members of the most effective kinship unit' (1953, p. 120). That is, we have to investigate the intricate network not only of general social interaction and shared concrete interests, but also the actual kinship relations among officers, directors, and principal shareholders, both in a single corporation and among the whole gamut of corporations (including banks and other financial firms).

This point is worth underlining, for it is crucial to our argument. To reveal the actual centers of corporate control, we must discover and delineate 'the most effective kinship unit.' Without research into the web of kinship relations binding apparently unrelated indviduals into a cohesive owning unit for purposes of control, analysis of the locus of control of the large corporation is hobbled at the outset. By proceeding from such an analysis it will also become possible to answer, on the most unambiguous empirical grounds, whether or not a capitalist 'class' exists in the United States or similar countries and to what extent and in what ways that class has really been 'decomposed' as the managerial theorists have assumed. As Joseph Schumpeter ([1923] 1955b, p. 113) rightly argues, 'the family, not the physical person, is the true unit of class theory.' Classes are constituted of freely intermarrying families variously located in the social process of production and system of property relations. People similarly located economically are more likely to associate with each other freely than with others, and, therefore, to freely intermarry. Particularly among the wealthy, a variety of specific institutions, from debutante balls to select social clubs, resorts, and assorted watering places, as well as the 'proper' schools, colleges (fraternities, sororities, and 'living groups'), assure their commingling and psychological compatibility – and, therefore, differential propensity to intermarry. Protection of the family's property (and 'good name'), which injects a further note of caution in the selection of proper marriage partners, merely increases this 'natural' social tendency (cf. Mills 1957; Baltzell 1966a, 1966b; Domhoff 1967, 1970, 1972). Our empirical investigations of the separation of ownership and control must lead us, therefore, to investigate the extent to which the families of the officers, directors, and principal shareowners of the large corporations are bound by interwoven kinship ties – the extent to which, in other words, those who own and control the decisive units of production freely intermarry to form a social class.[21] Particularly relevant here is Baltzell's conclusion: 'One of the functions of upper class solidarity is the retention, *within a primary group of families*, of the final decision-making positions within the social structure. As of the first half of the twentieth century in America, the final decisions affecting the goals of the social structure have been made primarily by members of the financial and business community' (1966a, pp. 183, 275, italics added).

Studies of the internal structure of capitalist classes will have to answer questions that include the following: what is the relationship between the 'new group of managers who are [supposedly] utterly different from their capitalist predecessors' and the old owning families – from whom they are said (Dahrendorf 1959, p. 46) to be increasingly moving apart? How are the different strata and segments of this class, and the incumbents of the new roles brought about by the 'decomposition of capital' and the growth of managerial functions, related? What role do the overlapping and interrelated interests of principal shareowning families in the large corporations play in class integration and corporate control? What is the relationship between formal authority in the bureaucratic adminis-trative apparatus, ownership interests, and kinship status? What role do the banks, as institutions, play in the control structure of the class? By whom are the banks owned and controlled? Do those who sit at the center of the web of interlocking directorates among corporations, or in the decisive posts which unite the banks and nonfinancial corporations, have a special position in the class? How, in sum, is the capitalist class internally differentiated and integrated?

To none of these questions do we have adequate answers. Important contributions have been made to our understanding of the formation of earlier historically dominant classes. Studies of such existing classes, however, are rare, and are usually limited to quantitative measurement of their social composition and to counting the social mobility of individuals. No studies have explored the relationships within an existing 'dominant' or 'upper' class, among its various types of constituent units: individuals, families, 'elites,' strata, and segments. Rather – with few exceptions – the structure of dominant classes has simply been ignored.[22]

Studies of dominant classes are necessary, among other reasons, so that we do not continue to 'read politics in an extraordinarily abstract fashion,' bereft of knowledge of the interaction and relationships among 'concrete interest groups, or classes.' I think it is correct, as Bell (1958, p. 240) argues, that, 'if the important considerations of power are *what people do with that power*, then we have to have more *particularized ways of identifying the groupings* than "institutionalized orders," "domains," "circles," etc.' (former italics in original; latter added). And this requires analysis of the internal relationships within the dominant or upper class – of the modes of articulation and association, as well as of differentiation among given interest groups, class segments, etc. – so that we are alerted to possible internal structural sources of class cohesion and conflict. 'Power,' as William Kornhauser has put it (1966, p. 213), 'tends to be patterned according to the structure of interests in a society. Power is shared among those whose interests converge, and divided along lines where interests diverge,' and this surely applies within a dominant class as it does in the society at large, though to what extent we can scarcely say, lacking such information as we are.

The separation of ownership and control has meant at the least, its proponents argue, that whatever the capacity for organized action of the 'full-blown capitalists' who constituted 'a homogeneous capitalist class' in the past, this situation has been superseded by the 'decomposition of capital' into a rather loose aggregate of fragmented groups having fundamentally different, often opposing, values and interests. 'This is a peculiar state of affairs,' in Dahrendorf's view (1959, p. 305) 'in which it is indeed virtually impossible to locate the ruling class.' Once America had a 'ruling class of businessmen [who] could relatively easily (though perhaps mistakenly) decide where their interests lay and what editors, lawyers and legislators might be paid to advance them,' as David Riesman has put the syllogism, but 'the captain of industry *no longer runs business*, no longer runs politics,' and that class has been replaced by 'an amorphous power structure.' Power in America has become 'situational and mercurial; *it* [sic] resists attempts to locate *it*' (Riesman *et al.* 1953, pp. 247, 242, 257, italics added). Certainly these are no more than assertions of the merely plausible; they are alleged social facts.

A contrary, and at least equally plausible, argument may be made that precisely because the individual capitalists of an earlier competitive era were compelled to struggle among themselves for economic survival, this also inhibited their acting in common, in comparison with the present relatively unified power and capacity for action possessed by those who own the principal portions and control the large corporations. Thus, for instance, Joseph Schumpeter ([1923] 1955a, pp. 80–1) attempted to explain in political economic terms what he considered the artificial conjuncture of capitalism and imperialism as the result of the emergence of 'monopoly capitalism' and the merger of formerly antagonistic 'capitalists and entrepreneurs.' In place of a 'mass of capitalists competing with one another,' there appeared what he termed 'organized capital': the structural integration of large industrial enterprises and the 'close alliance' of bankers and industrialists, 'often going as far as personal identity. . . . Here capitalism has found a central organ that supplants its automatism by conscious decision.' Therefore, it may be hypothesized that the social and economic interweaving of once opposed financial and industrial interests, increased economic concentration, the fusion of formerly separate large capitals, and the establishment of an effective organizational apparatus of interlocking directorates heightens the cohesiveness of the capitalist class and its capacity for common action and unified policies (see and compare Hilferding [1910] 1947, ch. 23). Whether, as Riesman might claim, such a theory applied to contemporary America is a spectral survival of an earlier time is an empirical question.

We cannot know what 'the capabilities and opportunities for cooperation among those who have similar interests, and for confrontation among those with opposing interest' (Kornhauser 1966, p. 213) are at the national level within the dominant class, unless we investigate the internal differentiation and integration of that class through the best available techniques of empirical inquiry. The fact is that there is far more systematic information available on the poor, on farmers, workers, and black Americans, than on the men and women of the rich and the well-born, on those who make up the 'upper strata' – if not the 'capitalist class' – of our society. Yet by now it ought to be apparent, if only from our most recent past, that we must discover as much as we can about those who occupy the upper reaches of American society if we are to understand

– and act effectively in – the present as history.[23]

Studies of contemporary dominant classes elsewhere, including not only 'advanced' but less developed and misdeveloped countries, are also essential. Aside from their intrinsic importance, such studies may help reveal theoretical gaps and errors, as well as inadequate methods, in the present body of research and writing, and allow us to clarify, elaborate, and specify a comparative theory of contemporary capitalist classes. It is bound to be more fruitful than the denial of their existence in managerialism, embodied in the 'astonishing consensus' among academic social scientists. In place of abstract models based on ostensible 'universal' elements in social structures, we need analyses of the structures of specific capitalist classes, related to the actual historical processes within which they have been formed.

Appendix 1

Baran and Sweezy (1966, ch. 2) discard the concept of 'interest groups' or 'communities of interest' binding together a number of corporations into a common system. They argue 'that an appropriate model of the economy no longer needs to take account of them.' Further, they also assert, without evidence, that it is appropriate to 'abstract from whatever elements of outside control may still exist in the world of giant corporations because they are in no sense essential to the way it works' (1966, pp. 18–20). To attempt to deal with this issue fully would take a new article, if not a full-length monograph, and space considerations preclude extended discussion here. Baran and Sweezy do not explain why they consider 'outside' or familial control irrelevant to understanding the American political economy, and it is not at all evident why they should be so insistent on this point.

The one piece of 'empirical evidence' they present about 'communities of interest' is on the alleged dissolution of the old Rockefeller group. But even if their 'evidence' for this *particular* group's dissolution were acceptable, which it is not, this would not warrant discarding the *concept* nor denying the *general* reality of other such groups (as this study has documented), some old, some new, some in the process of formation. As to the alleged dissolution of the Rockefeller group, Knowles persuasively argues, on the basis of detailed evidence, that the Rockefeller group – while now allied with other principal capitalists – continues to have a genuine (and measurable) impact on our economic life (Knowles 1973; cf. also Levine 1972).

To support their claim for the Rockefeller group's dissolution, Baran and Sweezy point out that Indiana Standard, once definitely Rockefeller controlled, had begun in the mid-1950s to aggressively attempt to penetrate foreign markets which had previously been delegated ('no doubt at Rockefeller behest') to Jersey Standard (1966, pp. 19–20). They note correctly that Indiana Standard had recently offered a 75 percent to 25 percent split of profits in favor of the host country, Iran, for a concession. It was, *Business Week* reported (October 25, 1958, p. 99), 'the first U.S. company to break openly with the 50–50 formula.' That Indiana Standard was now 'busily stealing markets' from Jersey Standard, an old Rockefeller firm, 'as well as from other non-Standard companies' illustrates, say Baran and Sweezy, the general theoretical point that 'the larger corporations' now enjoy 'independence from both bankers and dominant stockholders, and their policies accordingly [are] geared . . . each to its own interests rather than being subordinated to the interests of a group.' That is, among large corporations, they claim, 'the relevant line-ups are determined not by ties to outside control centers but by the rational calculations of inside managements' (1966, pp. 18, 20). On the contrary, however, the example of Indiana Standard demonstrates precisely the opposite.

Baran and Sweezy are right that Indiana's break with the cartel indicated that it was no longer subordinate to Rockefeller interests. But their *theoretical inference* concerning causation is *wrong*. For it was only after a new 'dominant stockholder' had suddenly appeared in Indiana Standard that the company began its struggle to penetrate markets previously controlled by the cartel in which Jersey Standard was then paramount. In 1954, after a 17-year court fight, and a still longer competitive struggle with the Rockefellers reaching back to 1932, the Blaustein family overcame the long attempt of Standard Oil to gain control, 'through a variety of intricate financial maneuvers,' of the Blaustein's own American Oil Company (AMOCO) (*New York Times*, November 16, 1970, p. 40). AMOCO was then merged with Indiana Standard; but 'far from having its own enterprise finally swallowed up in the old Standard Oil complex,' as *Forbes* explains, 'the Blaustein family ended up as the largest stockholder in Indiana Standard, the third largest unit of the old Rockefeller empire,' and the family head, Jacob Blaustein, joined Indiana's board. The Blaustein 'family and their various enterprises and trusts . . . own approximately . . . 3.6%' of Indiana Standard's stock (*Forbes*, September 15, 1968, pp. 28, 26). Immediately after Blaustein became Indiana Standard's principal stockholder, a 'drive' to reorganize its corporate structure was launched (*Business Week*, July 16, 1960, pp. 97–8) and it began 'racing all over the map . . . to obtain overseas concessions – as if it were making up for lost time' – and 'rankling' its competitors by 'the unorthodox methods [used] . . . to get a place in the sun overseas' (*Business Week*, October 25, 1958, p. 98).

Thus, the changed 'relevant line-ups' in the old Rockefeller group and Indiana Standard were determined *not* by 'the rational calculations of *inside managements*,' as Baran and Sweezy claim, but rather by a new 'outside control center,' i.e. by a new dominant stockholder who was responsible for Indiana Standard's new policies. Wrong on the one empirical case they cite to support their assertions about the irrelevance of 'interest groups' or 'communities of interest,' Baran and Sweezy simply neglect the theoretical question of how their continued existence would affect the central proposition of their theory of 'monopoly capitalism,' i.e. the ostensible 'tendency of surplus to rise.'

If, as they argue, (a) the large corporations tend, in their interaction, to produce a 'surplus' of investment funds in excess of private investment outlets, and (b) this disparity between a rising surplus and available investment outlets is a chronic threat of crisis under contemporary capitalism, how would this tendency of the rising surplus be affected if owning families still controlled the 'giant corporations'? How would this tendency be affected by 'interest groups' (or 'spheres of influence') able to coordinate the prices, production, sales, and investment policies of ostensibly independent corporations? Would not such interest groups or family spheres, rather than the 'giant corporation', as Sweezy argues (1971, p. 118), constitute the 'basic unit of capital'?

The large corporations are administrative units of 'social capital' in a class-controlled apparatus of private appropriation. Social capital may be organized in a variety of juridical and administrative forms of control on behalf of private capital. Thus, not 'giant corporations' but principal capitalists, engaged in the competitive struggle for profit and organized in various forms of alliance and combination – including corporations, family spheres of influence, 'Rinecon groups' (Zeitlin and Ratcliff 1988, pp. 7, 53–5, 98), pools, trusts, cartels, and other enlarged units of control of capital ('conglomerates' are a recent innovation) – constitute *the* 'basic units of capital.'

Baran and Sweezy's formulation tends to reify if not hypostatize 'giant corporations,' and to lead, as with the managerialists, to a sort of 'capitalism without capitalists.' Indeed, Baran and Sweezy themselves assert that 'the real capitalist today is not the individual businessman but the corporation' (1966, p. 43). In line with their formulation, a prominent Marxian historian, Eric Hobsbawm (1971, p. 19), takes this logic so far as to assert that 'the real members of the ruling class today are not so much real persons as organizations.' This sort of formulation is misleading, because it tends to displace the focus of analysis from the concrete classes, and their interrelations, of contemporary capitalism. It is, after all, merely a peculiar Marxian version of the view held by organizational and managerial theorists that 'organization' or 'power in its institutional form' has displaced and transcended the capital class and capitalism itself.

It is a shame that an original thinker like Sweezy fails to address these questions and contents himself with merely asserting their irrelevance. When he authored the NRC report on interest groups in 1939, he wrote: 'This study should be regarded as doing no more than posing the problem of the larger significance of the facts which it seeks to portray' (Sweezy 1953, p. 184). He ended his essay by two questions concerning their significance which, to my knowledge, he has yet to address: 'What is the significance of the existence of more or less closely integrated interest groups for the pricing process? What are its implications for the relation between economic and political activity?' These questions seem to me to be quite as relevant today as they were when Sweezy first asked them. Indeed, when he republished this study in 1953, nearly two decades after its original appearance, he wrote: 'No . . . study [of interest groups] . . . has been made in recent years, though there is an *obvious need* for one. I hope that the republication of this earlier attempt to deal with what was and *remains one of the crucial aspects of our whole social system* will stimulate the interest of younger social scientists and provide them with both a starting point and some useful methodological pointers' (1953, pp. 158–9, italics added). Perhaps I may immodestly hope that this article by a 'younger social scientist' will stimulate Sweezy to deal with the issues he has so far avoided, but which he once thought of paramount importance.

Appendix 2

Dahrendorf has taken certain formulations by Marx in volume 3 of *Capital* to support his own theses concerning the dissolution of capitalism as the result of the separation of ownership and control. Not only does Dahrendorf explicitly reject what I have termed the 'plain marxist' proposition that the functionaries of capital and the owners of capital (when they are not identical individuals) belong to the same social class, but he also asserts that this 'view is *clearly contrary* to Marx's own analysis' (1959, p. 43, italics added). In volume 3 of *Capital*, Marx briefly discusses the 'credit system' (stock market) and 'joint-stock companies,' whose economic importance in England was increasingly evident. He notes that (a) the 'joint stock companies' involve 'an enormous expansion of the scale of production and of enterprises, that was impossible for individual capitals' and that (b) capital is 'here directly endowed with the form of social capital [capital of directly associated individuals] as distinct from private capital.' But it is two additional propositions, in which Marx anticipates the debate about the separation of ownership and control, that Dahrendorf and others consider supportive of their own managerial theory. Marx also writes that (c) the corporations, being 'social undertakings as distinct from private undertakings,' mean 'the abolition of capital as private property within the framework of capitalist production itself.' (d) This also means the 'transformation of the actually functioning capitalist into a mere manager, administrator of other people's capital, and of the owner of capital into a mere owner, a mere money-capitalist' (Marx 1967, vol. 3, p. 436).

Now, as to the first two propositions there can be no debate. Few would disagree that Marx correctly anticipated the profound significance of the corporation for large-scale production and rapid economic development. And the second point is an unexceptionable description of the obvious fact that pooling individual capital allows 'undertakings' which smaller individual capitalists could not undertake separately. As to the third proposition, it is what I mean by 'confusing Hegelian comments.' For myself, its meaning is clear; for others, it has been confusing (e.g. Bernstein, Schmidt, Bell, Dahrendorf, etc.). Marx had a penchant for Hegel's language and often used it precisely because he wished to honor that 'mighty thinker' when others were currently treating him as a 'dead dog.' Therefore, he 'coquetted with the modes of expression peculiar to him' (Marx 1967, vol. 1, pp. 19–20). One of Marx's oft-used Hegelian concepts is *aufgehoben* or *aufhebung*. In the volumes of *Capital* translated into English, this has usually been rendered 'abolition.' Yet this is clearly not its Hegelian meaning, nor the meaning Marx intended. As Ivan Soll explains, for Hegel, 'the understanding's finite categories must be both preserved and negated – or to use a term favored by Hegel just because it possesses this double meaning, *aufgehoben*.' Or in Hegel's own words '*Aufheben* exhibits its true double meaning. . . . It negates and preserves at the same time' (cited from Hegel's *Logic* by Soll 1969, p. 134). Reinhard Bendix has written to me in a private communication: 'The implication [of *aufheben*] is to *re-create* in the process of *abolishing* – which is one of those conundrums Hegelians thrive on and the rest of us mortals despair over.' Thus, the large corporation, as a new form of 'social capital,' re–creates 'private capital' while abolishing it. Certainly, this is Marx's intended meaning. For, in even greater apparent exaggeration, he goes on to say, 'This is the abolition of the *capitalist mode of production* within the capitalist mode of production itself' (1967, vol. 3, p. 438). This can only be jibberish in English (or at best 'confusing') unless it is understood in its Hegelian sense of preserving while negating, re-creating while abolishing. Marx makes this clear in another passage: 'However, this expropriation appears within the capitalist system in a contradictory form, as *appropriation of social property by a few*. . . . There is antagonism against the old form in the stock companies, in which the social means of production appear as private property; but the conversion to the form of stock still remains ensnared in the trammels of capitalism; hence, *instead of overcoming* the antithesis between the character of wealth as social and as private wealth, the stock companies merely *develop it in a new form*' (1967, vol. 3, p. 440, italics added).

Further, it is in this context that Marx refers to the development Hilferding was later to elaborate, as were many others, including Lundberg, Bonbright and Means, and then (though secondarily) Berle and Means. These authors laid out several types of control other than private ownership and management control. In these types, 'the separation of ownership and control' means that the large property owners, those who own the majority or predominant minority of shares in a corporation, directly or indirectly (pyramiding), appropriate control from the small shareowners. This is Marx's point when he states that the form of the stock company and of credit offers the capitalist 'absolute control within certain limits over the capital and property of others, and thereby over the labor of others' (1967, vol. 3, p. 439).

As to the fourth proposition, it, too, is quite consistent with 'plain marxist' class analysis. For Marx, in elaborating this point, states: 'Stock companies in general – developed with the credit system – have an increasing tendency to separate this work of *management as a function* from the *ownership* of capital, be it self-owned or borrowed. . . . Profit is henceforth received . . . as compensation for *owning capital* that now is entirely divorced from the *function* in the actual process of reproduction, just as this *function* in the person of the manager is divorced from ownership of capital' (1967, vol. 3, pp. 387–8, 436–7, italics added). This, it will be remembered, is also Weber's view of the matter. Further, from the standpoint of the analysis of social domination, class conflict, and surplus appropriation (exploitation), Marx's view as already quoted here and in the following passage has nothing in common with the managerialist doctrine that the ascendancy of the large corporation leads to 'satisficing,' a 'corporate conscience,' a 'post-capitalist society,' or a 'new industrial state,' or with the functionalist conception that it leads to the displacement of class exploitation by a rational occupational order. The emerging corporation and stock market system, Marx wrote, would 'develop the incentive of capitalist production, enrichment through exploitation of the labor of others, to the purest and most colossal form of gambling and swindling, and . . . reduce more and more the number of the few who exploit the social wealth' (1967, vol. 3, p. 441).

Notes

1 Bain (1966, p. 102) refers here to the United States, England, Japan, Sweden, France, Italy, and Canada, which were included in his study.
2 Merton 1959, p. xiii. The internal quote is from Claude Bernard.
3 'Plain marxists' (lower case) was C. Wright Mills's (1962, p. 98) phrase to characterize thinkers to whom Marx's 'general model and . . . ways of thinking are central to their own intellectual history and remain relevant to their attempts to grasp present-day social worlds.' He listed such varied thinkers as Joan Robinson, Jean Paul Sartre, and Paul M. Sweezy, as well as himself, as 'plain marxists.'
4 Domhoff (1967, pp. 47–62) and Kolko (1962, pp. 60–9), who may also be considered plain marxists, reject the doctrine of the separation of ownership and control within the large corporation and also argue that 'managers' belong to the same social class as 'owners.' Their books contain brief empirical studies of the ownership of stock (Kolko) and 'upper-class membership' (Domhoff) of large corporate directors. This

is also the view of Ferdinand Lundberg (1946, 1968), who, in particular, lays stress on the need to study the kinship relationships among the owners and executives – a point we discuss in some detail below.

5 Though it might not accord with their 'economic' theory (see appendix 1).

6 For a contemporary polemic against the views of Bernstein and Schmidt, written in 1899, see Luxemburg (1970, pp. 16–20). Several colleagues, including Robert Merton and Daniel Bell, who read this article in an earlier draft, urged me to discuss what I refer to as 'Marx's confusing Hegelian comments.' Those who are interested in this discussion will find it in Appendix 2 to this study.

7 If one corporation was controlled by another through ownership, but the latter itself was found to be under management control, it was classified by Berle and Means as 'ultimately management controlled.' If it was ultimately under the 'joint control' of a minority interest and management, or other combinations, they counted the corporation as one-half in each of the categories. Thus, the figure 88½ corporations under management control.

8 Berle and Means had used 20 percent as the minimum necessary for minority ownership interests to keep control. In a note to a new edition of their work, Berle and Means (1967) refer to Larner's original article in the September 1966 *American Economic Review* as 'a study [which] has duplicated the 1929 analysis for 1963, making only one significant change in concept' (p. 358), the reduced amount (10 percent) necessary for ownership control.

9 I do not include all 26 privately owned firms named by *Fortune* (Sheehan 1966) because when the estimated sales of these firms are taken into account and they are ranked (and the others on the original 500 list are re-ranked) by sales, only 17 fall in the top 500. If all 26 were included, and the number of 'proprietary' firms (179) figured among the 526, the proportion would be the same: 34 percent. By sales, the 26 privately owned firms are ranked as follows: top 100, none; 101–150, 3; 151–200, 1; 201–250, 2; 251–300, 1; 301–350, 3; 351–400, 1; 401–450, 3; 451–500, 3; 501–526, 9.

10 Larner also apparently has some doubts about the adequacy of the residual definition of management control as equivalent to less than 10 percent of the shares held by a single owner. He names five firms among the top 200 (and refers to 'several others among the top 500') which, though he classified them as management controlled, 'appear to be controlled, or at least strongly influenced, by a single family within their management. Yet these families owned only a very small fraction of the outstanding voting stock' (1970, p. 19). With these firms included, 216 (not counting the unenumerated 'several others'), or 43.2 percent, of the top 500 firms in the United States are visibly controlled by

identifiable individuals, families, or banks. We might note also that there are 335 industrial corporations among the top 500 nonfinancials. Of these, Larner found 89, or 27 percent, controlled through ownership; 19, or 6 percent, through ownership via a legal device; and another two, or 1 percent, 'unknown,' which he believes likely to be privately owned. Fourteen of the 'bank-controlled' corporations found by Patman among Larner's management-controlled corporations are industrials. Three of the firms that Larner classified under management control but suspects are family controlled are also industrials. All 17 of the *Fortune* (Sheehan 1966) privately owned firms are industrials. This makes 144. We do not know (nor would *Fortune* provide the information when I asked) the industrial classification of the 52 corporations *Fortune* found under proprietary control (Sheehan 1967). Were they all industrials, 196, or 59 percent, of the 335 top industrial corporations in the United States as of the mid-1960s would be classified as controlled by identifiable individuals, families, or banks.

11 The destruction of the constitutional government and parliamentary democracy of Chile, and the death of her Marxist president, Dr Salvador Allende, at the hands of the armed forces on September 11, 1973, has once again given Anaconda (and other foreign corporations) 'hope of compensation.' The military regime's foreign minister, Adm. Ismael Huerta, announced within a week of the coup, that the '"door was open" for resumption of negotiations on compensation for United States copper holdings nationalized by President Allende' (*New York Times*, September 30, 1973, p. 14).

12 Kennecott illustrates well our insistence on how important it is to know a corporation's history in order to disclose its locus of control. The Guggenheims bought control of the El Teniente copper mine from the Braden Copper Company in 1908; in 1915 they sold it to the Kennecott Copper Corporation, in which Guggenheim Brothers was the controlling stockholder. In 1923, Utah Copper, in which the Guggenheims had a minority interest, also purchased a large block of Kennecott's shares (Hoyt 1967, p. 263). Yet for Berle and Means only six years later (their data were for 1929) Kennecott was 'presumably under management control' (1967, p. 104). When World War II began, as a historian close to the Guggenheim family has written, 'the Guggenheims created a new Kennecott Copper Corporation, which would have three million shares. This corporation bought up the Guggenheim copper holdings,' including 25 percent of Utah Copper Company's stock and controlling interests in Copper River Railroad and other 'Alaska syndicate holdings' (Hoyt 1967, p. 263). Guggenheim Brothers also had (until purchased recently by the Allende government) the controlling interest in Chile's Anglo-Lautaro Nitrate Company, organized in 1931 out of previous nitrate holdings controlled by the Guggenheims (Lomask 1964, p. 281) and reorganized

in 1951 by Harry Guggenheim (a senior partner of Guggenheim Brothers), to bring in two other smaller Guggenheim-controlled firms. Guggenheim presided as board chairman and chief executive officer of Anglo-Lautaro until his retirement in 1962. Previously, he had been 'absent from the family business for a quarter of a century,' until in 1949 his uncle enjoined him to reorganize Guggenheim Brothers (Lomask 1964, p. 65). In 1959 the Guggenheim Exploration Company, one of whose partners was a director of Kennecott Copper Corporation in which 'the Guggenheim foundations' now also held large holdings, was also revived (Lomask 1964, p. 281). The son of one of the original Guggenheim brothers (Edmond A., son of Murry) 'maintained an active interest in Kennecott Corporation' as a director (Lomask 1964, p. 295), while Peter Lawson-Johnston, a grandson of Solomon Guggenheim, was, as of 1966, a partner in Guggenheim Brothers, a director of the advisory board of Anglo-Lautaro, a director of Kennecott, a director of Minerec Corporation, the vice-president of Elgerbar Corporation, and the trustee of three Guggenheim foundations (Hoyt 1967, p. 348). In the period from roughly 1955 to 1965, Burch (1972, p. 48) found that Kennecott had 'significant [Guggenheim] family representation as outside members of the board of directors,' and concluded that it was 'possibly' under Guggenheim family control. This is certainly a cautious understatement, in the light of the historical evidence just presented, drawn from works by two writers close to the Guggenheim family.

13 Similar findings are reported by Kamerschen (1968, 1969), Hindley (1970), and Lewellen and Huntsman (1970). Contrary findings, which show small but statistically significant differences in profit rates between allegedly owner-controlled and allegedly management-controlled corporations, appear in Monsen et al. (1968). The study by Lewellen and Huntsman (1970) differs from the others cited here, because no attempt was made to contrast performance by owner-controlled versus management- controlled corporations. They focus on the specific question of whether a corporation's profitability or its sales revenue more strongly determines the rewards of its senior officers. By means of a multivariate analysis, they found that 'both reported profits and equity market values are substantially more important in the determination of executive compensation than are sales – indeed, sales seem to be quite irrelevant – [and] the clear inference is that there is a greater incentive for management to shape its decision rules in a manner consonant with shareholder interests than to seek the alternative goal of revenue maximization' (1970, pp. 718–19). The use of multiple-regression analysis (Larner) or analysis of variance (Monsen) does not resolve the problem of causation (time order). It merely shows, at one point in time, how corporations classified under different types of control differ on selected variables. It might plausibly be argued that a control group, whether

an individual, family, or coalition of business associates, might gradually dispose of its holdings in a corporation precisely because its profit performance was not satisfactory over a period of time – for reasons not connected to how it was managed. This might be particularly the case for small control groups, to whom not the corporation's profits as such but the dividend yield and price appreciation of their stockholdings ('combined return') is primary. Thus, a finding that owner-controlled corporations were more profitable than management-controlled corporations (assuming the latter exist) might simply mean that control groups do their best to retain control of the more profitable corporations and get out of those that are less profitable. A genuine causal study requires information on changes over time in types of control and in corporate performance. Unfortunately, the nature of the data available probably precludes such a study. Are the same corporations that were once owner controlled more or less profitable once they come under management control? Take an extreme example. In 1923, Guggenheim Brothers sold control of Chile Copper Company, whose major asset was the Chuquicamata mine in Chile, to the Anaconda Copper Company, headed by John D. Ryan. The family was split over this issue: some of them thought that this would become an extraordinary profit-yielding asset – as it did; others were for accepting the immediate profits to be made by Ryan's offering price of $70 million for the controlling interest. The result was that, although they sold the controlling interest, the family retained a large block of stock as an investment (Hoyt 1967, pp. 258, 263). Did the loss of 'family control' and the Chile Copper Company's acquisition by Anaconda result in lessening effort at profit maximization in the Chile Copper Company? Posed in this way, the question appears (at least to me) to be rhetorical, though, of course, it is empirical.

14 Jones and Laughlin Steel was classified under 'management control' by Larner. Aside from the 6.9 percent Mellon National Bank holding, the Bank also has two directors on the Company's board. Koppers Company, in which *Fortune* (Murphy 1967) claims the Mellons held at least 20 percent, was also classified as under 'management control' by Larner, indicating the difficulty of locating 'control' without access to 'street knowledge' or insiders. This emphasizes again the secrecy in which holdings are shrouded and the fact that insufficient account of this is taken when considering 'findings' about control centers. Larner himself notes, though without considering its possible general significance, that the Alcoa mandatory 10–K report filed with the SEC in 1963 states that no shareholder has more than 10 percent of the outstanding common shares, although from the proxy report and other sources he concludes that Alcoa is under Mellon control. *Fortune* (Murphy 1967) and the *New York Times* (Jensen 1971) estimate Mellon interests in Alcoa at 30 percent.

15 Larner's own statements in his notes on sources occasionally suggest

how important, if not vital, such kinship information is in order to reveal the actual loci of corporate control. Thus, for instance, Larner refers to *Moody's Industrials* as the source of his information that in the Dow Chemical Company, which he classifies under 'minority control,' there were '78 dependents (plus spouses) of H. W. Dow [who] owned 12.6 percent of [the] outstanding common stock' (1970, p. 75). Larner makes similar references to the Newberry Company, Cabot Corporation, and R. R. Donnelly & Sons Company, in which the descendants and kindred through marriage of the original founder are taken into account in determining what amount of stock these families own. Clearly, systematic independent research of this type into the kinship interconnections of the principal shareowners, officers, and directors of the 500 largest corporations has not yet been done by anyone purporting to locate their centers of control. The outstanding recent unsystematic attempt to do this is the work of Ferdinand Lundberg (1968, chs. 4–6).

16 The 1963 rankings are given because this was the year of the House Select Committee's study. The source of the rankings is the *Fortune Directory* for 1963. The latest rankings by *Fortune* (July 1973) for 1972 are Mellon, 15; Chase, 3; First National City, 2; National Bank of Detroit, 18; National City Bank of Cleveland, 49.

17 Corporations may purchase their own shares for other reasons: (a) to maintain the price of their stock, (b) to prepare for possible mergers and acquisitions, (c) to allow them to convert bonds to shares, etc. Whatever the reasons, such holdings are of use in control, when necessary.

18 The evidence on other countries is not reviewed here, and few relevant studies exist. On England, see Florence (1961); on Australia, see Wheelwright (1957).

19 An example of a critical unwitting pseudofact appears in two articles by Daniel Bell (1958, 1961). In both articles, Bell refers to the 'X' family of 'Middletown' as an instance of the end of family control. '[B]y and large,' Bell writes (1958, p. 248; and similarly, 1961, p. 45), 'the system of family control is finished. So much so that a classic study of American life like Robert Lynd's *Middletown in Transition*, with its picture of the "X" family dominating the town, has in less than twenty years become history rather than contemporary life. (Interestingly enough, in 1957, the Ball family, Lynd's "X" family, took in professional management of its enterprises, since the family lineage was becoming exhausted.)' Perhaps Bell really knows who now dominates Muncie, Indiana, and what role the Ball family plays there, but as an instance of 'the breakup of family capitalism' and the end of family control, this is a singularly poor choice. Given the context in which Bell refers to the 'X' family, his statement is quite misleading, since Ball Brothers, Inc., which, according to *Fortune*, is probably among the 500 largest corporations, ranked by

sales, in the country today, continues to be privately owned and controlled. 'Edmund F. Ball, a founder's son, is chairman of the company, but he has employed plenty of non-family talent. . . . "Ours is still," says Edmund Ball, "essentially a closely held, privately owned business"' (Sheehan 1966, p. 343).

20 The phrase in double quotes is from Lipset and Bendix (1951, p. 248).

21 Diverse authorities on kinship have noted that the 'upper' classes everywhere, the United States included, tend to be characterized by an extended and tightly organized network of kin relations (see Cavan 1963; Goode 1963; Goode et al. 1971). Yet such findings have been ignored by sociologists in their discussions of the alleged 'breakup of family capitalism' and the separation of ownership and control. Bert Adams (1970, pp. 591–2) is one of the few sociologists specializing in kinship relations to call specific attention to the interrelationship between kinship and 'the entire debate regarding who rules or controls the U.S. economic system,' stating that 'the evidence points unquestionably to strong kin links among the extremely wealthy in the society.' He suggests that 'much exciting research lies ahead for those who would pursue the links between kinship and economics, not only in the middle and working classes, but among the wealthy or upper classes as well.'

22 Aside from the works cited already by Domhoff, Mills, and Baltzell, Hunter's work (1959) – although not using the concept of class – contributes important information on interaction between corporate executives on a national level. Studies by Perlo (1957), Rochester (1936), and Lundberg (1946), as well as Lundberg's latest relevant work (1968), which is a mine of excellent ideas worth researching, are important nonacademic contributions. Poulantzas (1973) has a useful and provocative analysis of what he terms 'fractions,' 'strata,' and 'social categories,' within and across social classes. Barber and Barber (1965) contains excellent short historical studies. Other notable historical studies of dominant classes are by Bailyn (1955), Barber (1955), Ford (1953), Forster (1960; 1963), Edwards Vives (1927), Heise Gonzales (1950), and Rabb (1967).

23 Several years ago I wrote that 'just as a society's class structure is a major basis of its political diversity and cleavage, so too is *intra*class social differentiation politically significant, and by exploring the structure of the working class it will be possible to locate fundamental sources of its political behavior. This does not mean that *inter*class differences, or conflicting class interests, are in any way secondary to the internal structure of the working class as the source of its politics. Quite the contrary. Any conflict between classes tends to erase or minimize the significance of *intra*class differences and to maximize *inter*class differences' (Zeitlin 1967, pp. 8–9). I take it as a working hypothesis that this statement applies equally well to a society's dominant class. A fine

recent work which is replete with historical sociological interpretations that rest on, or require, analysis of the internal differentiation and integration of specific dominant classes is that by Moore (1966, e.g. pp. 36–9 on England; pp. 162–5, 192, on Imperial China; pp. 237ff. on Japan).

References

Abels, Jules. 1965. *The Rockefeller Billions*. New York: Macmillan.

Adams, Bert. 1970. 'Isolation, Function, and Beyond: American Kinship in the 1960's.' *Journal of Marriage and the Family* 32 (November): 575–97.

Alchian, Armen. 1968. 'Corporate Management and Property Rights.' In *Economic Policy and the Regulation of Securities*. Washington, D.C.: American Enterprise Institute.

Bailyn, Bernard. 1955. *The New England Merchants in the Seventeenth Century*. Cambridge, Mass.: Harvard University Press.

Bain, Joe S. 1966. *International Differences in Industrial Structure: Eight Nations in the 1950's*. New Haven, Conn.: Yale University Press.

Baltzell, E. Digby. 1966a. '"Who's Who in America" and "The Social Register": Elite and Upper Class Indexes in Metropolitan America.' In *Class, Status, and Power*, edited by Reinhard Bendix and S. M. Lipset. 2nd edn New York: Collier-Macmillan.

—— 1966b. *Philadelphia Gentlemen: The Making of a National Upper Class*. New York: Macmillan.

Baran, Paul A., and Paul M. Sweezy. 1966. *Monopoly Capital*. New York: Monthly Review Press.

Barber, Eleanor G. 1955. *The Bourgeoisie in Eighteenth-century France*. Princeton, N.J.: Princeton University Press.

—— and Bernard Barber, eds. 1965. *European Social Class: Stability and Change*. New York: Macmillan.

Baumol, William J. 1959. *Business, Behavior, Value, and Growth*. New York: Macmillan.

Bell, Daniel. 1958. 'The Power Elite – Reconsidered.' *American Journal of Sociology* 64 (November): 238–50.

—— 1961. 'The Breakup of Family Capitalism.' In *The End of Ideology*, Ch. 2. New York: Collier.

Bendix, Reinhard. 1952. 'Bureaucracy and the Problem of Power.' In *Reader in Bureaucracy*, edited by R. K. Merton, Ailsa P. Gray, Barbara Hockey, and Hanan C. Selvin. Glencoe, Ill.: Free Press.

Berle, Adolph, Jr. 1954. *The 20th Century Capitalist Revolution*. New York: Harcourt, Brace.

—— and Gardiner C. Means. 1967. *The Modern Corporation and Private Property*. New York: Harcourt, Brace & World (originally published in 1932 by Macmillan).

Bernstein, Eduard. 1961. *Evolutionary Socialism*. New York: Schocken (originally published in Germany in 1899).

Bonbright, James C., and Gardiner C. Means. 1932. *The Holding Company*. New York: McGraw-Hill.

Burch, Philip H., Jr. 1972. *The Managerial Revolution Reassessed*. Lexington, Mass.: Heath.

Business Week 1971. 'The Board: It's Obsolete Unless Overhauled.' May 22: 50–8.

—— 1972. 'An Ex-Banker Treats Copper's Sickest Giant.' February 19: 52–5.

Cavan, Ruth. 1963. *The American Family*. New York: Crowell.

Dahl, Robert A. 1970. *After the Revolution?* New Haven, Conn.: Yale University Press.

Dahrendorf, Ralf. 1959. *Class and Class Conflict in Industrial Society*. Stanford, Calif.: Stanford University Press.

Domhoff, G. William. 1967. *Who Rules America?* Englewood Cliffs, N.J.: Prentice-Hall.

—— 1970. *The Higher Circles: The Governing Class in America*. New York: Random House.

—— 1972. *Fat Cats and Democrats*. Englewood Cliffs, N.J.: Prentice-Hall.

Dooley, Peter C. 1969. 'The Interlocking Directorate.' *American Economic Review* 59 (June): 314–23.

Drucker, Peter F. 1971. 'The New Markets and the New Capitalism.' In *Capitalism Today*, edited by Daniel Bell and Irving Kristol. New York: Basic.

Earley, James S. 1956. 'Marginal Policies of Excellently Managed Companies.' *American Economic Review* 46 (March): 44–70.

—— 1957. 'Comment.' *American Economic Review. Papers and Proceedings* 47 (May): 333–5.

—— and W. T. Carleton. 1962. 'Budgeting and the Theory of the Firm.' *Journal of Industrial Economics* 10 (July): 165–73.

Edwards Vives, Alberto. 1927. *La Fronda Aristocrática*. Santiago: Editorial del Pacifico.

Eisenbeis, Robert A., and Alan S. McCall. 1972. 'Some Effects of Affiliations among Savings and Commercial Banks.' *Journal of Finance* 27 (September): 865–77.

Etzioni, Amitai. 1968. *The Active Society*. New York: Free Press.

Fitch, Robert, and Mary Oppenheimer. 1970. 'Who Rules the Corporations?' *Socialist Revolution* 1 (1): 73–107; also 1 (5): 61–114; 1 (6): 33–94.

Florence, P. Sargant. 1961. *Ownership, Control and Success of Large Companies: An Analysis of English Industrial Structure and Policy, 1936–1951*. London: Sweet & Maxwell.

Ford, Franklin L. 1953. *Robe and Sword: The Regrouping of the French Aristocracy after Louis XIV*. Cambridge, Mass.: Harvard University Press.

Forster, Robert. 1960. *The Nobility of Toulouse in the Eighteenth Century*. Baltimore, Md.: Johns Hopkins University Press.

—— 1963. 'The Provincial Noble: A Reappraisal.' *American Historical Review* 68 (April): 681–91.

Galbraith, John K. 1967. *The New Industrial State*. New York: New American Library (also, 'Introduction,' 2nd edn, 1971). New York: Houghton Mifflin.

Goldsmith, Raymond W., and Rexford C. Parmelee. 1940. *The Distribution of Ownership in the 200 Largest Nonfinancial Corporations*. In *Investigations of Concentration of Economic Power*, Monographs of the Temporary National Economic Committee, no. 29. Washington, D.C.: Government Printing Office.

Goode, William J. 1963. *The Family*. Englewood Cliffs, N.J.: Prentice-Hall.

—— Elizabeth Hobbins, and Helen M. McClure, eds. 1971. *Social Systems and Family Patterns: A Propositional Inventory*. Indianapolis, Ind.: Bobbs-Merrill.

Gordon, Robert A. 1966. *Business Leadership in the Large Corporation*. Berkeley, Calif.: University of California Press (originally published in 1945 under the auspices of the Brookings Institution).

Heise Gonzales, Julio 1950. 'La Constitucion de 1925 y las Neuvas Tendencias Politico-sociales.' *Anales de la Universidad de Chile* 108 (80; 4th trimester): 95–234.

Hilferding, Rudolph. [1910] 1947. *Das Finanzkapital*. Berlin: Verlag J. H. W. Dietz.

Hindley, Brian V. 1970. 'Separation of Ownership and Control in the Modern Corporation.' *Journal of Law and Economics* 13 (April): 185–221.

Hobsbawm, Eric J. 1971. 'Class consciousness in history.' In *Aspects of History and Class Consciousness*, edited by I. Meszaros. London: Routledge & Kegan-Paul.

Hoyt, Edwin P. 1967. *The Guggenheims and the American Dream*. New York: Funk & Wagnalls.

Hunter, Floyd. 1959. *Top Leadership, U.S.A*. Chapel Hill, N.C.: University of North Carolina Press.

Jensen, Michael C. 1971. 'A New Generation Comes of Age.' *New York Times*. May 2, sec. 3: 1, 5.

Kahl, Joseph. 1957. *The American Class Structure*. New York: Rinehart.

Kamerschen, David R. 1968. 'The Influence of Ownership and Control on Profit Rates.' *American Economic Review* 58 (June): 432–47.

—— 1969. 'The Effect of Separation of Ownership and Control on the Performance of the Large Firm in the U.S. Economy.' *Rivista Internazionale di Schienze Economiche e Commerciali* 16 (5): 489–93.

Kaysen, Carl. 1957. 'The Social Significance of the Modern Corporation.' *American Economic Review* 47 (May): 311–19.

—— 1965. 'Another View of Corporate Capitalism.' *Quarterly Journal of Economics* 79 (February): 41–51.

Knowles, James C. 1973. *The Rockefeller Financial Group*. Warner Modular Publications, Module 393: 1–59.

Kolko, Gabriel. 1962. *Wealth and Power in America*. New York: Praeger.

Kornhauser, William. 1966. '"Power Elite" or "Veto Groups"?' In *Class*,

Status, and Power, edited by Reinhard Bendix and S. M. Lipset. 2nd edn. New York: Collier-Macmillan.

Larner, Robert J. 1970. *Management Control and the Large Corporation.* Cambridge, Mass.: Dunellen.

Lenin, Nikolai. [1917] 1967. 'Imperialism.' In *Lenin: Selected Works.* New York: International.

Levine, Joel B. 1972. 'The Sphere of Influence'. *American Sociological Review* 37: 14–27.

Lewellen, Wilbur G., and Blaine Huntsman. 1970. 'Managerial Pay and Corporate Performance.' *American Economic Review* 69 (September): 710–20.

Lintner, John. 1967. 'The Financing of Corporations.' In *The Corporation and Modern Society,* edited by E. S. Mason. New York: Antheneum.

Lipset, S. M., and Reinhard Bendix. 1951. 'Social Status and Social Structure: A Re-examination of Data and Interpretations.' Part 1. *British Journal of Sociology* 2 (September): 150–68.

Lomask, Milton. 1964. *Seed Money: The Guggenheim Story.* New York: Farrar, Straus.

Lundberg, Ferdinand. 1946. *America's Sixty Families.* New York: Citadel (originally published by Vanguard in 1937).

—— 1968. *The Rich and the Super-rich.* New York: Bantam.

Luxemburg, Rosa. 1970. *Reform or Revolution.* New York: Pathfinder (originally published in Berlin in 1899).

Manne, Henry. 1965. 'Mergers and the Market for Corporate Control.' *Journal of Political Economy* 72 (April): 110–20.

Marris, Robin. 1963. 'A Model of "Managerial" Enterprise.' *Quarterly Journal of Economics* 77 (May): 185–209.

—— 1964. *The Economic Theory of 'Managerial' Capitalism.* London: Macmillan.

Marx, Karl. 1967. *Capital.* Vols 1–3. New York: International (originally published in German in 1867, 1885, 1894).

Mason, E. S. 1967. 'Introduction.' In *The Corporation in Modern Society,* edited by E. S. Mason. New York: Atheneum.

Merton, Robert K. 1959. 'Notes on Problem-finding in Sociology.' In *Sociology Today,* edited by R. K. Merton, Leonard Broom, and Leonard S. Cottrell, Jr. New York: Basic.

Metcalf, Lee. 1971. *Congressional Record* 117, pt. 17: 22141.

—— and Vic Reinemer. 1971. 'Unmasking Corporate Ownership.' *The Nation,* July 19: 38–40.

Miliband, Ralph. 1969. *The State in Capitalist Society.* New York: Basic.

Mills, C. Wright. 1957. *The Power Elite.* New York: Oxford University Press.

—— 1962. *The Marxists.* New York: Dell.

Monsen, R. Joseph, Jr., J. S. Chiu, and D. E. Cooley. 1968. 'The Effect of Separation of Ownership and Control on the Performance of the Large Firm.' *Quarterly Journal of Economics* 82 (August): 435–51.

——, ——, and —— 1969. 'Ownership and Management.' *Business Horizons* 12 (August): 45–52.

Moore, Barrington. 1966. *Social Origins of Dictatorship and Democracy.* Boston, Mass.: Beacon.

Moran, Theodore H. 1973. 'Transnational Strategies of Protection and Defense by Multinational Corporations.' *International Organization* 27 (Spring): 273–87.

Murphy, Charles J. V. 1967. 'The Mellons of Pittsburgh.' Part 1. *Fortune* 75 (October): 120ff.

National Resources Committee (NRC). 1939. *The Structure of the American Economy.* Washington, D.C.: Government Printing Office. Reprinted in Paul M. Sweezy. 1953. *The Present as History.* New York: Monthly Review Press.

Nichols, W. A. T. 1969. *Ownership, Control, and Ideology.* London: Allen & Unwin.

O'Connor, James. 1971. 'Who Rules the Corporation?' *Socialist Revolution* 2 (January–February): 117–50.

Parsons, Talcott. 1953. 'A Revised Analytical Approach to the Theory of Social Stratification.' In *Class, Status, and Power*, edited by Reinhard Bendix and S. M. Lipset. Glencoe, Ill.: Free Press.

—— and Neil Smelser. 1957. *Economy and Society.* London: Routledge & Kegan-Paul.

[Patman] Staff Report. 1964. *Twenty Largest Stockholders of Record in Member Banks of the Federal Reserve System.* 5 vols. US Congress, House, Committee on Banking and Currency, Domestic Finance Committee. 88th Congr., 2nd sess. Washington, D.C.: Government Printing Office (cited as Patman Report).

—— 1966. 'Bank Stock Ownership and Control' (reprinted in Patman Report 1968, vol. 1).

—— 1967. 'Control of Commercial Banks and Interlocks among Financial Institutions' (reprinted in Patman Report 1968, vol. 1).

—— 1968. *Commercial Banks and Their Trust Activities: Emerging Influence on the American Economy.* US Congress, House, Committee on Banking and Currency, Domestic Finance Committee. 90th Congr., 2nd sess. Washington, D.C.: Government Printing Office (cited as Patman Report).

Perlo, Victor. 1957. *The Empire of High Finance.* New York: International.

Peterson, Shorey. 1965. 'Corporate Control and Capitalism.' *Quarterly Journal of Economics* 79 (February): 1–23.

Playford, John. 1972. 'Who Rules Australia?' In *Australian Capitalism*, edited by John Playford and Douglas Kirsner. Harmondsworth: Penguin.

Poulantzas, Nicos. 1973. 'On Social Classes.' *New Left Review* No. 78 (no volume listed) (March–April): 27–54.

Rabb, Theodore K. 1967. *Enterprise and Empire: Merchant and Gentry Investment in the Expansion of England, 1575–1630.* Cambridge, Mass.: Harvard University Press.

Riesman, David, Nathan Glazer, and Reuel Denney. 1953. *The Lonely Crowd.* Garden City, N.J.: Anchor.

Rochester, Anna. 1936. *Rulers of America.* New York: International.

Rose, Sanford. 1968. 'The Rewarding Strategies of Multinationalism.' *Fortune,* September 15: 101–5, 180, 182.

Schumpeter, Joseph. [1923] 1955a. 'Social Classes in an Ethnically Homogeneous Environment.' In *Imperialism and Social Classes.* New York: Meridian.

—— 1955b. 'The Sociology of Imperialism[s].' In *Imperialism and Social Classes.* New York: Meridian.

Sheehan, Robert. 1966. 'There's Plenty of Privacy Left in Private Enterprise.' *Fortune,* July 15: 224ff.

—— 1967. 'Proprietors in the World of Big Business.' *Fortune,* June 15: 178–83, 242.

Simon, Herbert A. 1957. *Administrative Behavior.* 2nd edn. New York: Macmillan.

Smith, Ephraim P., and Louis R. Desfosses. 1972. 'Interlocking Directorates: A Study of Influence.' *Mississippi Valley Journal of Business and Economics* 7 (Spring): 57–69.

Soll, Ivan. 1969. *Introduction to Hegel's Metaphysics.* Chicago, Ill.: University of Chicago Press.

Sorokin, Pitirim. 1953. 'What Is a Social Class?' In *Class, Status, and Power,* edited by Reinhard Bendix and S. M. Lipset. Glencoe, Ill.: Free Press.

Sweezy, Paul M. 1953. 'Interest Groups in the American Economy.' In *The Present as History.* New York: Monthly Review Press.

—— 1956. *Theory of Capitalist Development.* New York: Monthly Review Press (originally published in 1942).

—— 1971. 'The resurgence of finance capital: fact or fancy?' In *The Dynamics of U.S. Capitalism,* edited by Harry Magdoff and Paul M. Sweezy. New York: Monthly Review Press.

Tanzer, Michael. 1969. *The Political Economy of International Oil and the Underdeveloped Countries.* Boston. Mass.: Beacon.

US Congress, House, Select Committee on Small Business. 1963. *Chain Banking: Stockholder and Loan Links of 200 Largest Member Banks.* Washington, D.C.: Government Printing Office.

Vernon, Jack R. 1970. 'Ownership and Control among Large Member Banks.' *Journal of Finance* 25 (3): 651–7.

Villarejo, Don. 1961–2. *Stock Ownership and the Control of Corporations.* Ann Arbor, Mich.: Radical Education Project. Reprint of articles in *New University Thought* (Autumn 1961 and Winter 1962).

Walker, Robert. 1971. 'A Banker for Anaconda.' *New York Times,* May 23, sec. 3: 3, 11.

Weber, Max. 1965. *Theory of Social and Economic Organization,* edited by Talcott Parsons. New York: Free Press (originally published in German in 1925).

—— 1968. *Economy and Society*, edited by G. Roth and C. Wittich. New York: Bedminster (originally published in German in 1921).

Wheelwright, E. L. 1957. *Ownership and Control of Australian Companies*. Sydney: Law Book.

Williams, Robin, Jr. 1959. *American Society*. New York: Knopf.

Williamson, Oliver E. 1963. 'Managerial Discretion and Business Behavior.' *American Economic Review* 53 (December): 1032–57.

—— 1970. *Corporate Control and Business Behavior*. Englewood Cliffs, N.J.: Prentice-Hall.

Wrong, Dennis. 1968. 'Some Problems in Defining Social Power.' *American Journal of Sociology* 73 (May): 673–81.

Zeitlin, Maurice. 1967. *Revolutionary Politics and the Cuban Working Class*. Princeton, N.J.: Princeton University Press.

—— and Richard Earl Ratcliff. 1988. *Landlords & Capitalists: The Dominant Class of Chile*. Princeton, N.J.: Princeton University Press.

2

On class theory of the large corporation

[Writing from the standpoint of the prevailing 'interorganizational paradigm' in sociology, Michael P. Allen (1976) raises several objections to my analysis of corporate ownership and control (1974), which appears as chapter 1 in this volume. He argues, in particular, that the separation of ownership and control in the large corporation has been convincingly demonstrated, that management control varies directly with size, and that it is the rule not only among the very largest corporations but among the biggest commercial banks as well.]

'Management Control': Fact or Pseudofact?

To begin with, the three recent studies Allen cites do not 'consistently confirm the theory of the separation of ownership and control.' I presented an extensive analysis of the problems entailed in obtaining reliable and valid evidence on the actual ownership interests involved in a given corporation and concluded that the separation of ownership and control is probably a pseudofact. Allen presents no evidence or reasoning to alter that conclusion or to substantiate these studies' suspect findings. Further, Allen's assertion that 'each of the three researchers concludes that a majority of the 500 largest corporations are subject to management control' is not correct. Philip Burch, Jr. classifies only 124 of the top 300 under 'probably management control' (PM), whereas he put 48 under 'possibly family control' (F?) and 128 under 'probably family control' (PF) (1972, pp. 36ff.). Relying on 'less intensive study' of the firms ranked by sales from 301 to 500, Burch classifies them as follows: PM, 76; F?, 16; PF, 108 (pp. 160ff.), yielding a total for the 500 of PM, 200 (40 percent); F?, 64 (12.8 percent); and PF, 236 (47.2 percent) – an estimate Burch thinks exaggerates the extent of management control.

With exemplary scholarly caution, he classifies firms under F? when the evidence is not conclusive enough to classify them as PF but when 'one or more families have been identified as being prominently associated with the company in question' (1972, p. 34). Without explanation, Allen has simply recategorized Burch's 64 'possibly family controlled' firms under 'management' control, thereby creating a 'majority' in the latter category.[1]

Management Control and Corporate Size

If we take the 500 industrial corporations studied by Burch and retain his classification, we find only a modest relationship between size rank and type of control (C = 0.169). The relationship between size and management control is particularly weak. Within deciles, the relationship is anything but consistent. Moreover, of the three types of control, F? is most clearly associated positively with size rank, which probably means only that the *visibility* of controlling proprietary interests is negatively associated with size: the larger the corporation, *ceteris paribus*, the more difficult it is to *discover* the locus of control.[2]

Otherwise, a finding that size and management control are positively associated is meaningless, because there are cogent reasons to doubt the adequacy of the methods of analysis and data utilized by Robert Larner (1970) and Robert Sheehan (1966), and thus to question how valid and reliable their evidence on the locus of control is; and Burch's, while unquestionably superior, are also inadequate. After all, Larner himself presents a table that shows fewer management-controlled firms in the lowest assets groups (301–500); and he tabulates Berle and Means's own classifications and finds 'that management control . . . was concentrated among the larger firms' (1970, pp. 18–19). Would that not mean, by Allen's logic, that managerial 'theory' had already been confirmed by Berle and Means over three decades ago (despite the huge gaps in their data that I revealed earlier)?

Three aspects of the 'dispersion of ownership' are often confused: as the size of a corporation increases, there tend to be (a) an increasing number of shareholdings, (b) a decreasing proportion of shares held by management, and (c) a decreasing proportion of shares held by principal shareowners. Assuming their empirical validity, none of these developments necessarily means that proprietary interests lose control of the large corporation. In fact, dispersion among a multitude of shareholders, or a slight ownership interest by management, can be exactly what assures proprietary control. As Berle and Means themselves noted: 'The larger the company and the wider the distribution of its stock, the more difficult it appears to be to dislodge a controlling minority' (1967, p. 75). Consequently, as I argued in my earlier article, what potential for control inheres in a specific proportion of shares held cannot be discovered without a 'case study of the pattern of ownership within the given corporation [and] . . . [of] the system of intercorporate relationships in which the corporation is implicated' (1974, p. 1091 – this volume, ch. 1). I have since sought to demonstrate this in a study of the large corporation in Chile (Zeitlin et al. 1974a; see Zeitlin and Ratcliff 1988). Much as in the United States and England, the largest corporations are most likely to be classified under management control, following Berle and Means's methods and procedures. Rather, however, than take appearances for reality, we utilize a method of analysis that focuses on intercorporate relationships and the web of kinship and thereby reveals the actual controlling proprietary families and associates in 14 of the 15 firms originally classified under management control. Thus, a causal interpretation of the association between corporate size and management control is spurious.

Management Control and the Interlocking Directorate

Allen's evidence concerning the association between the frequency of corporate and financial interlocking and types of corporate control is consistent with what I suggested in my earlier article, namely, that the corporations classified under management control interlock more frequently than others with the 50 largest banks and insurance companies, as well as with other top 200 corporations. But since the largest corporations interlock more frequently, and also tend to be classified under management control more frequently, than others, the effect of corporate size on the association between type of control and interlocking has to be investigated. Assuming that the type of control, even taking size into account, is associated with a greater frequency of interlocks, the question is, what relevance does this have for the managerial versus the class theory of the large corporation? On this, Allen is silent.

He has shown indeed that one of the basic assumptions of managerial theory is false. In managerialist imagery, the large management-controlled corporation exists in a state of splendid autonomy, each one's management independent of the other, impregnable, and invulnerable to 'external authority.' Nary a word is uttered by managerialists about interlocking directorates. 'Management,' it is said, simply 'selects itself and its successors as an autonomous and self-perpetuating oligarchy' (Galbraith 1967, pp. 88, 409). Managerialists also argue, as Berle and Means (1967, pp. xiv–xv) put it, that, because of the 'changed origin of finance capital' (sic)[3] the large corporation is emancipated from control by principal owners of capital; its management, in consequence, gains 'complete decision-making power' over its capital. The result supposedly is that the large corporation, 'runs on its own economic steam. . . . Management thus becomes, in·an odd sort of way, the uncontrolled administrator of a kind of trust, having the privilege of perpetual accumulation.'

Now, if corporate managements were really 'uncontrolled administrators,' because of decreased and decreasing dependence on outside liabilities for financing (itself an assumption contradicted by the evidence (Lintner 1967, pp. 179–84; see also Kuznets 1961, pp. 248, 264, 268; Payne 1961, pp. 130–9)), we should certainly *not* expect to find, as Allen has, that 'management-controlled' corporations interlock more frequently with the largest financial institutions, as well as with other large corporations, than the family-controlled corporations do. These findings are contrary to the implicit hypotheses of managerial theory. (Elsewhere, Allen himself has 'disconfirmed' the implicit managerial hypothesis that the frequency of interlocks between large corporations and banks has 'declined through time, . . . because these corporations have attained an increased capacity to generate capital internally . . .' (1974, pp. 402–3, italics added).)

These findings, though contrary to managerial theory, are consistent with my own class theory of corporate control. In reality, 'management- controlled' corporations are not shorn of proprietary control; their ownership is merely relatively dispersed. Put very schematically, they tend to interlock more frequently with other large corporations and the largest financial firms for the following reasons. The corporate form multiplies the potential for control inherent in every unit of capital by permitting several corporations to have common principal shareowners as well as to own shares in each other. The interlocking directorate is one formal method of corporate combination that enhances the ability of owners of large blocks of stock in several corporations to assure that these corporations' actions do not adversely affect each other – or the common principal shareowners' investments in them. Further, the consolidation of small minority control may be enhanced by formal representation in management. The tendency for common principal shareowners in several corporations (even if those corporations are not under their control), as well as corporations that have intercorporate holdings, to attempt to place themselves or their representatives in those corporations' managements is thus reflected in a pattern in which the putatively 'management-controlled' corporations are more tightly interlocked than others with other large corporations.

This hypothesis, *mutatis mutandis*, also applies to Allen's finding that the 'management-controlled' corporations interlock more frequently than others with the largest banks and to his other finding that bank directors, particularly board chairmen, have a higher average number of directorships than other directors. (The latter data, as Allen notes, 'confirm the results presented by Zeitlin.') A large bank typically has principal interests in several large corporations, and usually plays a critical role in mergers, acquisitions, and reorganization. So it will strive to prevent those corporations from taking actions that might be adverse to the others' (and, thereby, to its own) interests. Diversification and conglomeration increase the extent to which the largest corporations are actual or potential competitors throughout the economy; as a result, a bank that has common dealings with several such corporations finds it even more pressing to try to coordinate their policies in the common corporate interest. The same bank can interlock several corporations in which it has interests (and which are prohibited in the United States from direct interlocks with each other) by placing a different representative in each. If several big banks form a lending syndicate for a given corporation, or if the banks interpenetrate in their ownership (see US Congress 1974, p. 7), they will find it even more imperative to coordinate their policies and reconcile their interests. Indeed, the large corporation's 'vulnerability to external authority' is greater if its stock is scattered among a multiplicity of small shareowners. Therefore, we should expect, as Allen finds, that ostensibly management-controlled corporations are more likely than other corporations to have representatives of the biggest banks on their boards. This allows, as J. P. Morgan once explained, 'a certain number of men owning property . . . [to] do what they like with it . . . and act toward mutual harmony' (*New York Tribune*, March 27, 1902).

Who Controls the Banks?

Although Allen also emphasizes the 'dominant position of financial institutions among the large corporations,' he doubts my hypothesis that the large banks are units in, and instrumentalities of, the system of propertied interests controlled by principal capitalist families. For him, the 'critical issue . . . is the extent of management control among the large commercial banks,' and he refers to the finding (which I discuss in my earlier article – this volume, ch. 1) that 75 percent of the 200 biggest commercial banks are under management control (Vernon 1970). But Allen ignores Burch's (1972) finding that, at most, only 24 of the top 50 commercial banks are management controlled. I suggest that studies utilizing appropriate methods and data would reveal that the other top banks are – behind the managerial veil protecting their proprietary modesty – also controlled by principal owners of capital.

But what if this were not so? What if, as Allen avers, the big banks were management controlled? What implications would this have for the hegemony of the capitalist class and for the US political economy? Allen states none. No longer under the control of specific owners, would the banks forsake the maximization of profit for 'satisficing' (sic) (Simon 1962) conduct? Would the executives of such management-controlled banks be transformed, as was hoped (Berle and Means 1967, p. 313) of their corporate counterparts, into a 'purely neutral technocracy' allocating 'the income stream on the basis of public policy rather than private cupidity'?

The startling fact is that bank trust departments 'manage assets substantially exceeding the assets of the 100 largest corporations in the United States' and have 'larger securities portfolios than all other institutional investors combined' (Lybecker 1973, p. 997). Whose investments are managed by the trust departments of the top banks? Generally, as of the 1960s, they would not administer personal capital of less than $100,000. Morgan Guaranty, for instance, today has a $200,000 minimum. Thus, these trust departments probably serve fewer than 1 percent of Americans (see Projector and Weiss 1966). What might these principal owners of capital do if the management-controlled banks pursued anything but profit-maximizing investment policies? Would these banks be long permitted to retain their trust (sic!)? Assuming for the moment, with Vernon, that most of the top commercial banks are management controlled, we can ask what investment policy their trust departments have pursued. It happens that 'they have leaned very heavily in the last few years' on a policy of trading in the 'market of a select few securities, usually with high price-earning ratios, so-called glamour stocks, . . . to the virtual exclusion of the other market' of less favored stocks (Loomis 1973, p. 83; US Congress 1974, p. 16).

Apparently the glamour has not gone out of the pursuit of profit, even for the management-controlled banks. Certainly, there would be far-reaching reverberations for a bank's survival if the principal owners of capital (whose trusts and investment portfolios constitute one of its prime sources of investment capital) found that the bank was giving them, on the average, a lower rate of return than other banks and consequently shifted their trusts elsewhere. This would set in motion a rapid succession of similar and related moves by major corporate clients, other large banks, and large depositors such that a general 'loss of confidence' by investors would drain the bank's funds, render it incapable of honoring its contractual obligations, and drive it into collapse. Thus the 'discipline of the market,' which reflects the investment decisions of principal individual and institutional owners of capital, requires the banks not to deviate significantly from profit-maximizing policies. To the extent, therefore, that the management-controlled banks are both the creditors and principal shareholders of the largest management-controlled corporations, and interlock tightly with them, these banks will in turn impose their own profit-maximizing requirements on them.

The 'Inner Group' and 'Finance Capitalists'

With this coalescence of financial and industrial capital, as I argued in my article (ch. 1), a new social type also tends to emerge, i.e. the 'finance capitalist.' Neither 'financiers' extracting interest at the expense of industrial profits nor 'bankers' controlling corporations, but finance capitalists represented on the boards of the top banks *and* largest corporations preside over the banks' investments as creditors *and* shareholders, organizing production, sales, and financing, and appropriating the profits of their integrated activities. Thus, even were certain banks and corporations to become so large that they were not ordinarily under the control of specific minority ownership interests, their autonomy would not mean that power had passed to the 'new princes' of the managerial realm (Berle and Means 1967, p. 116; and see Zeitlin et al. 1974a, pp. 113–17). Although the largest banks and corporations might conceivably develop a relative autonomy from particular proprietary interests, their autonomy would be limited by the general proprietary interests of the principal owners of capital.

To the extent that large banks and corporations constitute a new form of class property – of social ownership of the means of production by a single social class – the 'inner group' (US Congress 1965, p. 4 and *passim*) of interlocking officers and directors, and particularly the finance capitalists, become the leading organizers of this system of classwide property. That is why I hypothesize that they 'represent a special social type in contrast to other officers and directors of the largest corporations and banks' (this volume, chapter 1, or Zeitlin 1974, p. 1103; also see p. 1110). They should be far more likely than ordinary corporate executives to be drawn from the 'upper' or 'dominant' or 'capitalist' class – the social class formed around the core of interrelated principal owners of capital. . . (see chapter 4 and Zeitlin et al. 1974b).[4]

Profit Maximization and Management Control

Larner tested three interrelated propositions about the effect of management control on *level* of profit rates, on *variability* of profit rates (to measure 'risk taking'), and on executive compensation. His findings provided systematic negative evidence concerning the main managerial propositions. As he says, 'It appears that proponents of theories of managerial discretion have expended much time and effort in describing a phenomenon of relatively minor importance. Management-controlled corporations seem to be just about as profit oriented as are owner-controlled corporations. . . . No fundamental differences in the level or stability of profit rates which might be attributed to management control were found' (1970, pp. 29, 63). Although the finding on relative profit rates by Monsen el al. (1968) is the opposite of Larner's, I put more confidence in Larner's work because of its greater sophistication and reliability: he takes account of critical variables and interrelations that Monsen et al. ignore. Let me also note that while Monsen et al. emphasize the large differences found over a period of 12 years between the mean ratio of net income to net worth of 12.8 percent for owner-controlled versus 7.3 percent for manager-controlled firms, their appendix of findings (which they ignore) on other ratios that they think are 'less interesting for our purposes' reveals that they found far smaller differences between owner–controlled and manager-controlled firms on the mean ratio of net income to total assets, 7.65 percent versus 6.09 percent, and virtually the same mean ratio of net income to sales for both types, 5.86 percent versus 5.29 percent.

Econometric studies of managerial discretion test contending theories by comparing the reported differences in profit performance of putatively management-controlled versus owner-controlled firms (see chapter 3). But managerial theory rests on a theory of managerial motivation, and posits different motives for managers than for owners. 'Never,' as Ralf Dahrendorf has put it, 'has the imputation of a profit motive been further from the real motives of men than it is for modern bureaucratic managers' (1959, p. 46). Given this assumption, another method of inquiry focusing on 'motivation' is relevant. Thus, two British sociologists, R. E. Pahl and J. T. Winkler, systematically interviewed directors in depth, examined their daily work diaries, held short discussion groups with selected directors and unobtrusively observed each director of 19 firms (a 'rough quota sample of British industry') for a full day of his working life in order to discover how 'directors perceived and negotiated their role.' What they found is quite contrary to managerial theory. 'The argument that managers still operate in a capitalist market and hence must be just as oriented to the traditional capitalist goal, profit, as owners . . . was completely confirmed by our observations. . . . The professionals saw their *purpose* and their *legitimation* in improving profitability markedly compared with the last years of the family owners' management. In *all* cases we encountered, they were successful. Not only were they more *oriented* to profit, they were more capable of obtaining it' (1974, pp. 102, 118, italics added).

Notes

1 Allen does not mention and I also inadvertently omitted from my article (this volume, ch. 1) Chevalier's (1969) findings on corporate ownership and control. With 5 percent as the management control threshold, and 'dominant influence' (DI) referring to probable minority control, using public and numerous private sources, Chevalier classifies the control of the 200 top industrials as follows: management, 80; individuals (including directors) and families, 81 (plus 4 under DI); majority owned, 4; financial, 19 (plus 12 under DI). Chevalier himself thinks that this estimate exaggerates the number of large industrial corporations under management control.
2 A table showing the relationship between type of control and size has been omitted in this volume.
3 Berle, of course, is using the term 'finance capital' merely as a synonym for 'loan capital' and not in the specific sense in which, following but departing slightly from Hilferding (1910), I have defined it. See below.
4 Consistent with this hypothesis are the findings of an analysis of the directors of 'very large industrial companies' and 'large financial institutions' in England (Whitley, 1974). This analysis reveals that, not only are 'the "City" and "industry" . . . remarkably closely linked,' but also 'while *aristocratic kinship links* do not appear to be particularly relevant for the industrial companies considered alone, they are important in connecting these companies to financial institutions and in producing a large integrated network of the two groups combined. The directorship connections between industry and financial institutions, that is, are reinforced by, or alternatively can be seen as reflections of, kinship ties' (p. 77, italics added). (See also Zeitlin and Ratcliff 1988, ch. 3.)

References

Allen, Michael P. 1974. 'The Structure of Interorganizational Elite Cooptation: Interlocking Corporate Directorates.' *American Sociological Review* 39 (June): 393–406.

—— 1976. 'Management Control in the Large Corporation: Comment on Zeitlin.' *American Journal of Sociology* 81 (January): 885–94.

Berle, Adolph, Jr., and Gardiner C. Means. 1967. *The Modern Corporation and Private Property*. New York: Harcourt, Brace & World (originally published in 1932 by Macmillan).

Burch, Philip, Jr. 1972. *The Managerial Revolution Reassessed*. Lexington, Mass.: Heath.

Chevalier, Jean-Marie. 1969. 'The Problem of Control in Large American Corporations.' *Antitrust Bulletin* 14 (Spring): 163–80.

Dahrendorf, Ralf. 1959. *Class and Class Conflict in Industrial Society*. Stanford, Calif.: Stanford University Press.

Galbraith, John K. 1967. *The New Industrial State*. New York: New American Library.

Hilferding, Rudolph. [1910] 1947. *Das Finanzkapital*. Munich: Berlin: Verlag J. H. W. Dietz.

Kuznets, Simon. 1961. *Capital in the American Economy*. Princeton, N.J.: Princeton University Press.

Larner, Robert. 1970. *Management Control and the Large Corporation*. Cambridge, Mass.: Dunellen.

Lintner, John. 1967. 'The Financing of Corporations.' Pp. 166–201 in *The Corporation and Modern Society*, edited by E. S. Mason. New York: Atheneum.

Loomis, Carol J. 1973. 'How the Terrible Two-Tier Market Came to Wall Street.' *Fortune* 88 (July): 2–88, 186.

Lybecker, Martin E. 1973. 'Regulation of Bank Trust Department Investment Activities.' *Yale Law Journal* 82 (April): 977–1002.

Monsen, R. Joseph, Jr., J. S. Chiu, and D. E. Cooley. 1968. 'The Effect of Separation of Ownership and Control on the Performance of the Large Firm.' *Quarterly Journal of Economics* 82 (August): 435–51.

Pahl, R. E., and J. T. Winkler. 1974. 'The Economic Elite: Theory and Practice.' Pp. 102–22 in *Elites and Power in British Society*, edited by Philip Stanworth and Anthony Giddens. London: Cambridge University Press.

Payne, W. F. 1961. *Industrial Demands upon the Money Market, 1919–1957*. New York: National Bureau of Economic Research.

Projector, Dorothy, and Gertrude Weiss. 1966. 'The Distribution of Wealth in 1962.' Pp. 33–6, 98–9, in *Survey of Financial Characteristics of Consumers*, Federal Reserve System, as reprinted in *American Society, Inc.*, edited by Maurice Zeitlin. Chicago, Ill.: Markham, 1970, pp. 105–12.

Sheehan, Robert. 1966. 'There's Plenty of Privacy Left in Private Enterprise.' *Fortune*, July 15: pp. 224ff.

Simon, Herbert. 1962. 'New Developments in the Theory of the Firm.' *American Economic Review* 52 (1): 1–15.

US Congress, Senate Subcommittee on Anti-trust and Monopoly. 1965. Staff Report to the Anti-trust Subcommittee of the Committee on the Judiciary. 89th Congr., 1st sess. House of Representatives. *Interlocks in Corporate Management*. Washington, D.C.: Government Printing Office.

US Congress, Senate Subcommittee on Intergovernmental Relations, and Budgeting, Management, and Expenditures of the Committee on Government Operations. 1974. *Disclosure of Corporate Ownership*. 93d Congr., 2nd sess. Washington, D.C.: Government Printing Office.

Vernon, Jack R. 1970. 'Ownership and Control among Large Member Banks.' *Journal of Finance* 25 (3): 651–7.

Whitley, Richard. 1974. 'The City and Industry: The Directors of Large Companies, Their Characteristics and Connections.' Pp. 65–80 in *Elites and Power in British Society*, edited by Philip Stanworth and Anthony

Giddens. London: Cambridge University Press.

Zeitlin, Maurice. 1974. 'Corporate Ownership and Control: the Large Corporation and the Capitalist Class.' *American Journal of Sociology* 74 (March): 1073–119.

—— Lynda Ann Ewen, and Richard Earl Ratcliff. 1974a. ' "New Princes" for Old? The Large Corporation and the Capitalist Class in Chile.' *American Journal of Sociology* 80 (July): 87–123.

——, Lynda Ann Ewen, and Richard Earl Ratcliff 1974b. 'The "Inner Group": Interlocking Directorates and the Internal Differentiation of the Capitalist Class in Chile.' Paper presented at the Annual Meeting of the American Sociological Association, August 27, at Montreal.

—— and Richard Earl Ratcliff. 1988. *Landlords & Capitalists: The Dominant Class of Chile*. Princeton, NJ: Princeton University Press.

3

Management control, exploitation, and profit maximization in the large corporation: an empirical confrontation of managerialism and class theory

What has the transformative impact of the large corporation been on capitalist development? Has it wrought, as managerial theory contends, a 'silent revolution' in which the managers of the large corporation usurp their capitalist predecessors and abolish the profit imperatives of capitalism, thereby establishing a new 'post-capitalist society'? Has it rendered a class theory in which the exploitative relationship between the owners of capital and formally free wage workers is central, inapplicable to the United States, England and other such ostensibly 'post-capitalist' societies? Can class theory no longer explain or provide a fruitful source of hypotheses concerning the production and division of the social product, class conflict, social domination, political processes, or historical change in these countries or does managerialism merely mystify the essence of the large corporation and obscure the most basic class relationship on which capitalism, 'advanced' or not, continues to rest? These are the originating questions of the present analysis.

Specifically, this study attempts to pose a direct empirical confrontation between certain crucial propositions of *a* class theory of contemporary capitalism and of the managerial theory of post-capitalist society on this paramount issue: does the accumulation of capital constitute the mainspring of the social process, even with the large corporation's decisive ascendance? To appropriately situate this empirical confrontation, the intellectual origins, basic propositions, and critical flaws of managerialism are outlined briefly and the central elements of our class theory of the large corporation are counterposed. Several quantitative analyses are then presented which are designed to replicate earlier studies of the relationship between management control and profit maximization. These are followed by a multiple regression analysis which includes not only the conventional econometric variables but also ones designed to measure a 'rate of exploitation.' The aim of this study, then, is to empirically test the validity of hypotheses derived from the theory that the production process under the reign of the large corporation is also inherently a process of the exploitation of labor by capital.

Remarkably, the theory of managerialism originated within 'Marxism' itself, in its revisionist variant, among such leading German Social Democratic theoreticians as Eduard Bernstein (1961) and Conrad Schmidt. Writing at the turn of the century, they theorized that the capitalist class was being replaced by an administrative stratum no longer devoted to the interests of property, and that the corporate form of large-scale production presaged and was an integral basis of the gradual alteration in the essence of capitalism. The capitalist class, said Schmidt, was undergoing a process of 'expropriation by stages.' The 'decomposition of capital' was leading to the gradual extension of the rights of 'sovereignty' over property to society as a whole. The capitalist was being transformed 'from a proprietor to a simple administrator.'[1]

The theory was later reconstituted in the United States by such 'new liberals' as Sumner Slichter (1931, pp. 81–4, 887) and, principally, Adolph Berle, Jr., and Gardiner C. Means, in their work, *The Modern Corporation and Private Property*. 'The dissolution of the atom of property,' Berle and Means wrote, 'destroys the very foundation on which the economic order of the past three centuries has rested' (1967, p. 8). Subsequently, the theory has been reincarnated in a variety of closely related formulations, the most recent and influential being John Kenneth Galbraith's notion, the 'new industrial state' (1971).

In the managerial model, much as in the neo-Marxian, the large corporation is at the economic center; however, not merely a new phase of capitalist development, but a veritable social metamorphosis is the result: a new 'corporate system' (Berle and Means 1967) founded on 'citizen enterprises' (Donnadieu 1975) in the 'post-capitalist society' (Dahrendorf 1959) is said to emerge. The 'separation of ownership and control' in the large corporation – which managerialists consider an 'incontrovertible' fact – has, they claimed, severed the connection between the family and private property in the means of production and torn up the roots of the class structure and political economy of capitalism; a new stratum of bureaucratic functionaries or a congeries of economic 'elites' in control of the new forms of productive property displaces the capitalist class and, with it, capitalism itself. The consequence, it is said, is the emergence of an occupational system based on individual achievement, in which 'statuses' are ordered in accordance with their functional importance. The essence of social domination is no longer class ownership of the means of production, and no class 'rules' in any sense, economically or politically. 'The decisive power in modern society,' in Galbraith's representative formulation, 'is exercised not by capital but by organization, not by the capitalist but by the industrial bureaucrat' (1971, p. xiv).

With this decomposition of capital and bureaucratization of enterprise, profit maximization no longer shapes the conduct of the large corporation. As Carl Kaysen avers, 'no longer the agent of proprietorship seeking to maximize return on investment, management sees itself as responsible to stockholders, employees, customers, the general public, and, perhaps most important, the firm itself as an institution' (1957, p. 313). Much as Berle and Means saw control of the large corporation devolving on 'a purely neutral technocracy, balancing a variety of claims by various groups in the community and assigning to each a portion of the income stream on the basis of public policy' (1967, pp. 312–13), Galbraith now finds the 'technostructure' in control of 'the heartland of the modern industrial system,' in which large corporations constitute the 'basic planning units.'

The result is that 'the classical class struggle at the center of our industrial life is a dwindling phenomenon. . . . Capitalist goals,' Galbraith explains, 'are sharply juxtaposed to those of labor. Both capitalist and worker want revenue; speaking broadly, both want the same revenue. This is a condition well calculated to induce conflict. With the passage of power to the corporate bureaucracy, to what I have called the technostructure, the conflict is a good deal less stark. In degree the technostructure has the choice between allocating revenue to stockholders and to labor.' Hence, the 'concern for profit maximization' disappears, says Galbraith (1970, p. 464; 1971, p. 121), and 'the primary structural emphasis,' as Talcott Parsons sums up the essence of managerialism, 'no longer falls on the orientation of capitalistic enterprise to profit and the theory of exploitation, but rather on the structure of occupational roles within the system of industrial society' (1954, p. 324).

Class Theory of the Large Corporation

The central illusion of managerialism derives from a teleology of bureaucratic imperatives: bureaucratization is implicitly assumed to be an inexorable historical process before whose advance even the capitalist class has fallen. Class theory, in contrast, reveals the contradictory class relations beneath the veiling appearances of the large corporation: the extraction and appropriation of the surplus product of labor, albeit mediated by complex bureaucratic forms, remains the essence of the entire productive process. If the ascendance of the large corporation has meant the dissociation between ownership of capital and actual direction of production, capital retains control of the productive process as a whole, on three levels: (a) the large corporation continues to be controlled by ownership interests, despite their management by functionaries who may themselves be propertyless; (b) whatever the situation within any given large corporation, the 'owners' and 'managers' of the large corporations, taken as a whole, are merely elements of the same more or less unified social class; and (c) the conduct of the large corporation is largely determined by the imperatives of capital accumulation. Briefly put, the reasoning behind these propositions is as follows:

1 Managerialism is based on a conceptual conflation of ownership, control, and administration of capital, and the consequent 'empirical' illusion that control and administration are identical. It confuses (a) the existence of an extensive administrative apparatus in the large corporation, in which the proportion of managerial positions held by members of the principal proprietary families may well be negligible, and (b) the locus of control over that apparatus. If the varied functions of capital that were once largely united in the person of the individual capitalist are now institutionalized and split up among various bureaucratic roles and interdependent offices in the large corporation, control over that apparatus remains extrabureaucratic, and resides with capital.

'Control' refers here to the ability of a given proprietary interest to realize its corporate objectives over time, despite resistance; and this depends on the corporation's concrete structure of ownership and the constellation of intercorporate relationships in which it is involved. Control can certainly be exerted without the official presence of principal owners of capital within 'management' itself, by virtue of their ownership of the corporation's critical minority holdings, or specific financial arrangements. An individual's or group's capacity for control of any specific corporation varies with the number of other large corporations (including banks and other financial institutions) in which it has a dominant if not controlling position. The same proportion of stock may have a qualitatively different significance for a principal capitalist family whose sphere of influence radiates out among several large corporations and banks compared with a single individual who has no other institutions or resources to buttress his position.

Empirically, such connections and critical holdings tend to be invisible to the uninformed eye – and even to the careful researcher. Even the staffs at *Forbes*, *Fortune*, and *Business Week* rely heavily on gossip to estimate the holdings of even 'well-known' families in specific corporations in the United States, because the latter's holdings are hidden in a welter of brokers, dealers, foundations, street names, nominees, holding companies, and associates, as well as by a web of kinship that binds apparently unrelated individuals into cohesive owning units for the purposes of control. Even a subcommittee of the US Senate Committee on Government Operations tried for several years without success to penetrate the secrecy hiding corporate ownership, leading the senator chairing it to exclaim that the use of nominees results in a 'massive coverup' of the real principal owners and centers of control in large American corporations (US Congress 1974, p. 3).

Thus, the managerial notion of the separation of ownership and control within the large corporation scarcely has evidential support. Rather, it is almost certainly a 'pseudofact,' the result of persuasion by the deception of appearances. (See Zeitlin (1974, 1976), reprinted as chapters 1 and 2 in this volume, for a systematic review of the discrepant findings of numerous studies and of critical problems of method and measurement concerning the question.) Even the widely cited but seldom read work of Berle and Means (1967), it turns out, was based on information allowing them to classify as definitely under management control only 22 percent of the 200 largest corporations, and of the 106 industrials, only 3.8 percent! Recently, moreover, an outstanding research work, utilizing publicly available 'inside information' that appeared in the various business journals and financial press over several years, concluded, contrary to the ontological assumptions of managerialism, that the vast majority, or 60 percent, of the 500 largest industrial corporations in the United States are under 'possible' (64) or 'probable' (236) family control (Burch 1972, pp. 36ff.; 106ff.). Full access to the critical data would probably reveal a specific proprietary locus of control in the other corporations as well.

2   The heads of the largest corporations are the principal functionaries of capital. They occupy the command posts in the country's decisive units of production; and their personal careers, interests, and commitments are intricately bound up with the expansion of corporate capital. Although not typically among the principal shareowners in the corporations they direct, many are; and most own significant blocks of stock whose absolute combined worth not only constitutes a primary source of their income but also places them among the major owners of capital in the population. Typically, whatever the country in question, they move in the same more or less intimate social milieu as the principal owners of capital. A variety of specific institutions, from debutante balls to select social clubs, summer resorts and winter retreats, and assorted watering places, as well as the 'proper' schools and colleges (fraternities, sororities, and 'living groups'), assure their families' commingling and psychological compatibility, and sense of social solidarity – and therefore differential propensity to intermarry. The families of the officers, directors, and principal owners of capital in the largest corporations, therefore, are probably integrated both by intimate social ties and a complex pattern of entangling kinship relations into the same social class.

Thus, even were certain banks and corporations to become so large that they were not ordinarily under the control of specific minority ownership interests, it would not mean that power had passed to the 'new princes' of the managerial realm. Although large corporations (and banks) might conceivably develop a relative autonomy from particular proprietary interests, their autonomy would be limited by the general proprietary interests of capital. The large corporations are units in a class-controlled apparatus of private appropriation; and the whole gamut of principal functionaries and owners of capital – bound together by an ensemble of social relations, concrete interests, and overriding commitments – participate in varying degree, and as members of the same dominant class, in its direction.

3   Even if 'management' were in control of the large corporation, it would be compelled to engage in a 'systematic temporal search for highest practicable profits' (Earley 1957, pp. 333–5; 1956). The conduct of the large corporation is largely shaped by objective necessities and systemic imperatives inherent in the accumulation of capital, and varies with the nature of its investments, competitive relationships (now fundamentally global rather than national), and labor force. Growth, sales, technical efficiency, and a strong competitive position are at once inseparable managerial goals and the determinants of high corporate profits – which, in turn, are the determinants of high managerial income and status (Alchian 1968; Larner 1970). Whatever its motivations, management's decisions on the planning and organization of production and on pricing and sales must be measured against and not imperil corporate profitability. Significant deviation from profit maximization also would lead to the lowering of the market price of the corporation's stock and the constriction of its capital base, and make it an attractive and vulnerable target for takeover – and the displacement of the incumbent management (Manne 1965). Especially with the centralization of investment among a few large bank trust departments (in the United States, they manage assets greater than the assets of the 100 largest corporations (Lybecker 1973, p. 99)), which administer the personal capital of the wealthiest investors, far-reaching negative reverberations would result for a corporation whose management provided a lower rate of return than others. In addition, 'professional' management, particularly the use of 'scientific budgetary planning' and the emphasis on the 'time-value of money,' may strengthen rather than weaken the drive toward profit maximization (Earley 1956, 1957; Earley and Carleton 1962; Tanzer 1969, pp. 32–4). Thus, whether or not managers are actuated by the 'profit motive,' as a subjective intention or goal, corporations must seek the highest practicable profits because profits are both the only unambiguous criterion of successful managerial performance and the irreducible necessity for corporate survival.

To sum up, in contrast to the managerialist metamorphosis of the large corporation into the basic planning unit of the new post-capitalist society, class theory maintains that the large corporation is fundamentally a class-owned and class–controlled form of social capital that both administers production and commands labor in order to enforce the extraction of labor's surplus product, which, in turn, is appropriated by private capital. A full empirical confrontation between these theories of the large corporation, as our discussion indicates, would involve testing a complex set of interrelated hypotheses. Nonetheless, two hypotheses are central: (a) if there are real qualitative differences between corporations controlled by 'managements' (or technostructures) compared with ones controlled by owners, then there should also be significant quantitative differences in their actual rates of profit; and, above all, (b) if class ownership of the means of production and the appropriation of labor's surplus product remains the essence of social domination under advanced capitalism, then the rate of profit of large industrial corporations should vary primarily with the rate of exploitation.

'Management Control' and Profit Maximization

The oft-repeated managerialist thesis on profit maximization was not investigated empirically until recently; a number of econometric analyses have now attempted to gauge the effects of putative management versus ownership control on the profit performance of large American corporations. Using mainly proxy reports and official government Securities and Exchange Commission files, these studies have classified firms under management control if less than an arbitrarily specified percentage of the stock was visibly held by an individual, family, or group of identifiable associates (usually 10 percent is the cut-off); then the rate of return on 'invested capital' (or 'stockholders' equity') was simultaneously related to a number of variables deemed important determinants of profit performance in conventional economics, in order to see how the effects of these variables compared with the effects of different types of corporate control. The most sophisticated of these analyses, by Robert Larner (1970), using multiple regression analysis and taking into account assets, industrial concentration, official indices of economy-wide growth and fluctuation of profit rates, and equity–asset ratios, found that among the 500 largest nonfinancial corporations in the United States in 1963 the putatively management- and owner-controlled firms earned just about the same profit rate. In contrast, John Palmer (1973), using essentially the same methods of classification of types of control as Larner, also took into account three levels of 'monopoly power' (a weighted average of the barriers to entry (BTEs) in the industries in which a firm operated). By an analysis of variance, he found that the average rate of return on net worth was significantly lower for management-controlled firms than for owner-controlled firms among those with a high degree of monopoly power. Palmer interpreted these findings to mean that managers operate 'under two constraints – one from stockholders and one from competition in the market. Only if both constraints are very weak would one expect a significant divergence from profit-maximizing behavior, as was observed' (1973, pp. 298–9). Two other quantitative studies, one by Kamerschen (1968) and the other by Monsen et al. (1968), also resulted in conflicting findings: the first found no significant difference in the profit performance of management-controlled versus owner-controlled firms, and the second found higher profit rates among the latter.

An examination of these quantitative analyses indicates at least three important deficiencies, which future studies must remedy. First and foremost, similar superficial sources of information and residual definitional categories of classification of types of control cannot be used. There is little reason to believe, as we have emphasized, that firms are genuinely under 'management control' simply because no easily recognizable substantial proprietary interest appears in the data of official files or proxy reports. Second, the impact on the rate of return of the market structure and the firm's competitive position *vis-a-vis* other firms in the industry has to be taken into account (or 'held constant'). Third (following from the previous point), the analysis has to allow possible interaction effects between type of control and market power, and not merely assume additive effects for each.

In what follows, we present the results of a number of quantitative analyses intended to remedy these defects, based on the analysis of data on the 300 largest US industrial corporations of 1964. These we classified into the types of control revealed by Philip Burch, who can be credited with far more reliable and valid methods of investigation and results than any previous studies of corporate control in the United States. We did a separate analysis of variance, paralleling Palmer's, and a multiple regression analysis, paralleling Larner's (based on an earlier Hall and Weiss (1967) model), with seven main independent variables and the rate of return on stockholders' equity in 1964 as the dependent variable. The multiple regression model is based on typical assumptions in conventional economics – the so-called 'neoclassicist synthesis' – and includes measures for the firm's type of control, size, equity–asset ratio (as an indicator of risk incurred by stockholders), monopoly power, and 'leading-firm group' (to tap the effect of the combined relative market shares of the other leading firms in the industries in which the firm operates), growth, and a specific variable to measure the interaction effect of management control and high monopoly power. The same analysis was also done using Palmer's classification of firms by type of control, so as to replicate his analysis.

The results of these analyses do not provide support for the profits hypothesis derived from managerial theory. In detail, our findings are as follows.

Palmer, as we noted earlier, found that among firms with high monopoly power (i.e. firms located in industries with high BTEs), the putatively management-controlled firms had lower rates of return than did owner-controlled firms. He found the difference to be statistically significant (at the 0.05 level) when he compared the 'high monopoly' firms that were management controlled with those that were 'strong-owner' controlled, or when he compared the former with both classes of owner control (i.e. weak and strong owner) grouped together; the difference was not significant when he compared the management and weak-owner-controlled firms alone.

To replicate the crucial part of Palmer's analysis, 291 of the 300 firms in our universe for which data were available were classified according to Palmer's measures of 'type of control' and 'degree of monopoly power.' The results of this cross-tabulation appear in table 3.1, which gives the average rates of return of the firms in each category for 1964. It is important to note (and a point to which we shall return) that the rates of return seem to rise systematically with the height of BTEs, averaging 10.26 percent for the low BTE firms, 11.79 percent for the medium BTE firms, and 13.40 percent for the high BTE firms. No simple linear pattern seems to exist in the average rates of return across categories of control. To relate these findings to those of Palmer, the reader should focus especially on the top row of table 3.1. Of the 62 firms that were located in industries with high BTEs, the 48 putatively management-controlled firms averaged a 12.81 percent rate of return, which appears to be considerably lower than the 16.35 percent average return of the eight weak-owner firms, and also lower than the 14.17 percent average of the six strong-owner firms. However, an analysis of variance showed that these differences are not statistically significant at the 0.05 level.

Table 3.1 *Average reported rates of return, by Palmer's type of control and height of barriers to entry (number of firms in each category in parentheses)*

	Palmer's type of control			
Palmer's barriers to entry (monopoly power)	Management control	Weak-owner control	Strong-owner control	Total
High barriers	12.81 (48)	16.35 (8)	14.17 (6)	13.40 (62)
Medium barriers	11.56 (101)	13.52 (26)	10.80 (22)	11.79 (149)
Low barriers	10.29 (54)	10.41 (12)	10.01 (14)	10.26 (80)
Total	11.52 (203)	13.20 (46)	11.01 (42)	11.71 (291)

$\chi^2 = 2.79$ with four degrees of freedom.

Table 3.2 *Comparisons of average reported rates of return for different types of control, among firms located in industries with high barriers to entry*

Comparison	Mean difference	t value	Degrees of freedom	Significance probability
Management vs. weak owner	3.54	1.604	59	0.1141
Management vs. strong owner	1.35	0.541	59	0.5903
Management vs. all owners	2.60	1.489	50	0.1416

As the results reported in table 3.2 show, neither the comparison between management-controlled firms and each of the two categories of owner-controlled firms, nor that between the former and the two latter taken together, turned out to be statistically significant. (That is, there is more than 5 percent likelihood that differences such as those that were found could have been observed by chance.)

A number of reasons might account for the difference between our findings and Palmer's. First, Palmer's sample consisted of the leading 500 corporations of 1965, while the sample for the present study consisted of the leading 300 of 1964. As the absolute magnitudes of the difference in rates of return were comparable in the two studies, the larger size of Palmer's sample might itself be sufficient to produce a statistically significant result. Second, the dependent variable of Palmer's study was the average rate of return from 1961 to 1969, while our study uses only the rate of return for 1964 as the dependent variable. Palmer's results may therefore be more reliable on this score. On the other hand, it has to be emphasized that Palmer's measure of the type of corporate control is probably neither valid nor reliable. In any event, our replication raises serious doubts about the validity and reliability of Palmer's findings. It certainly indicates the need to utilize a more sophisticated model than Palmer's in any subsequent analysis of the impact of type of control on the profit rates of large corporations.

One final point should be made, however, before proceeding to such an analysis. We cross-tabulated the 292 firms on which we had data by Palmer's and Burch's classifications of types of control and compared the average rate of return on shareholders' equity in each resulting type. The critical comparisons, of course, are between the 'pure' cases, i.e. those firms which fall into the category of 'management control' by both Palmer's and Burch's measures compared with those which are owner or family controlled according to both classifications. For the 115 firms considered to be under management control by both Palmer and Burch, the rate of return is 12.02 percent. For the 42 firms considered under 'strong-owner control' and 'probably family control' by Palmer and Burch, respectively, the rate of return is 11.01 percent. There were also another 40 firms which fell in Palmer's category of 'weak-owner control' and Burch's 'possibly family control,' for which the rate of return is 13.5 percent. These findings, therefore, also reveal no consistent or significant difference in the profit performance of large industrial corporations which are allegedly under different types of control.

A Multiple Regression Analysis of Type of Control and Profit Performance

Our multiple-regression analysis uses data on the top 300 industrial corporations of 1964; the model utilizes variables drawn from conventional economics and managerial theory. It may be stated as follows:

$$RR = a + b_1M + b_2S + b_3R + b_4HMP + b_5GP + b_6GRO + b_7M.HMP + e_1$$

where,

RR is the rate of return on shareholder's equity, 1964
M is management control (dummy variable; Burch or Palmer to be indicated)
S (size) is the inverse logarithm of assets
R (risk) is the equity–asset ratio
HMP is high monopoly power (dummy variable)
GP (leading-firm group) is the combined market shares of the other firms in the leading firm group
GRO (growth) is the percent change in total sales from 1955 to 1964
M·HMP is an interaction dummy variable for Burch or Palmer, as indicated (management control and high monopoly power)

A detailed description of how each variable was measured appears in the appendix. The model is discussed in greater detail below, in connection with the question of measuring the rate of exploitation.

According to the predictions of these theories, regression coefficients b_1, b_2, b_3 and b_7 should be expected to be negative, b_4 and b_6 should be positive, and b_5 might be either negative or positive, depending on one's reasoning.

The results are reported in table 3.3. The four separate equations were needed to test the main and interaction effects of each of the two measures of management control. Thus, equation (3.1) includes Burch's management control variable; equation (3.2) includes this as well as an interaction variable between it and a measure of high monopoly power; equation (3.3) uses Palmer's measure of management control; and equation (3.4) reports the results for the latter and its interaction variable. Results reported in this table were computed by replacing missing data with a means algorithm.

These regression findings are not consistent with the profits hypothesis of managerial theory. The regression coefficients for Burch's measure of management control (which, for reasons noted above, is probably far more valid than Palmer's) are very small and positive; those for Palmer's measure are small and negative. None

Table 3.3 *Management control and the rate of return in the 300 largest industrial corporations in the United States, 1964[a]*

Variable	Equations			
	(3.1)	(3.2)	(3.3)	(3.4)
Management control (M, Burch)	0.068[b] (1.2384)[d] 0.7051[c]	0.061 0.6339 (1.0701)		
Management control (M, Palmer)			−0.058 −0.6744 (−1.0494)	−0.043 −0.4983 (−0.7444)
Inverse log of assets (S)	0.008 0.6692 (0.1442)	0.008 0.6890 (0.1483)	−0.029 −2.5073 (−0.5203)	−0.032 −2.7726 (0.7924)
Equity–asset ratio (R)	0.033 1.2861 (0.5859)	0.035 1.3398 (0.6085)	0.048 1.8952 (0.8392)	0.045 1.7921 (0.7924)
High monopoly power dummy (HMP)	0.268 5.5795 (4.8649)	0.246 5.1188 (3.3003)	0.260 5.5564 (4.7128)	0.333 7.1064 (3.5083)
Leading-firm group (GP)	−0.095 −3.6558 (−1.7159)	−0.093 −3.5912 (−1.6793)	−0.092 −3.6447 (−1.6619)	−0.102 −4.0546 (−1.8131)

	(1)	(1)	(2)	(2)	(3)	(3)	(4)	(4)
Growth (GRO)	0.192	−0.3229 (3.3910)	0.191	0.3221 (3.3773)	0.196	0.3394 (3.4668)	0.195	0.3379 (3.4512)
Interaction dummy (M, Burch × HMP)			0.034	0.9741 (0.4419)				
Interaction dummy (M, Palmer × HMP)							−0.090	−2.3013 (−0.9412)
Constant		10.3572 (4.0152)		10.3211 (3.9938)		12.2005 (4.5262)		12.4113 (4.5877)
Coefficient of multiple determination (R^2)	0.1297		0.1303		0.1260		0.1286	
Corrected coefficient of multiple determination ($\bar{R}^2$)	0.1119		0.1094		0.1081		0.1077	

[a] Missing data replaced with means algorithm.
[b] Standardized regression coefficient.
[c] Unstandardized regression coefficient.
[d] t ratio.

of the coefficients, whether for the main effects or for the interactions with high monopoly power, are statistically significant at the 0.05 level. Nor does the addition of the interaction variable to either 'main effects' equation add to the proportion of variation in rate of return accounted for by the respective equations. On the basis of these findings, it has to be concluded that so-called management control has no measurable effect on the rate of return of the large corporation. Nor is there any discernible impact on the rate of return which is attributable to the interaction effect of monopoly power and management control.

The foregoing regression analyses account for some 12 or 13 percent of the variation in the rate of return. Most of this is attributable to the effects of two variables: high monopoly power and the growth of the firm over the previous decade. Having a high degree of monopoly power (i.e. with high BTEs in the industry and a weighted average market share for the firm of 25 percent or more) in particular allows firms to enjoy a more than 5 percent higher average rate of return than firms which lack this degree of monopoly power. This positive relationship agrees with those found by Shepherd (1972, 1975), Gale (1972) and – though they used concentration ratios as measures of market power – Hall and Weiss (1967). (The positive regression coefficient for the concentration ratio in Larner's analysis was not statistically significant at the 0.05 level (1970, p. 30)). None of the remaining variables show any statistically significant relationship to the rate of return. With the data used for this study, firm size, risk, and the combined market shares of the other leading firms show no significant relationship to a firm's rate of return.

Accounting for about one-eighth of the variation in the dependent variable is not a notable achievement, particularly in a cross-sectional analysis using data of this type. Although these findings do support one of the cardinal hypotheses of oligopoly theory – that relative monopoly power enables a firm to achieve a higher rate of return than others – the relationship is quite disappointing if the aim is to adequately comprehend the differences in the rate of return among different firms. Of course, this may be the result of inadequacies in the construction of the variables themselves. But in comparison with previous empirical analyses of these hypothesized relationships, the measures used here appear equally valid and reliable (and in the case of the management control variable, far more valid than any used in previous studies). In fact, the fault may lie not with the measures, but with the basic theory from which the hypotheses have been derived. Managerial theory is simply wrong; and even conventional oligopoly theory is quite incomplete. The question is, can categories and measures informed by Marx's theory of exploitation significantly improve our understanding and prediction of profitability in the large corporation?

Measuring the Rate of Exploitation

Exploitation, i.e. the extraction and appropriation of the 'surplus labor' or 'surplus product' of the direct producers by the dominant class, takes profoundly different historical forms in precapitalist and capitalist modes of production. Under capitalism, the relationship between 'necessary labor' and 'surplus labor' is mediated by the commodity form, and the surplus product appears as 'surplus value,' i.e. the 'mere congelation of surplus labor-time, . . . materialized surplus labor.' Thus, surplus value is the difference between the socially necessary labor time embodied in the commodities produced by the workers and that embodied in their wages (variable capital). The ratio of surplus value to variable capital is defined as the rate of exploitation (Marx 1967, vol. 1, ch. 9 *passim*, especially pp. 217–20; also ch. 10, especially sec. 2). It is this ratio which is the most condensed expression of capitalism's primary class relationship and of the production process as a whole; for the production process is simultaneously a process of appropriation by capital of the labor power of, and consequently the surplus value produced by, the working class. The rate of exploitation is the underlying source of the rate of profit. But, as Marx put it, 'the conditions of direct exploitation and those of the realization of surplus value are not identical.' Its realization is limited 'by the proportional relations of the various lines of production and by the consuming power of society,' which is 'based on antagonistic conditions of distribution' and 'restricted by the tendency to accumulate.' Thus, the rate of exploitation and the actual rate of profit cannot be identical. Furthermore, if 'the rate of profit is no mystery, so soon as we know the laws of surplus value,' the second critical determinant of the rate of profit is the 'organic composition of capital': the ratio of the socially necessary labor time embodied in the means of production used by labor in the productive process (constant capital) to that embodied in wage goods (variable capital).

Marx represented the rate of surplus value as s/v; the organic composition of capital as c/v; and the rate of profit as $s/(c+v)$. Logically then, as a simple algebraic manipulation familiar to students of Marx's theory shows, the rate of profit ought to vary directly with the rate of exploitation and inversely with the organic composition of capital:

$$\frac{s}{c+v} = \frac{\dfrac{s}{v}}{\dfrac{c+v}{v}} = \frac{\dfrac{s}{v}}{\dfrac{c}{v}+\dfrac{v}{v}} = \frac{\dfrac{s}{v}}{\dfrac{c}{v}+1}$$

$$= \frac{\text{rate of surplus value}}{\text{organic composition of capital} + 1}$$

The question is, can we 'really' measure the rate of surplus value and submit this logical deduction from Marx's theory to a genuine empirical test? For some so-called 'Marxists,' the mere posing of this question already indicates that Marx's theory has suffered an 'empiricist' contamination. This notion we reject as contrary to Marx's own example, and his methodological precept of 'rising from the abstract to the concrete as the only way in which thought appropriates the concrete' (1970, p. 101). If 'Marxian categories are not just ideas,' as Geoff Hodgson correctly argues, but '. . . correspond to real relations and parameters in the capitalist system' (1974, p. 70), then hypotheses using these categories must be amenable to verification. No doubt 'conventional statistics are not always well suited' to test such hypotheses because their 'conceptual basis' differs (Rowthorn 1976, p. 65). Without an effort to devise empirical indicators for that purpose, however, Marxian 'theory' will be merely the peculiar form of radical neoscholasticism it has already become in some hands.

Several methodological problems are involved in attempting to devise an empirical measure of the rate of exploitation and to gauge its impact on the rate of profit. Conceptually, two problems present themselves immediately. First, Marx was trying to demonstrate how the 'law of value' was both the basis of exchange relations between commodities and determined the production and division of the social product under capitalism. Throughout, therefore, Marx's principal categories are expressed in 'value' terms rather than in 'price' terms, i.e. in terms of what he called 'abstract labor,' or units of homogeneous unskilled labor time. For Marx, 'labor is the substance and the immanent measure of value.' Thus, to measure the rate of exploitation, it would be necessary to find data which approximate his concept of 'socially necessary labor time.' Second, there is the distinction between 'productive' and 'unproductive' labor.[2] Theoretically, under capitalism only labor that functions in the sphere of production and directly creates surplus value (or capital) is productive. In contrast, labor involved in the circulation of capital, i.e. in the mere formal transfer of rights of ownership of the product from one person to another, or in the 'realization' of value already produced, is 'unproductive.' Yet in the concrete labor carried out in the process of circulation, there are intermixed 'real functions' which actually enhance the value of the product, such as storage, preservation, packing, transport, etc. How, then, can these real and formal functions, and therewith productive and unproductive labor, be separated not merely conceptually but in actual empirical analysis?

To approximate a solution to the first problem of measurement, we sought data that would permit figures on production and on wages and salaries to be expressed in terms of some common unit of expenditure of social labor time in the production process. Marx himself often employed the concept, 'the collective working-day.' This he defined as 'the number of workmen simultaneously employed' by the same capitalist multiplied by the number of hours in 'the working-day of each individual' employed. 'For example, let the working-day of each individual be 12 hours. Then the collective working-day of twelve men simultaneously employed, consists of 144 hours' (1967, vol. 1, p. 323). This, it seems to us, is essentially an adumbration of the now common unit of measure of labor time in production used in censuses of production in the United States and other advanced capitalist countries, namely, 'production worker manhours.' From a publication of the US Department of Commerce (1971), we were able to obtain systematic data for each major industry (categorized by the four-digit Standard Industrial Classification, SIC) on total annual production worker manhours, in terms of which the following are stated: total annual wages of 'production workers'; total annual payroll for 'all employees on the payroll of operating manufacturing establishments [including] . . . salaries of officers of these establishments, if a corporation, [but excluding] . . . payments to the proprietor or partners, if an unincorporated concern'; and 'value added in production.' The derivation of a rate of exploitation from these figures is discussed in a moment.

To the second problem of measurement of 'productive' versus 'unproductive' labor, our solution is rather to circumvent than to solve. The problem is less insurmountable, given the objectives of our analysis, than if we were attempting to operate on the level of the system as a whole, where the increased significance of employment in the 'public' sector, and of the myriads of commercial and financial employees, especially complicates distinguishing between productive and unproductive labor. Our analysis is confined to manufacturing industries, where labor may be assumed to be predominantly productive. True, as Gillman (1957) and Baran and Sweezy (1966) have persuasively argued, the 'sales effort' has penetrated ever more deeply into industrial production itself under advanced capitalism; therefore, even a portion of the labor time of 'production workers' is probably, from a formal point of view, 'unproductive,' and such wages would properly have to be deducted from the total wage bill and added to the category of surplus value. Similarly, a portion of the salaries of engineers, scientists, production managers, designers, etc., whose 'real functions' are productive would have to be added to the wages of production workers to constitute the sum of variable capital. On the other hand, the salaries of top corporate executives are probably more accurately considered as part of surplus value than of variable capital. Since doing such additions and subtractions is impossible with the data now available, our practical solution, for this particular analysis, has been to construct two different rates of exploitation, one utilizing the wages of production workers and the other the payroll of all employees in 'operating manufacturing establishments.' An accurate estimate of the bearing of 'the' rate of exploitation on the rate of return probably lies somewhere between the results obtained using the two different measures. Hence, both sets of results are reported below.

Our procedure for measuring *a* rate of exploitation is as follows. 'True value added in production' is the academic economics term for 'exactly the sum of . . . [a firm's] wage, interest, rent and profit costs' (Samuelson 1961, p. 217). Therefore, assuming that in each industry 'value added per production worker manhour' equals $s+v$ per manhour; and that wages per production worker manhour (or – separately – payroll of manufacturing employees per manhour) equals v per manhour, then

$$\frac{\text{value added per production worker manhour}}{\text{minus wages per production worker manhour}} = \frac{(s+v)-v}{v} = \frac{s}{v}$$

We do not think that this procedure provides us with a measure of *the* 'real' rate of surplus value. But we do consider that, for the analytical– empirical purposes at hand, it allows a first approximation to measuring *a* rate of exploitation of workers employed by the largest US industrial corporations. Also, our data are expressed in price units rather than value units, but our measure is, at least, consistent with Marx's concepts.

In any attempt to measure the effect of the rate of exploitation on the rate of profit, the effect of the organic composition of capital also has to be considered. This problem we also propose to circumvent rather than try to solve – in a manner similar to Marx's own procedure. Although Marx surely knew that the extent to which labor uses materials and machinery in the productive process varies considerably from industry to industry in which entirely different commodities are produced by entirely different methods, he ignored (or abstracted from) these differences in the first two volumes of *Capital*. By assuming the organic composition of capital to be constant (or 'equal to zero') (1967, vol. 1, pp. 213–18), this allowed him to fully explore the logic of his basic propositions that commodities exchange at their values and the rate of exploitation primarily governs the rate of profit. Accordingly, even if an adequate measure of the organic composition of capital were available (which it is not, because data on depreciation for each industry are not available, and depreciation statements themselves are notoriously unreliable), this variable would have to be held constant in the empirical analysis. As a very crude surrogate for the organic composition of capital, we introduced into our equations the 'book value of assets per employee' in each industry. This certainly is not anything more than a rough indirect indicator of the ratio of constant to variable capital within each industry.[3] For our present purposes, however, it should suffice, since we are not trying to ascertain this ratio's effect on the rate of profit but only to use it as a means of holding c/v constant, as it were, so as to measure the independent effect of the rate of exploitation. Note also that assigning this particular industry characteristic to the individual firms within it poses no special conceptual problem, since the largest firms within the same industry do probably tend, in fact, to have the same organic composition of capital.[4]

Assigning to the individual firms in an industry the aggregate rate of surplus value in that industry also is probably a valid simplifying assumption. In any case, it is a necessary procedure because appropriate data are not available for individual firms. The extent of unionization of the various large firms within the same industry probably is sufficiently alike, and the relative mobility of labor between them sufficiently high, to justify this procedure.

Another empirical problem, though, is how to assign some firms to a specific industry, given the wide-ranging diversification and conglomeration now characteristic of the largest firms. We assigned each firm to the specific four-digit SIC 'industry' in which the highest percentage of its domestic manufacturing employees are located. Some firms are so diversified, however, that even using the industry in which the highest proportion of a firm's manufacturing employees is located to assign it to that industry may be inaccurate and misleading, because that figure may actually represent only a minor percentage of its total domestic manufacturing employees. Since many of the largest firms are also multinationals, whose phases of production actually cut across geographical boundaries, it may be surmised that this even further complicates matters.

To find out whether or not our procedure might be misleading, we took the group of 106 firms among the top 300 that had at least half of their domestic manufacturing employees in the four-digit SIC to which they were assigned, and ran the regression equations, whose results are about to be reported, on this subsample alone; similarly, we also ran these equations on a subsample of the 57 firms that had at least half of their worldwide employees in the four-digit SIC to which they were assigned. In both runs, in fact, the coefficients for the two measures of a rate of exploitation, and the proportion of the total variation in the rate of return accounted for, were higher than those to be reported for the entire population of firms.[5] If anything then, it could be argued that our method of assigning firms to industries probably underestimates the strength of the real relationship investigated here.

Given the conceptual and empirical difficulties discussed, we want to emphasize again that the measure of a rate of exploitation constructed for the present analysis is a reasonable approximation rather than a precise measure of *the* 'real' rate of surplus value. The task of such measurement is considered 'well nigh impossible' by some theorists, because of the 'practical difficulties involved' (Yaffe 1973, p. 50). We claim only that we constructed our empirical measure with the maximum feasible fidelity to Marx's original concepts, given the types of data available. This is, after all, a virtually unprecedented effort not only to measure the rate of exploitation of industrial workers, but also to analyze its effect on the rate of profit of the largest corporations in an advanced capitalist country, while simultaneously taking into account several other theoretically relevant variables; so it is to be hoped that any criticism of the present empirical analysis will aim at replicating it by improved methods.[6]

Finally, it also should be emphasized that no attempt has been made here to devise a measure of the theoretical rate of profit defined by Marx in his formula $s/(c+v)$. Instead, the 'rate of return on shareholders' equity' (or on 'invested capital') is the dependent variable utilized in the regression equations. It is a measure found acceptable and used by some Marxian economists in their analyses. For instance, Paul Bullock and David Yaffe (1975, p. 12), having questionably asserted that 'the rate of profit in the Marxist sense cannot be measured,' employ this rate of return as an index. Similarly, Robert Rowthorn (1976, p. 71) specifically refers to the rate of return on shareholders' equity as an indicator of the share of surplus value received by industrial capital.

The two main theoretically relevant independent variables in our final multivariate model, then, are 'management control' and 'rate of exploitation.' Through them managerialism and a class theory of exploitation symbolically confront each other empirically, by an assessment of the simultaneous impact of these independent variables on the dependent variable, the rate of return on shareholders' equity. Several other independent variables are also included in the model, either because they are important variables that, from some relevant theoretical standpoint, should be held constant in the analysis of the impact of the main structural variables, e.g. the assets–employee ratio or 'organic composition of capital,' or because the findings of previous econometric analyses show, and/or neoclassical or Marxian economics predicts, that they directly affect profitability. Of the latter, two variables in particular, namely, growth and monopoly power, have quite different predictable effects on the rate of return from the standpoint of contemporary managerialism as opposed to both conventional neoclassical and Marxian economic theory.

Paul M. Sweezy argues that monopoly power indirectly redistributes surplus value through monopoly pricing and the consequent deduction from the profit of other capitalists and/or, to the extent that the commodities with monopoly prices are consumed by the working class, by a deduction from the workers' real wages. Hence, 'the equal profit rates of competitive capitalism are turned into a hierarchy of profit rates,' in Sweezy's words, 'highest in the most completely monopolized industries, lowest in the most competitive' (1956, pp. 272–4, 285). More or less the same argument has been made by oligopoly theorists. 'Where there are few sellers and high entry barriers,' as Willard F. Mueller explains, 'the price leaders may set prices that yield a monopoly return,' at the expense of either 'consumers' or 'weaker competitors' (1970, pp. 86–90; 97–101; also see Hall and Weiss 1967; and Shepherd 1975).

In contrast, contemporary managerialists either dismiss or ignore the problem of monopoly power. It is considered of no great consequence because of the supposed shift of corporate control from capital to bureaucracy or 'organized intelligence.' Guided by 'satisficing' (Simon 1962) rather than profit-maximizing principles, the market power of the large corporation is used merely to minimize uncertainty and unreliability of markets so as to maximize technical efficiency and 'effective planning.' With the passage of power to the technostructure, it is doubtful, says Galbraith, that firms which have 'the power commonly associated with monopoly . . . will seek as large a profit as possible,' since profit maximization is not the technostructure's 'goal.' In any event, 'consumers do not seriously complain of exploitation' by large firms that have 'the market power associated with monopoly' (1971, pp. 76, 110–11). Thus, if both a class theory of the large corporation and conventional oligopoly theory predict that relative monopoly power should increase a given large corporation's rate of return, contemporary managerialism predicts no association between these variables.

As to 'growth,' the managerialist thesis is that it takes priority over profits as a managerial goal, because it both minimizes risk and maximizes firm size and, thereby, the power and prestige of management itself (Baumol 1959; Marris 1964). The Galbraithian variant is that growth is the primary goal of the technostructure because 'expansion of output means expansion of the technostructure itself.' In either case, so Galbraith says, 'business is being taken, not for its profit, but "to hold the organization together"' (1971, pp. 171, 173). It follows, therefore, that quantitative analysis should reveal no association or even an inverse association between the rates of growth and return. In contrast, if our argument is correct that growth is, in fact, not merely a managerial 'goal' but an objective determinant of high corporate profits, then there should be a direct association between it and the rate of return. In particular, if growth were equivalent to internal accumulation of capital, it would be closely associated with the rate of profit. However, in practice expansion also can occur through acquisitions and mergers, as well as through pricing tactics that sacrifice immediate profits so as to assure market security and long-term profit stability. Therefore, growth and the rate of return may be only weakly associated at any given time, if these aspects of growth are not distinguished in the analysis – and they are not in ours. The final model, then, stands as follows:

$$RR = a_0 + b_1M + b_2S + b_3R + b_4HMP + b_5GP + b_6GRO + b_7(s/v) + b_8(c/v) + e_2$$

Where:

RR is the rate of return on shareholders' equity, 1964
M is management control (dummy variable, Burch)
S (size) is the inverse logarithm of assets
R (risk) is the equity–asset ratio
HMP is high monopoly power (dummy variable)
GP (leading firm group) is the combined market shares of the other
    firms in leading-firm group
GRO (growth) is the percent change in total sales from 1955 to 1964
s/v is 'rate of exploitation' (for production workers or all manufactur-
    ing employees, as indicated)
c/v is 'organic composition of capital,' asset–employee ratio

The precise measures of all variables in the model are described in detail in the appendix.

The reasons for the inclusion in the model of the main theoretically relevant variables, namely, 'management control' and the 'rate of exploitation,' as well as of growth, 'monopoly power,' and the 'organic composition of capital' have already been discussed in detail. Very briefly, the reasons for the inclusion of the other variables (which several recent analyses of the rate of return have also included) are as follows:

Size The hypothesis is that the size of investment necessary to enter an industry constitutes a 'capital requirements' BTE, which would afford larger firms a higher rate of return. Yet absolute size could raise average costs, even if competitive constraints were tight, and sales maximization to secure larger market shares could be at the expense of short-term rates of return. Academic economics does not predict the net effect of these opposed forces (Hall and Weiss 1967; Shepherd 1972).

Risk   A low equity–asset ratio (high leverage) implies high risk, which in conventional theory should yield a higher rate of return for the firm than low risk (Hall and Weiss 1967; Larner 1970).

Leading-firm group   The hypothesis is that the combined relative market shares of the other leading firms in the industries in which the firm operates have a negative effect on the firm's own rate of return 'if dominant firms profit at the expense of their lesser rivals. An orthodox Chamberlinian hypothesis would instead be that the group's benefits are shared by all members,' and this variable should vary directly with the firm's rate of return (Shepherd 1972, p. 26).

What, then, does our multiple-regression analysis reveal concerning the effects of 'management control' and the 'rate of exploitation' on the rate of return in the largest US industrial corporations? The results are presented in table 3.4 overleaf.[7] (See table 3.5 for the correlation matrix.) Depending on which measure of a 'rate of exploitation' is used – based on wages of production workers or payroll for all manufacturing employees – the model as a whole accounts for between a fourth and a fifth of the variation in the rate of return on shareholders' equity, which is roughly twice as much as was accounted for with the same model excluding the 'rate of exploitation.' Most important, it is precisely the 'rate of exploitation' itself that has by far the strongest direct effect on the rate of return. The only other variables in the model with significant direct effects on the rate of return are – contrary to managerialism, and as we predicted – growth and relative monopoly power. But the rate of exploitation of production workers accounts for about twice as much of the variation in the rate of return as either of these variables. Moreover, 'management control' (as well as the interaction term combining it with high monopoly power) has no significant measurable effect on the rate of return.

Therefore, insofar as this multiple-regression analysis has permitted an empirical confrontation of the two main contending theories of the impact of the large corporation on the profit imperatives of contemporary capitalism, it is clear that the most basic proposition of a class theory of exploitation under advanced capitalism has been empirically confirmed: the rate of exploitation is the primary determinant of the rate of profit. Behind the bureaucratic appearances of the large corporation is the inherently exploitative relationship between capital and labor upon which advanced capitalism continues to rest. Today, as in Marx's time, the workers' 'productive power . . . when working in cooperation, is the productive power of capital' (1967, vol. 1, p. 333).

Appendix

Unless otherwise specified, the analysis reported here is based on data on the top 300 industrial corporations in the United States in 1964, ranked by sales, as listed in *Fortune* (1965). For present purposes, this list is quite adequate. There is no official list of the largest US firms, ranked by assets, profits, or sales, and even Senate investigations in recent years have relied on *Fortune's* 500 as their primary source of a list of which corporations to investigate. The only quasi-official list was compiled three decades ago by the Temporary National Economic Committee (1940), and this covered only the 200 largest nonfinancial corporations. The *Fortune* list has an unknown number of large firms missing. In 1966, *Fortune* disclosed for the first time that over the years since it had been publishing its list it had been omitting 'privately owned or closely held companies that do not publish certified statements of their financial results.' On the basis of *Fortune's* information, it now named 26 companies which it believed 'had sufficient sales in 1965 to qualify for the 500 list' (*Fortune*, July 15, 1966, pp. 224ff.) Obviously, then, the real number of identifiable owner-controlled firms is higher than estimates based only on *Fortune's* list. But this does not affect the present analysis because the profit performance of the firms on the list is not affected by the omission of these other privately owned or closely held firms. Of course, from the standpoint of any generalizations concerning the proportion of owner-controlled versus management-controlled firms among the largest corporations, the omission of such firms and any others which may still have escaped notice is a critical deficiency of the list.

The variables were measured as follows:

Rate of Return on Invested Capital (Shareholder's Equity) Equity is book value of equity plus retained earnings, 1964, as compiled by *Fortune*. The rate of return is measured by net income after taxes as a percentage of equity. Accounting practices are known to introduce some variation in reporting, but this cannot be adjusted on the basis of data available. Academic economists commonly agree that in theory the rate of return on equity should tend toward equality between industries under perfect competition, whereas there is disagreement concerning the tendency of the rate of return on assets. In particular, because managerialists raise the issue

Table 3.4 *The rate of exploitation, management control, and the rate of return in the 300 largest industrial corporations in the United States, 1964*[a]

	Production workers (unweighted)		Production workers (weighted)		All employees (unweighted)		All employees (weighted)	
Management control (M, Burch)	0.088[b]	0.9151[c] (1.7164)[d]	0.083	0.8767 (1.6385)	0.079	0.8443 (1.5046)	0.074	0.7756 (1.4162)
Inverse log of assets (S)	−0.043	−3.6364 (−0.7663)	−0.042	−7.2274 (−1.5160)	−0.060	−5.1963 (−1.0405)	−0.034	−5.8763 (−1.2062)
Equity-asset ratio (R)	0.028	1.0873 (0.5247)	0.055	2.0204 (0.9603)	0.028	1.1024 (0.5030)	0.039	1.4298 (0.6607)
High market power dummy (HMP)	0.173	3.6061 (3.2330)	0.168	3.4919 (3.1758)	0.176	3.7562 (3.1852)	0.181	3.7561 (3.3186)
Leading-firm group (GP)	−0.091	−3.5132 (−1.7515)	−0.098	−3.5923 (−1.8844)	−0.102	−4.0545 (−1.9151)	−0.113	−4.1261 (−2.1094)
Growth (GRO)	0.194	0.3271 (3.6727)	0.196	0.3365 (3.7556)	0.205	0.3543 (3.7729)	0.199	0.3428 (3.7314)
'Rate of exploitation,' production workers	0.351	0.6853 (6.5949)	0.329	0.6730 (6.2654)				

	Model 1[b][c]	Model 2[b][c]	Model 3[b][c]	Model 4[b][c]
'Rate of exploitation,' all employees			0.297; 1.4399 (5.1622)[d]	0.280; 1.3286 (4.8467)[d]
Asset–employee ratio	-0.110; -0.0028 (-1.9025)[d]	-0.143; -0.0033 (-2.3828)[d]	-0.167; -0.0043 (-2.7124)[d]	-0.182; -0.0042 (-2.8413)[d]
Square root of the log of assets		0.177; 11.7782 (4.8186)[d]		0.183; 12.1352 (4.8457)[d]
Constant	10.5023 (4.1270)[d]		11.8297 (4.4474)[d]	
Coefficient of multiple determination (R^2)	0.2452	0.9365	0.2046	0.9332
Corrected coefficient of multiple determination ($\bar{R}^2$)	0.2245	0.8770	0.1827	0.8709

[a] Missing data replaced with means algorithm.
[b] Standardized regression coefficient.
[c] Unstandardized regression coefficient.
[d] t ratio.

Table 3.5 *Correlation matrix*

	1a	1b	2	3	4	5	6	7a	7b	8a	8b	9	10
1a Management control (M, Burch)	(0.4932)												
1b Management control (M, Palmer)	0.476	(0.4596)											
2 Inverse log of assets (S)	−0.076	−0.157	(0.0607)										
3 Equity–asset ratio (R)	0.036	0.022	−0.029	(0.1319)									
4 High monopoly power dummy (HMP)	0.045	−0.017	−0.024	0.107	(0.3453)								
5 Leading-firm group (GP)	0.019	0.050	−0.103	0.062	0.023	(0.1858)							

6 Growth (GRO)	−0.054	0.022	0.027	−0.233	0.055							−0.089 (3.1992)
7a Interaction dummy (M, Burch × HMP)	0.231	0.086	−0.032	0.031	0.663	−0.034	0.053					(0.2480)
7b Interaction dummy (M, Palmer × HMP)	0.112	0.153	−0.068	0.057	0.796	−0.085	0.055	0.742				(0.2893)
8a 'Rate of exploitation,' production workers (s/v)	−0.051	−0.168	0.017	0.083	0.237	0.031	−0.017	0.055	0.096			(2.9624)
8b 'Rate of exploitation,' all employees (s/v all)	−0.015	−0.054	−0.085	0.170	0.228	0.112	−0.072	0.117	0.174	0.671		(1.2249)
9 Asset-employee ratio (c/v)	0.016	0.049	−0.404	0.143	−0.091	0.159	−0.094	−0.061	−0.072	0.097	0.298	(228.43)
10 Rate of return on equity, 1964 (RR)	0.072	−0.057	−0.013	0.024	0.276	−0.100	0.206	0.219	0.192	0.361	0.269	−0.100 (5.2604)

$N = 300$; misssing data replaced with means algorithm. Standard deviations in parentheses.

as to how shareholders' interests are affected by management control, this is the appropriate variable for both theoretical reasons.

Management Control   Two different measures of management control or owner control were used for this analysis. Burch (1972) presents the most careful recent study of the type of control in large corporations; his study did not rely exclusively on data reported to governmental agencies by the firms themselves, or on proxy reports. Instead, Burch examined the business press (i.e. *Fortune, Forbes, Time, Business Week*, and the business section of *The New York Times*) from 1950 to 1971 for references to the 300 leading industrials (as well as the next 200, though in less detail, and the 50 leading merchandising firms, the top 500 transportation companies, and the top 50 commercial banks). On the basis of this publicly available 'inside information' supplemented by *Moody's* manuals, *Standard and Poor's Corporation Records*, and the Securities and Exchange Commission's *Official Summary of Securities Transactions and Holdings* (whose data he found less accurate than those he culled from the business press, p. 27), Burch categorized each corporation according to its apparent type of control 'as of the mid-1960's' (p. 27). He assigned firms to the 'probably family control' class if both of the following criteria were met: (a) 'that approximately 4–5 percent or more of the voting stock was held by a family, group of families, or some affluent individual'; and (b) that he found evidence of membership 'on the part of a family on the board of directors of a company, generally over an extended period of time' (pp. 29–30). If only one of these two criteria was met, firms were classified as under 'possibly family control'; if neither was met, firms were regarded as under 'management control.' Using these classifications, the 300 firms in the present sample were categorized by a dichotomous variable which equals 1 if Burch judged them to have been under management control and 0 if Burch regarded them as under probable or possible family control. For the purpose of comparison, the classification of firms by Palmer (1973) was also used in this analysis, though also as a dichotomous variable equal to 1 if Palmer considered a firm to be under management control or 0 if he classified it under weak- or strong-owner control. The product moment correlation coefficient between the two dichotomous variables is 0.476. Palmer's classification, it should be noted, closely approximates Larner's (1970), modified in part by the classifications of Monsen et al. (1968); so by using Palmer's variable we are also replicating Larner's analysis to a great extent. Palmer generously provided his classification of firms for our use.

Size   Following Hall and Weiss (1967) as did Larner (1970); size is measured by the reciprocal of the logarithm to the base 10 of the total year-end assets expressed in millions of dollars. Hall and Weiss used the logarithmic form of asset size, because they reasoned that raising 1 percent additional assets is more nearly comparable between firms of different sizes than raising a specific absolute amount. The reciprocal was used because they reasoned that a larger firm would find it easier to raise another percentage addition to assets than a smaller one.

Risk   Again, following Hall and Weiss, and Larner, the equity–asset ratio is used as a measure of risk (or leverage).

High Monopoly Power   A dichotomous variable was constructed to indicate a firm's possession or not of a high degree of monopoly power. A firm was classified as having high monopoly power if both of the following conditions were met: (a) the weighted average of BTEs in the industries in which the firms operate was judged to be 'high' by Palmer (1973); and (b) its 1961 weighted average market share in these industries was estimated by Shepherd (1972) to have been 25 percent or more. Shepherd (1975) considers a market share of 25 percent as substantial, and Gale (1972) suggests 0.15 standard deviations above the mean of market share as a cutoff for high values. In the present population of firms, a market share of 25 percent meets this criterion. The present measure of monopoly power appears to be preferable to the concentration ratio (whether four-firm or eight-firm) of the firm's principal industry because it combines a contextual feature of the industry in which the firm operates (BTEs) and a specific feature of the firm itself, i.e. its market share in that industry. Firms were assigned to the industry in which the highest percentage of their employees were located, as is discussed in the text. Market share data were generously provided by William Shepherd.

Leading-firm Group   Following Shepherd (1972), this variable is constructed by subtracting a firm's average market share from the average four-firm concentration ratio of the industries in which it produces. It is meant to tap the effect of the combined relative market shares of the other leading firms in the industries in which a firm operates.

Growth   This is measured by the percent change in the firm's total sales between 1955 and 1964, i.e. revenues in 1964 minus revenues in 1955, divided by revenues in 1955. This both follows Shepherd (1972) and is specifically the measure of growth proposed by managerial theorists. Thus, Galbraith says that the technostructure's goal is 'to achieve the greatest possible rate of corporate growth as measured in sales' (1971, p. 171).

Management Control with High Monopoly Power   Following Palmer (1973), this variable was used to test for a possible interaction effect between relative monopoly power and management control. Two variables have an 'interaction effect' if the effect of independent variable on a dependent variable varies with the level of the independent variable. A dichotomous variable was constructed in which a firm with both high monopoly power and management control was scored 1, and others 0. Two variables, one using Burch's classification and the other using Palmer's, were used in separate runs.

Correcting for Heteroskedasticity   As in previous studies with similar data on firms, the variance of the dependent variable, i.e. the rate of return, was found not to be uniform across categories of size. (Hall and Weiss (1967) assumed the variance of the rate of return to be proportional to the inverse of assets; Shepherd (1972) assumed it to be proportional to the inverse of the logarithm assets; while Gale (1972) assumed it to be proportional to the square root of market share.) To correct for this heteroskedasticity, each variable in the equation was multiplied by a weighting factor (the square root of the logarithm of assets), the weighting factor itself was added to the equation as an additional independent variable, and the regression curve was constrained to pass through the origin. Table 3.4 reports the results for the weighted and unweighted regressions.

Notes

1 For a fine contemporaneous polemic against the views of Schmidt and Bernstein, see Luxemburg ([1899] 1970, pp. 16–20).
2 A brief note on productive labor appears in Marx's *Capital*, vol. 1, ch. 16, and is elaborated in his *Theories of Surplus Value* (1956, p. 380ff.). A fine exposition of these concepts appears in the recently translated work, originally published in Leningrad in 1928, by Isaak T. Rubin (1972, ch. 19).
3 Cogoy (1973) also uses this index of capital per employed worker in his analysis of the purported rise of the organic composition of capital. Since this ratio does not indicate anything concerning the productivity of labor, it would have to be divided by some index of manhours in production or, better, labor productivity for it to approximate a measure of value ratios. While this is a serious deficiency in any analysis of historical changes in the organic composition of capital, it is not in the present analysis, because, at any given time, labor productivity probably tends to be the same for the largest firms in the same industry. Therefore, this ratio probably usefully serves as an indirect indicator of the industry's real value ratio. It gives us 'a rough guide to the amount of investment per job required in a given industry and of the capital intensity of individual industries' (US Department of Commerce 1971, p. vii).
4 The equation of 'value added' with $s+v$ may not be correct for other than conceptual reasons, for although it can be argued that 'true value added' as Paul Samuelson defines it, conceptually approximates $s+v$, in practice it may be derived by procedures that make value added a closer equivalent to $s+v$ plus a major component of c: depreciation. In the Department of Commerce's procedures, value added 'is derived by adding

the values of shipments to the net change, between the beginning and the end of the year, in inventories of finished goods and work in process (may be plus or minus), and subtracting the cost of materials. The value of shipments includes the value of product shipments, receipts for services for others on their materials, miscellaneous receipts (repair work, scrap sales, etc.) and sales of products bought and resold without further manufacture, processing, or assembly. The cost of materials includes the cost of materials [sic], components, parts, containers, fuels, purchased electricity, products bought and sold without processing and the cost of contract work done by others. 'Value added' avoids the duplication in the 'value of shipments' figure which results from the use of products of some establishments as materials by others. Consequently, it is useful for comparing the relative economic contributions of the manufacturing process among industries and geographical areas' (US Department of Commerce 1971, p. viii). If it is assumed, then, that this measure of 'value added' more closely approximates $s+v$ plus the portion of constant capital consisting of depreciation than it does only $s+v$, our procedure in this particular analysis would be unchanged. That is, since we would not be able to really deduct a measure of this component of c from the figure for value added, we would, at least, have to employ the present procedure of controlling for its presence anyway, by utilizing our very crude index of c/v in the regression equations predicting the rate of return.

5 It was not possible to assign to an industry 66 of 300 firms.

6 Gillman (1957), Mage (1963), and Perlo (1974) have all attempted to measure the rate of surplus value, but none used industries or firms as analytic units, and none attempted to simultaneously measure the effects of several different variables on the rate of profit. Nonetheless, of course, these are all valuable pioneering efforts at empirical verification of Marx's hypothesis.

7 See the appendix.

References

Alchian, Armen. 1968. 'Corporate Management and Property Rights.' In *Economic Policy and the Regulation of Securities*. Washington, D.C.: American Enterprise Institute.

Baran, Paul A., and Paul M. Sweezy. 1966. *Monopoly Capital*. New York: Monthly Review Press.

Baumol, J. 1959. *Business Behavior, Value and Growth*. New York: Macmillan.

Berle, Adolph, Jr., and Gardiner C. Means. 1967. *The Modern Corporation and Private Property*. New York: Harcourt, Brace & World.

Bernstein, Eduard. 1961. *Evolutionary Socialism*. New York: Shocken (originally published in Germany in 1899).

Bullock, Paul, and David Yaffe. 1975. 'Inflation, Crisis and the Post-war Boom.' *Revolutionary Communist* 3–4 (November): 5–45.

Burch, Philip H., Jr. 1972. *The Managerial Revolution Reassessed*. Lexington, Mass.: Heath.

Cogoy, Mario. 1973. 'The Fall of the Rate of Profit and the Theory of Accumulation.' *Bulletin of the Conference of Socialist Economists*, Winter: 52–67.

Dahrendorf, Ralf. 1959. *Class and Class Conflict in Industrial Society*. Stanford, Calif.: Stanford University Press.

Donnadieu, Gerard. 1975. *Citoyens dans l'Entreprise*. Paris: Resma.

Earley, James S. 1956. 'Marginal Policies of Excellently Managed Companies.' *American Economic Review* 46 (March): 44–70.

—— 1957. 'Comment.' *American Economic Review. Papers and Proceedings* 47 (May): 333–5.

——, and W. T. Carleton. 1962. 'Budgeting and the Theory of the Firm.' *Journal of Industrial Economics* 10 (July): 165–73.

Galbraith, John K. 1970. 'What Happened to the Class Struggle?' *Washington Monthly* 2 (February), as reprinted, pp. 463–9, in *American Society, Inc.*, edited by Maurice Zeitlin. Chicago, Ill.: Rand McNally, 1977.

—— 1971. *The New Industrial State*, 2nd edition. Boston, Mass.: Houghton Mifflin.

Gale, Bradley T. 1972. 'Market Share and Rate of Return.' *Review of Economics and Statistics* 54 (November): 412–23.

Gillman, Joseph. 1957. *The Falling Rate of Profit*. London: Dobson.

Hall, Marshall, and Leonard W. Weiss. 1967. 'Firm Size and Profitability.' *Review of Economics and Statistics* 49 (August): 319–31.

Hodgson, Geoff. 1974. 'The Theory of the Falling Rate of Profit.' *New Left Review* 84 (March–April): 55–82.

Kamerschen, David R. 1968. 'The Influence of Ownership and Control on Profit Rates.' *American Economic Review* 58 (June): 432–47.

Kaysen, Carl. 1957. 'The Social Significance of the Modern Corporation.' *American Economic Review* 47 (May): 311–19.

Larner, Robert J. 1970. *Management Control and the Large Corporation*. Cambridge, Mass.: Dunellen.

Luxemburg, Rosa. 1970. *Reform or Revolution*. New York: Pathfinder (originally published in Berlin in 1899).

Lybecker, Martin E. 1973. 'Regulation of Bank Trust Department Investment Activities.' *Yale Law Journal* 82 (April): 977–1002.

Mage, Shane H. 1963. 'The Law of the Falling Tendency of the Rate of Profit.' Unpublished Ph.D. dissertation, Columbia University.

Manne, Henry. 1965. 'Mergers and the Market for Corporate Control.' *Journal of Political Economy* 72 (April): 110–20.

Marris, Robin. 1964. *The Economic Theory of 'Managerial' Capitalism*. New York: Free Press.

Marx, Karl. 1956. *Theories of Surplus Value*. Moscow: Foreign Languages Publishing House.

—— 1967. *Capital*, vols. 1–3. New York: International.

—— 1970. *The Grundrisse*. Harmondsworth, Middlesex: Penguin.

Monsen, R. Joseph, Jr., J. S. Chiu, and D. E. Cooley. 1968. 'The Effect of Separation of Ownership and Control on the Performance of the Large Firm.' *Quarterly Journal of Economics* 82 (August): 435–51.

Mueller, Willard F. 1970. *A Primer on Monopoly and Competition*. New York: Random House.

Palmer, John. 1973. 'The Profit Performance Effects of the Separation of Ownership and Control in Large U.S. Industrial Corporations.' *Bell Journal of Economics and Management Science* 4: 293–303.

Parsons, Talcott. 1954. *Essays in Social Theory*. Glencoe, Ill.: Free Press.

Perlo, Victor. 1974. *The Unstable Economy*. New York: International.

Rowthorn, Robert. 1976. '"Late Capitalism."' *New Left Review* 98 (July–August): 59–83.

Rubin, Isaak T. 1972. *Essays on Marx's Theory of Value*. Detroit, Mich.: Black and Red.

Samuelson, Paul. 1961. *Economics*, 5th edn. New York: McGraw–Hill.

Shepherd, William G. 1972. 'The Elements of Market Structure.' *Review of Economics and Statistics* 54 (February): 25–37.

—— 1975. *The Treatment of Market Power*. New York: Columbia University Press.

Simon, Herbert. 1962. 'New Developments in the Theory of the Firm.' *American Economic Review* 52 (1): 1–15.

Slichter, Sumner. 1931. *Modern Economic Society*. New York: Holt.

Sweezy, Paul M. 1956. *Theory of Capitalist Development*. New York: Monthly Review Press.

Tanzer, Michael. 1969. *The Political Economy of International Oil and the Underdeveloped Countries*. Boston, Mass.: Beacon.

Temporary National Economic Committee. 1940. 'The Distribution of Ownership in the 200 Largest Nonfinancial Corporations,' in *Investigations of Concentration of Economic Power*, Monograph No. 29. Washington, D.C.: Government Printing Office.

US Congress, Senate Subcommittee on Intergovernmental Relations, and Budgeting, Management, and Expenditures of the Committee on Government Operations. 1974. *Disclosure of Corporate Ownership*. 93rd Congr., 2nd sess. Washington, D.C.: Government Printing Office.

US Department of Commerce, Bureau of Domestic Commerce. 1971. *Industry Profiles, 1958–1969*. Washington, D.C.: Government Printing Office.

Yaffe, David S. 1973. 'The Crisis of Profitability.' *New Left Review* 80 (July–August): 45–62.

Zeitlin, Maurice. 1974. 'Corporate Ownership and Control: The Large Corporation and the Capitalist Class.' *American Journal of Sociology* 79 (March): 1073–119.

—— 1976. 'On Class Theory of the Large Corporation.' *American Journal of Sociology* 81 (January): 894–903.

4

Finance capital and the internal structure of the capitalist class in the United States

A handful of immense banks, concentrating within their coffers the bulk of the assets and deposits of the entire banking system and providing much of the loans and credits for industry, are the decisive units in the circulation of capital in contemporary capitalist economies.[1] With this consolidation of oligopoly in banking itself, the amount of loans and credits granted by the leading banks actually determines the amount of money deposited with them, because what they lend flows back to them as deposits. They can, within fairly wide limits, 'vary at will the supply of credit or short-term capital available at any given time...' and thus determine the price of (or rate of interest on) loan capital.[2] As C. Wright Mills (1942, p. 46) aptly remarks, 'not violence, but credit may be a rather ultimate seat of control within modern societies.'

The leading banks are also structurally interconnected – through long-standing business associations, financial arrangements, inter-locking directorates, and overlapping and interpenetrating owner-ship – with the top nonfinancial corporations. Thus, if our originating question is how this affects the dynamics of contemporary capitalism, this study focuses, in particular, on the inner structure of the capitalist class itself, and involves the following questions. Do the interconnections between the major financial institutions (banks, insurance companies, and other financial firms) and large industrial corporations constitute institutional means of intraclass power? Do the men who sit simultaneously in the managements of both of them play a distinctive role in the corporate world? Are they, in a phrase, 'a special social type in contrast to other officers and directors of the largest corporations and banks'? (Zeitlin 1974, pp. 1103, 1110 – this volume, ch. 1; also 1976, pp. 900–1 – this volume, ch. 2).

The Contending Theories

'Historically,' as a US congressional antitrust subcommittee notes, *'interlocking relationships between bank managements and the directors of other corporations have been of special significance* [because of the potential] . . . misuse of the power to control money and credit from financial institutions' (see US Congress 1965, p. 164; also Federal Trade Commission 1951; US Congress 1978). In recent years, several sociologists and economists have conducted informative but essentially descriptive studies and 'network analyses' of interlocking directorates.[3] But the critical theoretical issues and empirical questions addressed in this study have been all but entirely neglected, primarily, perhaps, because they cannot be posed within the regnant academic paradigms in the social sciences.[4]

Remarkably, despite its explicit focus on the impact of the large corporation on contemporary society, even managerial theory simply discounts, when it does not ignore, the major bank as a decisive locus of economic power; its authors (e.g. Galbraith 1967, p. 68) dismiss the 'bankers' themselves with witticisms concerning their ostensible 'dwindling social magnetism.' For although banking functions persist, these functions are supposedly no longer vital in 'the new industrial state' or 'post-capitalist society.' Rather, in managerial theory, because the large corporation exists in a state of splendid – and self-perpetuating – autonomy, generating earnings 'wholly under its own control,' and running 'on its own economic steam,' it no longer depends on 'financial capital.'[5] 'Management thus becomes,' as Berle and Means (1967, pp. xiv–xv) put it, 'in an odd sort of way, the uncontrolled administrator of a kind of trust, having the privilege of perpetual accumulation.' Freed from the dictates of capital and the control of its major shareowners, and thereby of the imperatives of profit maximization, the large corporation is thus, in managerial doctrine, the embodiment of economic rationality. The large corporation's management (or 'technostructure'), deriving its 'decisive power' not from capital but from organization, is said to administer social investment much as if it were a 'purely neutral technocracy,' allocating 'the income stream on the basis of public policy rather than private cupidity.'[6]

Sociological analyses of the large corporation, whether or not they explicitly accept such managerialist notions, tend to have the same implicit premises. In the 'interorganizational paradigm,' for instance, the large corporation is also conceptualized essentially as merely one sort of complex organization operating 'within a larger environment comprised of other organizations' (Allen 1974, pp. 393, 403; 1976). In this paradigm, too, neither the imperatives of capital accumulation nor the private ownership of capital is considered of decisive relevance. Instead, what impels the interaction of the large corporations is supposedly an 'interorganizational' dynamic based on their efforts to 'avert threats to their stability or existence' as autonomous organizations and to anticipate and control 'environmental contingencies' (Thompson 1967, p. 35; Allen 1974, p. 393; also see Pennings 1978, 1980, pp. 7–10). It is also this same dynamic that accounts, in particular, for the pattern of interlocking among the large corporations and major banks (Pfeffer 1972; Allen 1974, 1976; Pennings 1980, pp. 67, 107ff.).[7]

Thus, although managerialism dismisses or ignores interlocking directorates, and the men who fill them, both among large corporations and between them and the major banks,[8] while 'interorganizational theory' actually *focuses* on these interlocks, the paradox is that they share the identical paradigmatic presupposition: the major banks and large corporations are assumed to be, as Richard E. Ratcliff observes (1980b, p. 557), more or less 'distinct islands of self-interest.' Neither theory attaches any significance to the so-called 'outside interests' (let alone controlling interests) of ownership, or considers the possibility that the so-called 'outside directors' who interlock the big banks and top industrial corporations are bearers of decisive *extra-organizational powers*. Both the interorganizational and managerial theories assume that the management of the large corporation or leading bank is, in Galbraith's phrase (1967, pp. 88, 409), 'invulnerable to external authority,' and 'selects itself and its successors as an autonomous and self-perpetuating oligarchy.' For both theories, the basic unit of analysis is the 'firm,' i.e. the corporate *organization* itself, as it interacts with other organizations to maximize its security and minimize its uncertainty.

In our conception of class theory, however, the top nonfinancial corporations and leading banks are considered 'units in a class controlled apparatus of appropriation, and the whole gamut of functionaries and owners of capital participate in varying degrees, and as members of the same social class, in its direction' (Zeitlin 1974, p. 1079 – this volume, ch. 1). This means that the relevant analytical unit in an adequate explanation of the significance of the interlocking directorate is not merely the corporation or the bank as an 'organization' or even as a 'firm,' but rather the internal structure of the *class* that owns and controls them both. The central proposition of this analysis, then, is that it is not a process of autonomous self-selection or of 'interorganizational elite cooptation' that underlies the pattern of interlocking and the selection of the interlocking directors themselves, but rather a process of intraclass integration, coordination, and control.

For, if managerialism poses a false problem and provides a false solution, the ascendancy of the large corporation surely has altered the structure of the capitalist class, to the extent that, within the large corporation itself, the ownership of capital has become partly dissociated from the control of production. 'With the dispersion of shares,' as Rudolf Hilferding long ago observed ([1910] 1947, pp. 155–6), 'capitalist property has been converted increasingly into a limited form of property which merely gives its owners a simple title to surplus value without in itself permitting them to intervene decisively in the productive process. . . . The effective control of production is in the hands of persons who provide only a part of the capital involved. The owners of the means of production no longer exist in isolation, but rather constitute an economic association [*Gesellschaft*] in which the individual has a right only to an aliquot share [i.e. proportional to the stockholding] of the profits.'

The critical theoretical issue, then, is how the dissociation of these once unified functions of capital affects the inner structure of the capitalist class. This, in turn, necessitates recognizing and specifying the different locations occupied in the accumulation (and appropriation) process by various types of 'owners' and 'managers,' and analyzing their implications. The so-called 'managers' themselves do not constitute a homogeneous category of functionaries identically situated in the accumulation process or in the capitalist class itself. The crucial empirical question is thus how the various types of higher executives – these leading *functionaries of capital* – are related to the principal *capital-owners* themselves in the actual ensemble of intraclass social relations.

If the large corporation has partly dissociated the functions of capital-ownership and corporate control, it has also unified functions of capital that were dissociated before the corporation's ascendancy – functions that used to constitute ' *a qualitative division*' both of 'the total capital' and of 'the entire class of capitalists.' As Marx argued a century ago (1967, vol. 3, pp. 379, 372–8, italics added), 'interest-bearing capital as such has . . . productive capital for its opposite.' The 'money-capitalist' confronts the 'industrial capital-ist . . . as a special kind of capitalist,' i.e. they confront each other 'not just as legally different persons but as *persons playing entirely different roles in the reproduction process*.' In their hands, 'the same capital really performs a two-fold and wholly different movement. The one merely loans it, the other employs it productively.' The 'capitalist working on borrowed capital' ends up with only a 'portion of profit,' i.e. 'profit minus interest.' Thus, in Marx's time, as he saw it (1952, p. 86), 'money capitalists' and 'industrial capitalists' constituted, as did 'merchant capitalists' also, 'rival fractions . . . of the appropriating class.' They were, in our conceptual terms, separate and opposed 'class segments' occupying – despite their common ownership of the means of production – relatively distinct locations in the processes of accumulation and appropriation of capital, and, consequently, possessing inherently contradictory interests.[9]

Under the domain of large corporations and major banks, and the consequent interpenetration of industrial, commercial, and loan capital, however, there emerges a new historical form of capital and, with it, a new coalesced class type: 'finance capital' and the 'finance capitalist.' The big banks and top industrial corporations, as we noted earlier, have both proprietary and organizational interconnec-tions. The big banks are not only major creditors of the top corporations, but also simultaneously own or administer some of their principal shareholdings. And the top corporations (which in the United States are themselves being transformed into 'conglomerates' spanning all economic sectors) tend, in turn, to own or control substantial blocks of stock in the leading banks.

Aside, however, from such reciprocal institutional shareholdings and financial connections, the big banks and top nonfinancial corporations also tend to have the very same individuals and families among their principal owners. In the United States, for example, such prominent wealthy families as the Mellons, Rockefellers, Stillmans, Duponts, Fishers, Weyerhausers, Rosen-walds, Motts, Fords, and Hannas have identifiable principal owner-ship interests in some of the largest industrial corporations *and* leading commercial banks (Zeitlin 1974, p. 1102 – this volume, ch. 1; Black and Goff 1969; Knowles 1973; White 1978; Dunn 1979; Domhoff 1983, pp. 60–3). But, in all likelihood, these wealthy families are merely well-documented instances of the general tendency of the principal capital-owning families to have interests overlapping finance, industry, and commerce. They illustrate the critical theoretical question of the extent to which it is at all valid to think of the various firms to which these families are attached as independent 'organizations,' whatever their formal or legal status. Rather, these firms tend, as Ratcliff puts it well (1980b, p. 557), to be 'interconnected points of decision-making within larger networks of class interests.' The big banks, other financial institutions, and top nonfinancial corporations tend, that is, to be 'units in, and instrumentalities of, the whole system of propertied interests controlled by these major capitalist families' and their entire class (Zeitlin 1976, p. 901 – this volume, ch. 2). (See the fine analyses, using a similar approach to Scotland and England, by Scott (1979), and Scott and Griff (1984).)

Under these circumstances, the interlocking directorates tying together the major banks and top nonfinancial corporations take on a crucial political-economic role in integrating the simultaneous and potentially contradictory financial, industrial, and commercial interests of the wealthiest families, whose various investments span these ostensibly separate sectors. Those who sit at the conjoined managerial helms of the big banks or other financial institutions and top industrial corporations as the functionaries of 'finance capital' are, to this extent and in this limited sense – by virtue of their simultaneous administration of loan and productive capital – themselves 'finance capitalists.' In short, we suggest that the interlocking of the leading banks or other financial institutions and top industrial corporations is an organizational expression of the inner transformation of the capitalist class itself. 'Neither "financiers" extracting interest at the expense of industrial profits nor '"bankers" controlling corporations, but finance capitalists on the boards of the largest banks *and* corporations preside over the banks' investments as creditors *and* shareholders, organizing production, sales, and financing, and appropriating the profits of their integrated activities' (Zeitlin 1974, p. 1102 – this volume, ch. 1).

With this coalescence of banking and industrial capital, however, the contradictions between them are not eliminated, nor are the claims of the former to a share of the profits extracted by the latter. Rather, this form, i.e. 'finance capital,' now contains as 'constitutive contradictions' within itself (Poulantzas 1975, p. 130) the contradictory interests once dividing qualitatively different coexisting segments within the capitalist class. In Hilferding's (1947, p. 299) ironic imagery: 'Industrial capital is the Father that sired commercial and banking capital as its Son, and money is the Holy Spirit. They are three but only one in finance capital.' Put more mundanely, in the words of a leading econometrician (Kuh 1963, p. 16), the 'financial policies of industrial enterprises should be meshed with their investment behavior, but exactly how remains an open question.'

'Meshing' these potentially contradictory investments, then, is the special double role of the finance capitalist, who, as James O'Connor observes, 'combines and synthesizes the motives [and functions] of the merchant, industrialist, and banker.'[10] As the representative of the nonfinancial corporation's lenders and bondholders, the finance capitalist must favor higher interest rates but, as the representative of its principal shareowners, he must strive to assure maximum industrial profits. In other words, the coalescence of banking and industrial capital produces a *self-contradictory intraclass location*: as a result, the individual higher executives who personify this coalescence must continually try, in practice, to reconcile the irreconcilable – these contradictory interests of loan and productive capital. If this reconciliation can never be assured, interlocking directorates between the leading banks and top nonfinancial corporations are nonetheless the singular 'interorganizational means of administration' with which to attempt it.

To the extent that propertied individuals and families have major investments and principal shareholdings both in financial institutions and industrial corporations, they have a special and heavy stake in trying to harmonize their broad policies and reconcile the contending interests involved in them. And to the extent that actual participation in management is necessary (and it may not be) for them to be able actively to shape a business strategy that they think will best accommodate their own specific self-contradictory interests, they should also seek (and be sought) to occupy precisely those directorships that interlock the leading financial and industrial corporations. Faced with the need to coordinate the business strategies of the various business units in which they have substantial interests in order to try to maximize this entire *system*'s profits, irrespective of the profits earned by each of its separate financial or industrial units, these men of property may well wish to provide an added measure of assurance that such coordination actually occurs in practice, by sitting personally on the boards of these companies.[11]

For these reasons, our major hypotheses are as follows. (a) Finance capitalists, who are simultaneously represented on the boards of top industrial corporations and major banks or other financial institutions, should tend, by virtue of the greater number of directorships held, to have a more extensive role than other directors in coordinating the policies of the top industrial corporations. (b) They should also tend, in particular, to have a more extensive role in coordinating the policies of those top industrial corporations that are the dominant and most centrally located ones in the economy. (c) Thus they should also be more likely than other directors to be drawn from the nation's leading propertied families.

Data, Concepts, Indicators

We analyze these interrelationships on the basis of data gathered on the men occupying the directorships of the top 200 US industrial corporations of 1964, ranked by sales (on the *Fortune 500* 1965 list). Data for 1964 were utilized both because of the comparisons such data allow to the findings of related studies and because several of these studies also provided relevant data to supplement our own analysis. To our knowledge, nine studies have been done of corporate control of large nonfinancial corporations in the United States, spanning the period from 1959 through 1970. Of these nine studies, five presented case by case evaluations of the locus of control in specific corporations, and were thus useful secondary sources for our own analyses of corporate control. Two of the latter studies were based on 1964 data and one on 1963 data (Soref 1979, pp. 219–37; James and Soref 1981, p. 5).

From the top 200 industrials, 40 were selected as 'sampling units.' The 200 industrials were ranked by the number of their directors and divided into 20 strata, from each of which two companies were selected, without replacement. Then, from these 40 companies, 300 directors were selected. The two-stage sampling design introduced the possibility of a bias toward directors of companies with large boards. Thus, the stratified sampling was done to minimize any such bias.

The unweighted sample was a sample of directorships, i.e. of the 'offices' or positions, not of directors. A sample of directors would be taken from a list of directors on which every individual appeared only once. In our sample, however, a man who sat on the board of three different top 200 industrials, i.e. who held three directorships, had three times the probability of being selected as a man having only a single directorship on a top 200 industrial. Accordingly, cases were weighted for the quantitative analysis, so that a man having one directorship was assigned a weight of unity, a man with two top 200 directorships was assigned a weight of 0.5, and so on. For most tabulations, the total N is 235 from a sample size of 273. (For details on procedures, see Soref 1979, pp. 87–94).)

Information on the various directorships occupied was drawn from such standard sources as *Who's Who in America, Who's Who in Commerce and Industry, Poor's Register of Corporations, Executives and Directors, Moody's Manual*, and *Who's Who in Canada*. To qualify as a 'finance capitalist' in the present analysis, a director of a top 200 industrial also had to be either a partner of a leading investment bank or a director of one of the top 50 commercial banks, top 50 insurance companies, or of another major financial company: 47 of the 235 directors in the sample are, by this definition, finance capitalists.

We identified the directors who belong to a leading propertied family, and defined three types of propertied families: two are defined by specific information on their capital-ownership *in the 40 industrials analyzed*, whom we call 'dominant owners' and 'outside owners'; one is defined by information on their 'membership' in the national status-community of the very rich, whom we call members of the 'establishment.' Conceptually, all three types of propertied families belong to the capitalist class, specifically the segment of corporate capital, based on the ownership and control of the nation's leading corporations.

The 'principal owners' in the present analysis are defined by their personal or family holdings *in the 40 industrials analyzed*. The findings presented here are based on a secondary analysis of the ownership and control of each of these companies as of the mid-1960s by Michael Soref; he used information provided on them in several studies (Villarejo 1961–2; Sheehan 1966, 1967; Lundberg 1968; Chevalier 1970; Larner 1970; Burch 1972; Pederson and Tabb 1976; Kotz 1978), as well as in various government publications and periodicals. He also scrutinized citations concerning his sample companies and all source articles cited by the other authors, and consulted the periodical files of the North American Congress on Latin America, the Securities and Exchange Commission's *Official Summary*, the *Foundation Directory*, company and family histories, and various biographical reference works (see Soref 1979).

A 'dominant owner' is a director who either personally has a principal holding in or belongs to a family that controls an industrial corporation in the sample of the 'top 40' companies. An 'outside owner' is a director identified as the representative of another company (whether financial or nonfinancial) with a controlling interest in an industrial corporation in the 'top 40' sample, when the locus of control of the controlling company itself was not ascertained. In what follows, for convenience, we speak in the present tense, referring, however, to the situation as of the mid-1960s.

'Dominant owners' included among our directors, for example, are Samuel Mosher, August A. Busch, Jr., and Thomas Mellon Evans. In 1958, when he was chairman of the board, Mr Mosher reportedly held 75 percent of the voting securities of Signal Company. The 1965 proxy gave Mr Mosher only 11.3 percent of Signal's stock (*Fortune* 1958; Chevalier 1970, appendix II). But Burch (1972, p. 47) found that the Mosher family held at least 39.6 percent of Signal's stock, as of the mid-1960s. Mr Busch, chairman of the board of Anheuser-Busch, Inc., is the grandson of Adolphus Busch, the brewery's co–founder. *Business Week* reports (1968, p. 104) that the combined Anheuser and Busch family holdings exceed 40 percent, and, according to an earlier report in *Time* (1955, p. 85), Mr Busch himself held 22 percent at the time. Among his listed financial directorships are those in General American Life Insurance and First National Bank of St. Louis. Mr Evans (a Mellon relative) probably personally controls the Crane Company, with 16.8 percent of the voting stock and 15.6 percent of the voting securities, according to the 1965 proxy report. (A member of the original owning family, Emily Crane Chadbourne, also has a substantial Crane holding. Larner, citing the 1964 proxy report, notes that she holds 11.1 percent of Crane's stock, but Mr Evans is clearly 'in charge,' according to insiders (e.g. Sheehan 1967, p. 182).)

Examples of 'outside owners' included among our directors are Plato Malozemoff in Continental Oil, and Arthur K. Walton and Charles M. Odorizzi on the board of Whirlpool. Mr Malozemoff, president of Newmont Mining, probably represents its 4.15 percent interest (reported in the 1965 proxy) in Continental Oil. Mr Walton, a Sears vice-president, represents the Sears group's substantial interests in Whirlpool, which amount as of 1965 to at least 7.5 percent (held among Allstate, Sears savings and profit-sharing pension fund, the Sears Foundation, and Allstate Foundation, according to *Moody's*). Sears also has 27 percent of Whirlpool's 4.25 percent cumulative convertible preferred stock, according to the 1965 proxy report. With Sears since 1931, Mr Walton represents it in several of its subsidiaries also. Among Mr Walton's listed financial directorships are the Sears Bank and Trust Company. Mr Odorizzi, an executive vice-president of RCA, which he joined in 1949, probably represents its substantial interest in Whirlpool. Villarejo (1961–2) found that RCA held 18.65 percent of Whirlpool's stock but subsequently RCA disposed of a significant portion of this holding; in 1962 it sold about a million of its Whirlpool shares and still held about 167,000 shares, or 3.1 percent, as of 1965, according to data in the Securities and Exchange Commission's *Official Summary*. Sears and RCA are not the only elements involved in the control of Whirlpool; other directors in the sample representing substantial ownership interests but not enough to be classified as 'dominant' owners are a member of a Cleveland financial family (Boynton Murch) and a member of one of Whirlpool's founding families (Steve Upton).

Now, of course, many of the directors of the 40 industrials in our sample not identified as dominant or outside owners *of these 40 industrials* probably belong to capital-owning families who have principal ownership interests elsewhere. That some directors are from prominent owning families is immediately obvious to a relatively informed observer; among these directors, for example, are Thomas Watson, Jr., Gilbert W. Humphrey, and Ogden Phipps. Mr Watson sits on the board of *Time* and Mssrs Humphrey and Phipps on that of Texaco, two of our sample of 40 industrials. The three sons of Thomas Watson, Sr., who presided over IBM's rise, hold, as of the mid-1960s, perhaps 6 percent of the stock of IBM, of which Thomas, Jr., is chairman. His brothers Arthur and Richard also are in IBM's top management, and the Watsons probably control the company (Burch 1972, table 3–1; Rodgers 1974, pp. 235–46). Mr Humphrey's father, George M. Humphrey, leads a coalition of four Cleveland families (Hanna, Humphrey, Weir, Love) that, as of the mid-1960s, controls several major industrial companies, including Chrysler, Consolidation Coal (which merged in 1965 with Continental Oil), National Steel, and M.A. Hanna Company, as well as National City Bank of Cleveland (Black and Goff 1969; Chevalier 1970; Burch 1972). Mr Humphrey is also married to a Hanna, Louise Ireland. Ogden Phipps, chairman of Bessemer Securities, is the grandson of Henry Phipps – a partner of Andrew Carnegie and the founder of the family fortune. Bessemer Securities is a 'family office' that holds and manages the Phipps stock portfolio, amounting to some $550 million in 1967. Other Phipps assets are held by other such family offices (Mahon 1978, p. 4; Dunn 1979, p. 9).

Despite the fact that these three directors, i.e. Mssrs Watson, Humphrey, and Phipps, are members of three of the nation's most prominent capitalist familes, they have *not* been defined here as dominant or outside owners, because they neither hold nor represent identifiable principal ownership interests in any of the 'top 40.' Obviously, then, to the extent that such men of property appear among the directors of the 40 industrials but have not been identified as such by our limited analyses and procedures, the latter underestimate the number of directors who are, in fact, principal owners of capital. It was simply not feasible to investigate such other ownership interests systematically; it was already a formidable research task to reveal and specify the ownership interests involved in the sample of 40 industrials and to discover the connections of their directors to these interests.

As something of a surrogate for such research, however, publicly available information was utilized to identify the directors belonging to the integrated core of older, more established, families of the capitalist class; i.e. the families whose diversified holdings probably span finance and industry. For want of a better term, they are identified here as members of the 'establishment.' The three criteria used to identify a director as a member of the 'establishment' were (a) listing in the *Social Register*, (b) attendance at one of a few exclusive preparatory schools, or (c) membership in one of a few exclusive men's clubs. These schools and clubs are considered by G. William Domhoff (1970, pp. 21–4) as usually indicative of 'upper class' membership.[12] Using these criteria, Mssrs Watson, Humphrey, and Phipps, as well as Mosher, Busch, and Evans, but not Malozemoff or Odorizzi, qualify as members of the 'establishment.' All told, 100 of the 235 directors qualify as members of the 'establishment,' while only 23 qualify as principal (dominant or outside) owners. Also, as will be seen in the following analysis, 14 men are both principal owners and members of the establishment.

Using such criteria as attendance at an exclusive school, membership in such a club, or a *Social Register* listing to indicate whether or not a director belonged to an established propertied family obviously may have resulted in the inclusion in the 'establishment' of some men whose families, though prominent and enjoying considerable 'status,' are not among the nation's principal capital-owning families. The vast majority of such families, however, probably belong to a self-conscious national 'status group' high within the American capitalist class. As Max Weber (1946, pp. 187–8) long ago pointed out, stimulated in part by his observations during his trip to the United States in 1904, 'status groups are normally communities' self-defined by a 'social estimation of honor.' But, if the relationship between social honor and property varies, and a tension may exist between their claims, property tends historically to be the basis of such communities of 'social honor': '. . . property as such is not always recognized as a status qualification, but in the long run it is, and with extraordinary regularity.' In any case, even when the 'pretensions of sheer property' and of social honor may stand opposed to each other, the *institutions* of the establishment, in Baltzell's apt phrase, 'carry authority' and serve as gatekeepers for admission to the community of families of old, established wealth, at the core of the American capitalist class.

The 'Inner Group' and Finance Capitalists

The interlocking directorate, as C. Wright Mills rightly remarks, 'is no mere phrase: it points to a solid feature of the facts of business life, and to a sociological anchor of the community of interest, the unification of outlook and policy, that prevails among the propertied class.' The men who sit at the interlocking managerial helms among the top corporations are, then, in a very concrete sense, the leading organizers of the corporate system of 'operating classwide property' (Mills 1956, pp. 122–3). Compared with other higher executives, the authority of the directors in this 'inner group' ranges further, and their responsibility is far broader, whether in attempting to protect and enhance the common interests of the same principal owning families dispersed among the interlocked corporations or to reconcile the opposed interests of the contending major investors involved in them.[13] In short, the men in this inner group bear a special class burden: they have a disproportionate responsibility for managing the common affairs of the entire 'business community.'

Finance capitalists, we have suggested, because they preside over the contradictory confluence of loan and productive capital, also play a special role in coordinating and integrating the classwide interests embodied in the top industrials. And insofar as their occupancy of multiple industrial directorships is an indicator, this is precisely what we find: among the directors who sit on the board of only a single industrial, a mere 15 percent are finance capitalists;

in sharp contrast, a majority of those who hold multiple seats (51 percent of those who sit on two industrial corporation boards and 59 percent of those who sit on three or more boards) are finance capitalists. Thus, finance capitalists predominate within the inner group. The same pattern repeats itself if we take into account the relative assets size of the industrial corporation: the more seats a director occupies in the biggest industrials among the top 200, with assets of a $0.5 billion or more, the more likely that he is a finance capitalist: of the 116 directors without a seat in a $0.5 billion or bigger corporation, 15 percent are finance capitalists; of the 108 with a single such seat, 21 percent, and of the dozen who hold seats in two or more of the biggest industrials, 52 percent are finance capitalists.

Conversely, the contrast is also sharp between finance capitalists and other directors in the number of directorships they hold in the top 200 industrial corporations, especially the largest of them; the finance capitalists are far more likely than other directors to hold multiple directorships of both kinds: 34 percent of the finance capitalists but only 8 percent of the other directors hold seats on the boards of two or more of the top 200. By no means as sharp but still substantial is the difference in the seats held in the largest corporations, ranked by assets: 62 percent of the finance capitalists compared with 48 percent of the other directors in the sample hold directorships in industrial corporations having assets of a $0.5 billion or more.

In manufacturing, certain 'key' industries might be said to constitute the industrial nucleus of all manufacturing, because of their close technical and their close market interdependence (Averitt 1968, pp. 38–44). They consist of the manufacturing industries that produce the most important capital goods; that have backward and forward linkages to other industries (i.e., accounting for a high proportion of their output and input) or have a high price–cost effect on them; that are characterized by considerable 'technological convergence' (e.g. machine tools, chemicals, electronics); or are leading 'growth' or innovative industries. For these reasons, i.e. given their place 'in the hierarchy of economic importance,' the corporations in the 'key' industries 'at the heart of manufacturing' (Averitt 1968, pp. 2–3) might also be expected to have their boards disproportionately engrossed by finance capitalists. This is more or less what we find: the more corporate boards in the 'key' industries a man sits on, the more likely it is that he is a finance capitalist.

Of the men who hold either no seats or a single seat on the board of a company in a 'key' industry, 15 percent are finance capitalists, but of those with two such seats, 29 percent, and of those with three or more such seats, 44 percent are finance capitalists. Conversely, finance capitalists are far more likely to sit on multiple boards in 'key' industries than are other directors of the top 200 industrial corporations: for instance, of the 47 finance capitalists, 17 percent hold two and 19 percent hold three or more directorships in companies in 'key' industries but, of the 188 other directors, 11 percent hold two and only 6 percent hold three or more such 'key' directorships.

In sum, finance capitalists not only establish a form of 'personal union,' as Hilferding called it, between the leading financial institutions and top industrial corporations, but also are the preeminent embodiment of the interlocking community of interest formed among the top industrial corporations themselves. So they are uniquely located to try to coordinate and harmonize the policies of the financial institutions and industrial corporations in order to maximize the net return of the entire system of large-scale production and investment under their command.

'Bureaucracy' and Property in the Managerial Realm

But who are they, in sociological terms? Leaving aside their personal predilections, their individual character, talents, and skills, what sort of men are socially selected and recruited to exercise the decisive powers in the interlocking managerial realms of finance and industry? Do these finance capitalists represent 'a special social type' (Zeitlin 1974, pp. 1103, 1110 – this volume, ch. 1) compared with the other industrial directors? No single indicator is sufficient to answer this question, but information concerning their own propertied interests and their place within the nation's community of established families of property is surely critical.

We find that, by both their concrete ownership interests in the corporations they direct and their membership in the 'establishment,' the finance capitalists stand out as distinctively men of property. The overwhelming majority (69 percent) of the finance capitalists ($N = 47$) are in the establishment compared with just over a third (36 percent) of the other industrial directors ($N = 188$). Similarly, the finance capitalists are roughly three times more likely than other directors to be principal owners of 'their' corporation. Conversely, 32 percent of the establishment directors ($N = 100$) but only 11 percent of those who are not in the establishment ($N = 135^*$) are finance capitalists; and 41 percent of the principal owners ($N = 23^*$) are finance capitalists compared with 18 percent of the non-owners ($N = 212$) among the directors. (An asterisk here and in the following indicates rounding error in weighted cases.)

How, then, does the combination of a man's being both a principal owner of a corporation of which he is a director *and* belonging to an established family affect the chances that he will also be a finance capitalist? Is this 'establishment owner' more likely than other directors to occupy the strategic seat of power of a finance capitalist? And, conversely, what is the relative likelihood that a finance capitalist as compared with an ordinary industrial director will be an establishment owner? Once again the finance capitalist stands out as a distinctive class type: the 'establishment owners' are the most likely of all directors to be finance capitalists and the nonestablishment nonowners, by far, are the least; indeed, proportionately five times as many of the former as the latter are finance capitalists: 45 percent of the establishment owners ($N = 15^*$) but only 9 percent of the nonestablishment nonowners ($N = 127$) are finance capitalists (35 percent of the nonestablishment owners ($N = 9^*$) ($N = 9^*$) and 30 percent of the establishment nonowners are finance capitalists.) Conversely, finance capitalists have a much higher proportion than ordinary industrial directors of each of the types of directors that are either in the establishment or principal owners or both. But among the ordinary directors, the nonestablishment nonowners overwhelmingly pre-dominate: three-fourths of the finance capitalists ($N = 47^*$) are either principal owners or in the establishment, but some three-fifths of the other industrial directors are *neither* (table 4.1).

The finance capitalists and the inner group, as we have seen, overlap considerably, for the men in the inner group – sitting as they do at the center of a web of interlocking directorates among the top industrials themselves – are probably charged with serving not only the particular interests of specific companies or families but the broader community of interest of the principal owners with investments among the variously interlocked industrial corporations. But, for this same reason, we might expect that the men in the inner group would also be drawn more heavily than single-firm directors from propertied families. Mere 'business administrators,'

Table 4.1 *Percentage of finance capitalists and other directors of the top 200 industrial corporations who are in the establishment or principal owners, both, or neither*

	Establishment outside owners	Non-establishment outside owners	Establishment dominant owners	Non-establishment dominant owners	(N)
Finance capitalists	7	6	7	0	(47)
Other directors	1	1	4	2	(188)
All directors	2	2	4	2	(236)[a]

	Establishment owners	Non-establishment owners	Establishment nonowners	Non-establishment nonowners	(N)
Finance capitalists	14	6	55	25	(47)
Other directors	4	3	32	61	(188)
All directors	6	4	36	54	(236)[a]

[a] Rounding error in weighted cases.

however gifted and fitted for such responsibility they might be, are not as likely to be entrusted with such broad class responsibility, we suggest, as are men whose family's own privileges and prerogatives rest on their extensive principal ownership of the top industrials.

So, it is necessary to hold constant the number of directorates on which they sit while comparing the relative intraclass situation of finance capitalists and other industrial directors. For it is possible that it is not their location at the conjoined financial and industrial managerial helms but rather their longer reach throughout the interlocked top industrials alone that accounts for the apparent intraclass specificity of the finance capitalists. Put differently, the 'null hypothesis' is that it is not that they are finance capitalists but rather that they are in the inner group that explains the difference in propertied interests between them and ordinary industrial directors. If this reasoning is correct, then with the number of directorships in the top 200 industrial corporations held constant, finance capitalists should be indistinguishable in their property ownership from ordinary industrial directors, while inner group members should stand out in comparison with single-firm directors as distinctively men of property.

As an investigation of the range of possible relationships among the directors of the top 200 industrial corporations reveals, however, this is not what happens. Rather, compared with other top 200 directors, the finance capitalists consistently stand out as members of established propertied families or as among the principal owners of the corporations they direct. With the number of directorships held constant, finance capitalists are far more likely than ordinary directors to belong to the establishment or be principal owners.

Thus, for instance, 61 percent of the finance capitalists ($N = 31$) but only 36 percent of the other directors with a single directorship ($N = 174$) are in the establishment; the contrast between them is even sharper among the men in the inner group, i.e. among those who hold two or more seats: 84 percent of the finance capitalists ($N = 16^*$) but only 33 percent of the other directors ($N = 14^*$) are in the establishment. Similarly, 19 percent of the finance capitalists ($N = 31$) but only 7 percent of the other directors ($N = 174$) with a seat on only one board ($N = 174$) are principal owners; and among the men in the inner group, the difference is also sharp: 22 percent of the finance capitalists ($N = 16^*$) but only 10 percent of the other directors ($N = 14^*$) are principal owners.

Conversely, with the number of directorships held constant, proportionately far more of the men in establishment families than in other families are finance capitalists: among those with a single directorship, 23 percent of the establishment directors ($N = 82$) but only 10 percent of the others ($N = 123$) are finance capitalists; among those in the inner group, the comparable figures are 74 percent of the establishment directors ($N = 18^*$) but only 21 percent of the nonestablishment directors ($N = 12^*$). And again, the pattern is much the same comparing owners and nonowners. Among the men sitting only on one board, 33 percent of the principal owners ($N = 18$) but only 13 percent of the nonowners ($N = 187$) are finance capitalists; and for those in the inner group, the comparable figures are 70 percent ($N = 5^*$) versus 49 percent ($N = 25^*$).

These figures also reveal that, as expected, whether they are finance capitalists or ordinary directors, the men of the inner group are typically more likely than those outside it, i.e. holding only a single directorship, to be either members of establishment families or principal owners. The converse relationship also tends to hold: whether or not they are in the establishment or are principal owners, the men in the inner group are more likely than those outside of it to be finance capitalists.

Table 4.2 *Percentage of finance capitalists and other directors of the top 200 industrial corporations who are in the establishment or principal owners, both, or neither, by the number of top 200 directorships held*

	Establish-ment owners	Non-establish-ment owners	Establish-ment nonowners	Non-establish-ment nonowners	(N)
		Single top 200 directorship			
Finance capitalists	13	7	48	32	(31)
Other directors	5	2	32	62	(174)
All directors	6	3	34	57	(205)
		Two or more top 200 directorships			
Finance capitalists	16	6	69	9	(16)
Other directors	0	10	33	56	(14)
All directors	8	8	52	32	(31)[a]

[a] Rounding error in weighted cases.

Finally, the pattern tends to repeat itself when we take into account the combination of establishment membership and principal ownership, while controlling for the number of top 200 directorships held (table 4.2). Both within the inner group and outside it, finance capitalists are more likely than ordinary directors to be establishment owners; similarly, they are far less likely to be *non*establishment *non*owners. The pattern, however, is not entirely consistent; the finance capitalists in the inner group are not more likely than other directors to be nonestablishment owners. Most striking, however, they are by far the *least* likely of all types to be *non*establishment *non*owners: a mere 9 percent of the finance capitalists in the inner group but 62 percent of the other directors holding only a single top 200 directorship neither belong to established families nor are themselves principal owners.[14]

If we take into account the relative economic centrality and size of the corporations, the finance capitalists continue to stand out as the incarnate representatives of their class, even in this already rarified atmosphere of the top 200 industrials in the corporate world. Or, put conversely, the established families of property and principal owners are much more likely than nonestablishment or nonowning families to have their members or representatives at the interlocking financial industrial helms, both in the 'key' manufacturing industries, which constitute the nucleus of all manufacturing and other industries, and in the bigger and smaller of the top 200 industrials.

Thus, among the men with directorships in corporations in 'key' industries, 79 percent of the finance capitalists ($N = 33$) are in the establishment and 20 percent are principal owners, but only 39 percent of the other directors ($N = 131$) are in the establishment and 7 percent are principal owners; while among those in other industries, 48 percent of the finance capitalists ($N = 15^*$) are in the establishment and 21 percent are principal owners versus, respectively, 30 percent and 8 percent of the other directors ($N = 57$).

Conversely, among those with directorships in 'key' industries, 33 percent of the establishment directors ($N = 76$) but only 8 percent of the nonestablishment directors ($N = 88$) are finance capitalists; in other industries, the respective figures are 29 percent ($N = 24$) and 16 percent ($N = 48$). Similarly, 42 percent of the principal owners ($N = 16^*$) but only 18 percent of the nonowners ($N = 148$) with directorships in corporations in 'key' industries are finance capitalists, and in other industries the respective percentages are almost identical: 40 percent ($N = 8$) and 18 percent ($N = 64$). If we also control for the assets size of the corporation, the same pattern of relationships holds in both 'key' and other industries (but space limitations preclude running through them here).

Finally, if we examine the various combinations of being a principal owner or a member of an established family, these relationships tend once again to be recapitulated (tables 4.3 and 4.4). In the 'key' industries and in other manufacturing, in the

Table 4.3 *Percentage of finance capitalists and other directors of the top 200 industrial corporations in 'key' and other industries, who are in the establishment or principal owners, both, or neither*

	Establish- ment owners	Non- establish- ment owners	Establish- ment nonowners	Non- establish- ment nonowners	(N)
	Directorships in corporations in 'key' industries				
Finance capitalists	11	9	68	12	(33)
Other directors	4	3	35	58	(131)
All directors	5	4	41	49	(164)
	Directorships in corporations in other industries				
Finance capitalists	21	0	28	52	(15)
Other directors	5	3	25	68	(57)
All directors	8	2	25	64	(72)

corporations with assets of a $0.5 billion or more and in the smaller ones, the finance capitalists stand out sharply in comparison with other directors as peculiarly men of property: indeed, while the vast majority of the ordinary industrial directors in these categories are neither members of established propertied families nor principal owners, this is true of only a small fraction of the finance capitalists (except among those in *non*-'key' industries). The contrast in the intraclass situations of the finance capitalists in the 'key' industries and in other manufacturing is thus especially striking: in the 'key' industries, the overwhelming majority (88 percent) of the finance capitalists are either in the establishment or are principal owners, but in the other industries this is so for only slightly less than half (48 percent) of the finance capitalists. (See tables 4.3 and 4.4.)[15]

Table 4.4 *Percentage of finance capitalists and other directors of the top 200 industrial corporations who are in the establishment or principal owners, both, or neither, by the assets size of the corporations in which they hold directorships*

	Establish-ment owners	Non-establish-ment owners	Establish-ment nonowners	Non-establish-ment nonowners	(N)
			Assets of US$0.5 bn plus		
Finance capitalists	10	5	59	26	(29)
Other directors	2	2	34	62	(90)
All directors	4	3	40	53	(119)[a]
			Other corporations		
Finance capitalists	20	8	50	22	(18)
Other directors	6	4	30	61	(98)
All directors	8	4	33	55	(116)

[a] Rounding error in weighted cases.

Conclusion

This empirical analysis has been guided by a class theory of the relations between various conceptually defined types of 'managers' of major financial institutions and top industrial corporations and their 'owners' under conditions of the high concentration, centralization, and coalescence of both loan capital and productive capital in the large corporation. With the consequent emergence of the self-contradictory historical form of 'finance capital,' a specific class type or distinctive class segment also emerges, namely, the 'finance capitalist,' representing and embodying that form in the interlocking directorates between big banks and other financial institutions and large industrial corporations.

Probing systematically into the comparative intraclass situations of the various types of directors of the top industrials reveals that the finance capitalists, sitting simultaneously on the boards of financial and industrial corporations, do indeed have a special and extensive directorial role in the higher industrial world and constitute a genuine class type within the capitalist,class itself. These leading organizers of the corporate system of classwide property and private appropriation preside over the coalescence of financial and industrial capital, and bear the specific intraclass burden of coordinating and attempting to reconcile the self-contradictory interests inherent in the interpenetrating ownership and interlocking credit and investment relationships of the major financial institutions and large industrial corporations; and they are drawn heavily, and disproportionately compared with other directors of the top 200 industrial corporations, from among the nation's established families of property and principal owners of capital. The finance capitalists are indeed the virtual personification of the fusion of the family and property systems in the so-called bureaucratic and interorganizational managerial realm of the large corporation.[16]

From the standpoint of managerial theory, in general, and of 'interorganizational theory,' in particular, the findings in this study are inexplicable, and directly contradict some of their most basic assumptions and central propositions. In both these theories, the large corporation appears as no more than another complex organization in an uncertain environment constituted of other organizations, and administered by propertyless 'managers' who even take on a semblance of being a 'purely neutral technocracy' or 'technostructure.' Neither the private ownership of capital nor the imperatives of capital accumulation determine their conduct or the dynamics of the large corporation and its interrelations with other corporations and major financial institutions.

In short, neither managerialism nor interorganizational theory would predict the systematic findings presented here and neither theory can account for them. These findings show conclusively that not 'organization' but capital, and not the 'mere administrator' or bureaucratic manager, but the finance capitalist, representing and personifying the coalescence of financial and industrial capital, exercises the decisive power in the nation's top industrial corporations. Not a process of supposed 'interorganizational elite cooptation' but rather discrete, specific intraclass relations and concrete propertied interests explain the selection and recruitment of the men who fill the strategic seats of power interlocking the managerial helms of the leading financial institutions and largest industrial corporations in our country.[17]

Notes

1 As of 1964, the 100 largest commercial banks in the United States held 46 percent of all the deposits of the 13,775 commercial banks in the country. The 14 largest alone held 24 percent of all commercial bank deposits. (See Patman Report 1966, p. 804.) Germany's dominant 'Big Three,' the Deutsche, the Dresdner, and the Commerz, have long dominated its banking system. In England, this has been so of the 'Big Five': Lloyds, Westminster, Midland, Barclays, and National Provincial; they already controlled three-fourths of all funds deposited in British banks by the eve of World War II (Eaton 1949, p. 143). The United States, despite its concentration, is unusual in the *number* of competing banks. England has 11 clearing banks and 24 'joint stock' banks, and Canada has eight chartered banks, for instance, compared with the nearly 14,000 commercial banks in the United States (Nadler 1968, p. 167). Also see Sayers (1962).

2 Strachey (1956, pp. 273–5), concerning the theory of John M. Keynes. Limited research on the relationship between banking concentration and interest rates in the United States shows that, when regional and local market conditions and differences in loan characteristics are held constant, there is a significant relationship between banking concentration in metropolitan areas and loan rates. The Chicago Federal Reserve Board's own studies have shown that 'the greater the number of banks or the lower the percentage of deposits held by the largest bank in the study, the lower were effective interest rates charged on loans. . . . Higher banking concentration was also associated with greater pre-tax earnings on assets' (Fischer 1968, p. 369).

3 For a review of the issues and evidence presented in several of the most influential studies, see Glasberg and Schwartz (1983).

4 Earlier formulations of these questions and several hypotheses on the 'inner group' and 'finance capitalists' in the United States appear in Zeitlin (1974, 1976 – this volume, chs 1 and 2). Cf. also Ratcliff (1980a, 1980b), Soref (1980), and Mintz and Schwartz (1985).

5 Galbraith 1967; Berle and Means 1967, pp. xiv-xv. Berle uses the phrase 'financial capital' as a synonym for 'loan capital,' *not* with the specific conceptual content elaborated here concerning 'finance capital.'

6 Galbraith 1971, p. xix; Berle and Means 1967, p. 313. Galbraith's concept of 'technostructure' was adumbrated three decades earlier by Berle and Means' 'technocracy.'

7 These authors are rather vague about what they think are the meaning

and implications of 'financial interlocks.' A very recent systematic analysis of the corporate network of American business also rejects this interorganizational paradigm and argues, to the contrary, that 'hegemonic relations organized around the interests of financial institutions, are the main organizing principles of the business world' (Mintz and Schwartz 1985, p. 249).

8 Gordon (1966, p. x), for instance, simply notes, in a new preface to his study of American corporations in the late 1930s, the extensive interlocking between the banks and corporations, and suggests that this is a 'far cry from what was once meant by "financial control",' but suggests no possible implications. 'Interorganizational' theorists often make reference to the 'interorganizational *context*,' as well as 'characteristics of the organization,' but the 'unit of study ... [is] construed as an individual organization,' and the 'context' as other organizations (see Pennings 1980, pp. 9–10). The so-called 'interorganizational context' never involves even the concrete interests of principal shareowners and major investors, let alone the class and intraclass relations within which these 'organizations' – the major corporations – operate.

9 For analyses of the historical and social relevance of class segments, see Zeitlin (1984), Zeitlin and Ratcliff (1988). Although Weber, unlike Marx, focuses in his conception of class on so-called 'market relations' rather than on 'production relations,' he also differentiates the propertied according to the specific form in which they appropriate their portions of the social product, and underlines the contradictions between the industrialist, on the one side, and 'the rentier ... and the banker,' on the other; the latter's 'cash boxes,' writes Weber, are filled with '"unearned" gains' taken from 'the pockets of the manufacturers.' (Weber 1946, pp. 181–6, 301).

10 O'Connor (1968, p. 31), referring to 'corporate capital,' which he substitutes for the term 'finance capital' because, he says, the latter is often confused with bank capital, i.e. the notion that the banks control the corporations or dominate the economy. Hilferding occasionally appears to lapse into this, perhaps because of the specific situation at the time in Germany, when the ascendancy of the big banks seemed indisputable. But whatever his occasional tendency to speak of industry as under bank control, this is not the overall theoretical thrust of *Das Finanzkapital*. Lenin's formulation of the concept of finance capital ([1917] 1967, vol. 1, pp. 710–11) was borrowed explicitly, with slight modification, from Hilferding. We think that referring, as O'Connor does, to the decision-makers in simultaneous charge of the leading banks and large nonfinancial corporations as 'corporate capitalists' deflects attention from the critical theoretical focus on the contradictions inherent in the coalescence of loan and productive capital.

11 'Men' because very few women yet occupy these corporate commanding

heights, and only two (one of whom was Vera Heinz on the board of Heinz) did in our sample of 40 top industrials of 1964.

12 Domhoff developed the lists of (a) clubs and (b) preparatory schools to fill in the gaps which would be left by exclusive reliance on (c) the *Social Register*. He tried to narrow down the lists of clubs and preparatory schools to those composed almost entirely of establishment members (thus excluding Andover and Exeter from the list of preparatory schools, for example). We classified a director as belonging to the establishment if he met any *one* of the three criteria, i.e. (a) clubs, (b) preparatory schools, or (c) *Social Register*. We used the 1965 edition of the *Social Register Locator* to check *Social Register* listings for the sample. The *Social Register Locator* is a master list of the names listed in the various *Social Register* volumes. Each of 12 cities has its own volume. As Domhoff (1967, p. 15) suggests, men listed only in the Washington, D.C. edition of the *Social Register* were not classified as members of establishment families. Domhoff also used the 'blue books' of several other cities (the *Detroit Social Secretary*, the *Houston Social Register*, the *Los Angeles Blue Book*, the *New Orleans Social Register*, and the *Seattle Blue Book*), but these volumes were not available for our research. It also was less thorough than Domhoff's in that listings for parents, siblings or wives were not checked, which probably resulted in a few misclassifications. E. Digby Baltzell (1958, 1964) considers private schooling an even better index of 'upper-class' membership than the *Social Register*. Information on schooling came from entries on directors in *Who's Who in America*, or *Who's Who in Commerce and Industry* (or other collective biography information). In some cases, the only biographical information available was in *Poor's Register of Corporations, Executives, and Directors*, which gives only information on college attendance. Membership in specific exclusive clubs is perhaps *the* mark of acceptance into the establishment (Domhoff 1967, pp. 18–20, 34–6). The list of clubs covered most of the country, unlike the *Social Register* criterion and the preparatory school criterion (the schools on Domhoff's list are concentrated in the northeast); most of the nation's big cities had at least one club on Domhoff's list of 40 clubs. Directors' *Who's Who* biographies generally listed directors' club memberships. Directors for whom there was only a *Poor's* entry and who were not listed in the *Social Register* were classified as nonestablishment, even though there was no way to know whether or not they belonged to a club on Domhoff's list or had attended a preparatory school on Domhoff's list. Domhoff set out two additional criteria for membership in the upper class that were not used here (1970, pp. 24–7), because a trial sample using them revealed that the number of directors misclassified as nonestablishment would not justify the additional research. See Soref (1976, p. 362; 1979, pp. 282–3) for an estimate of false negatives in the present sample.

13 The *term* 'inner group' has been around for decades in the United States, and recurs, for instance, throughout US Congress (1965). But I and my students first delineated the concept of the inner group and elaborated a theory of the internal relations of the capitalist class and of the inner group's place within them, particularly in intraclass leadership and political hegemony. (See Zeitlin et al. 1974b, 1974c; Zeitlin 1976, pp. 900–1 – this volume, ch. 2). Since then, Useem (1978; 1979; 1980; 1983) has taken our theory of the inner group as the basis of his own fine work. Cf. also Domhoff (1983, pp. 70–2), who presents evidence on the inner group but wrongly attributes the original concept and propositions on intraclass differentiation to Useem.

14 The numbers in the relevant cells here are too small for reliable percentages to be computed in order to show the converse relationships.

15 Here, too, the converse relationships cannot be shown because the numbers in the relevant cells are too small for reliable percentages to be computed.

16 Mintz and Schwartz analyze the role of financial institutions in intercorporate relationships but do not consider the role of the capitalist class itself or of the place of specific segments within it. They argue, however, that 'class can be introduced into this analysis' by focusing both on the 'inner group' and 'finance capitalists' and integrating such an 'analysis of individuals with the theory of finance capital. . . .' Based on my elaboration of that theory for analysis of the internal structure of the capitalist class, and related empirical analyses (Zeitlin 1974, 1976 – this volume, chs 1 and 2; Zeitlin et al. 1976; Ratcliff 1980a, 1980b), Mintz and Schwartz (1985, pp. 253–4) conclude that 'combining . . . inner-group analysis with the theory of finance capital, [suggests] that business leadership accrues to a special social type: a cohesive group of multiple directors . . . who sit on bank boards as representatives of capital in general. . . . [D]ecisions on capital allocation are affected by the needs of this inner group of finance capitalists . . . and conditioned by the class networks they create and inhabit.' Thus, if finance capitalists are constrained and limited in their conduct by the imperatives of capital accumulation and by the centrality of banks in this process, 'they must also make real choices about which investment options to pursue [as Ratcliff has shown]. . . . Without their input, capital would be allocated in different ways and in response to different pressures. Like everyone else, the capitalist class makes decisions but not under conditions of its own choosing.'

17 Analysis of the internal structure of the dominant class in Chile by Zeitlin and Ratcliff (1988, ch. 3) has yielded findings that are strikingly like the ones reported here. Based both on the analysis of far richer data on ownership and on a detailed and systematic analysis of kinship relations among the families of the higher executives and principal

owners of capital in the top corporations and banks owned and controlled by Chileans, they also find that finance capitalists constitute a special class type, both in terms of the extensiveness of their role in coordinating the common business affairs of their class and in their integration within its central core of principal capital-owning families.

References

Allen, Michael P. 1974. 'The Structure of Interorganizational Elite Corporation: Interlocking Corporate Directorates.' *American Sociological Review* 39 (June): 393–406.

—— 1976. 'Management Control in the Large Corporation: Comment on Zeitlin.' *American Journal of Sociology* 81 (January): 885–94.

Averitt, Robert T. 1968. *The Dual Economy*. New York: Norton.

Baltzell, E. Digby. 1958. *Philadelphia Gentlemen: The Making of a National Upper Class*. New York: Macmillan.

—— 1964. *The Protestant Establishment*. New York: Random House.

Berle, Adolph, Jr., and Gardiner C. Means. 1967. *The Modern Corporation and Private Property*. New York: Harcourt, Brace & World (originally published in 1932 by Macmillan).

Black, Edie, and Fred Goff. 1969. *The Hanna Industrial Complex*. Berkeley, Calif.: North American Congress on Latin America.

Burch, Philip H., Jr. 1972. *The Managerial Revolution Reassessed*. Lexington, Mass.: Heath.

Business Week. 1968. 'Brewing His Own Formula for Success.' July 13: 104–6.

Chevalier, Jean-Marie. 1970. *La Structure Financière de l'Industrie Americaine et le Problème du Controle dans les Grandes Sociétés Americaines*. Paris: Cujas.

Domhoff, G. William. 1967. *Who Rules America?* Englewood Cliffs, N.J.: Prentice-Hall.

—— 1970. *The Higher Circles: The Governing Class in America*. New York: Random House.

—— 1983. *Who Rules America Now? A View for the '80s*. Englewood Cliffs, N.J.: Prentice-Hall.

Dunn, Marvin. 1979. 'The Family Office as a Coordinating Mechanism Within the Ruling Class.' *The Insurgent Sociologist* Fall–Winter: 8–23.

Eaton, John. 1949. *Political Economy*. New York: International.

Federal Trade Commission. 1951. *Report of the Federal Trade Commission on Interlocking Directorates*. Washington, D.C.: Government Printing Office.

Fischer, Gerald C. 1968. *American Banking Structure*. New York: Columbia University Press.

Fortune. 1958. 'West-coast Wheeler Dealer.' November: 69.

Galbraith, John K. 1967. *The New Industrial State*. New York: New American

Library. (Also, 'Introduction,' 2nd edn. 1971. New York: Houghton Mifflin.)

Glasberg, Davita S., and Michael Schwartz. 1983. 'Ownership and Control of Corporations.' *Annual Review of Sociology* 9: 311–32.

Gordon, Robert A. 1966. *Business Leadership in the Large Corporation.* Berkeley, Calif.: University of California Press (originally published in 1945 under the auspices of the Brookings Institution).

Hilferding, Rudolf. 1947. *Das Finanzkapital: Eine studie uber die jungste Entwicklung des Kapitalismus.* Berlin: Verlag J. H. W. Dietz (reprint of the original 1910 edition).

James, David, and Michael Soref. 1981. 'The Unmaking of the Corporation President: Profit Constraints on Managerial Autonomy.' *American Sociological Review* 46: 1–18.

Kotz, David M. 1978. *Bank Control of Large Corporations in the United States.* Berkeley, Calif.: University of California Press.

Kuh, Edward. 1963. *Capital Stock Growth: A Micro-Econometric Approach.* Amsterdam: North-Holland.

Larner, Robert J. 1970. *Management Control and the Large Corporation.* Cambridge, Mass.: Dunellen.

Lenin, Nikolai. [1917] 1967. 'Imperialism.' In *Lenin: Selected Works.* New York: International.

Lundberg, Ferdinand. 1968. *The Rich and the Super Rich.* New York: Bantam.

Mahon, Gigi. 1978. 'War of Fortunes: The Wealthy Phipps Clan is Rent by Strife.' *Barron's,* July 31: 4–5, 16.

Marx, Karl. 1952. *The Civil War in France.* Moscow: Foreign Languages Publishing House.

—— 1967. *Capital.* vols. 1–3. New York: International.

Mills, C. Wright. 1942. 'Review of the Social Life of a Modern Community.' *American Sociological Review* 7 (April): 264–71. (Pp. 39–52 in *Power, Politics and People: The Collected Essays of C. Wright Mills,* edited by I. L. Horowitz. 1963. New York: Oxford.)

—— 1956. *The Power Elite.* New York: Oxford University Press.

Mintz, Beth, and Michael Schwartz. 1985. *The Power Structure of American Business.* Chicago, Ill.: University of Chicago Press.

Nadler, Paul S. 1968. *Commercial Banking in the Economy.* New York: Random House.

O'Connor, James. 1968. 'Finance Capital or Corporate Capital?' *Monthly Review* 20 (October): 3–35.

[Patman] Staff Report 1966. 'Bank Stock Ownership and Control', reprinted in Patman Report 1968. *Commercial Banks and Their Trust Activities: Emerging Influence on the American Economy,* vol. 1. US Congress, House, Committee on Banking and Currency, Domestic Finance Committee. 90th Congr., 2nd sess. Washington, D.C.: Government Printing Office.

Pederson, Lawrence, and William Tabb. 1976. 'Ownership and Control of

Large Corporations Revisited.' *Antitrust Bulletin* Spring: 53–6.

Pennings, Johannes. 1978. 'Interlocking Relationships: The Case of Interlocking Directorates.' Paper presented at the Annual Meeting of the American Sociological Association, August at San Francisco, Calif.

—— 1980. *Interlocking Directorates: Origins and Consequences of Connections Among Organizations and Boards of Directors*. San Francisco, Calif.: Jossey-Bass.

Pfeffer, Jeffrey. 1972. 'Size and Composition of Corporate Boards of Directors: The Organization and Its Environment.' *Administrative Science Quarterly* 17 (June): 218–28.

Poulantzas, Nicos. 1975. *Classes in Contemporary Capitalism*. London: New Left Books.

Ratcliff, Richard E. 1980a. 'Banks and the Command of Capital Flows: An Analysis of Capitalist Class Structure and Mortgage Disinvestment in a Metropolitan Area.' Pp. 107–32 in *Classes, Class Conflict, and the State*, edited by Maurice Zeitlin. Boston, Mass.: Little, Brown.

—— 1980b. 'Banks and Corporate Lending: An Analysis of the Impact of the Internal Structure of the Capitalist Class on the Lending Behavior of Banks.' *American Sociological Review* 45 (August): 553–70.

Rodgers, William. 1974. *Think: a Biography of the Watsons and IBM*. New York: Mentor.

Sayers, R.S., ed. 1962. *Banking in Western Europe*. London: Oxford University Press.

Scott, John. 1979. *Corporations, Classes and Capitalism*. London: Hutchinson.

—— and Catherine Griff. 1985. *Directors of Industry: The British Corporate Network 1904–1976*. Cambridge, England: Polity Press.

Sheehan, Robert. 1966. 'There's Plenty of Privacy Left in Private Enterprise.' *Fortune*, July: 224–5, 327, 328, 334, 343, 348.

—— 1967. 'Proprietors in the World of Big Business.' *Fortune*, June 15: 178–83, 242.

Soref, Michael. 1976. 'Social Class and a Division of Labor Within the Corporate Elite: A Note on Class, Interlocking, and Executive Committee Membership of Directors of U.S. Industrial Firms.' *Sociological Quarterly* 17 (Summer): 360–8.

—— 1979. 'The Internal Differentiation of the American Capitalist Class.' Ph.D. dissertation, Department of Sociology, University of Wisconsin, Madison.

—— 1980. 'The Finance Capitalists.' Pp. 62–82 in *Classes, Class Conflict, and the State*, edited by Maurice Zeitlin. Boston, Mass.: Little, Brown.

Strachey, John. 1956. *Contemporary Capitalism*. New York: Random House.

Thompson, James D. 1967. *Organizations in Action*. New York: McGraw-Hill.

Time. 1955. 'The Baron of Beer.' July 11: 82–6.

US Congress, Senate Subcommittee on Anti-Trust and Monopoly. 1965.

Interlocks in Corporate Management. Staff Report to the Anti-trust Subcommittee of the Committee on the Judiciary. House of Representatives. 89th Congr. 1st sess. Washington, D.C.: Government Printing Office.

US Congress, Senate Committee on Governmental Affairs. 1978. *Interlocking Directorates Among the Major U.S. Corporations.* Washington, D.C.: Government Printing Office.

Useem, Michael. 1978. 'The Inner Group of the American Capitalist Class.' *Social Problems* 24 (February): 225–240.

—— 1979. 'The Social Organization of the American Business Elite and Participation of Corporation Directors in the Governance of American Institutions.' *American Sociological Review* 44: 553–72.

—— 1980. 'Which Business Leaders Help Govern?' Pp. 199–225 in *Power Structure Research*, edited by G.W. Domhoff. Beverly Hills, Calif.: Sage.

—— 1983. *The Inner Circle: Large Corporations and the Rise of Business Political Activity in the U.S. and U.K.* New York: Oxford University Press.

Villarejo, Don. 1961–2. 'Stock Ownership and Control of Corporations.' New England Free Press reprint of a two-part article published in *New University Thought*, Autumn, 1961, and Winter, 1962.

Weber, Max. 1946. *From Max Weber: Essays in Sociology*, edited by H.H. Gerth and C. Wright Mills. New York: Oxford University Press.

White, Shelby. 1978. 'Cradle to Grave: Family Offices Manage Money for the Very Rich.' *Barron's*, March 20: 9, 18, 20–1.

Zeitlin, Maurice. 1974. 'Corporate Ownership and Control: The Large Corporation and the Capitalist Class.' *American Journal of Sociology* 79 (March): 1073–119.

—— 1976. 'On Class Theory of the Large Corporation.' *American Journal of Sociology* 81 (January): 894–903.

—— 1984. *The Civil Wars in Chile (or the bourgeois revolutions that never were).* Princeton, N.J.: Princeton University Press.

—— and Richard E. Ratcliff. 1988. *Landlords and Capitalists: The Dominant Class of Chile.* Princeton, N.J.: Princeton University Press.

—— Lynda Ann Ewen, and Richard E. Ratcliff. 1974a. '"New Princes" for Old? The Large Corporation and the Capitalist Class in Chile.' *American Journal of Sociology* 80 (July): 87–123.

——, Lynda Ann Ewen, and Richard E. Ratcliff 1974b. 'The "Inner Group": Interlocking Directorates and the Internal Differentiation of the Capitalist Class in Chile.' Paper presented at the Annual Meeting of the American Sociological Association, August 27, at Montreal.

—— W. Lawrence Neuman, Richard E. Ratcliff, and Lynda Ann Ewen. 1974c. 'Politics and the Capitalist Class in Chile: The "Inner Group" and the State.' Paper presented at the Annual Meeting of the American Sociological Association, August 27, at Montreal.

——, W. Lawrence Neuman, and Richard E. Ratcliffe. 1976. 'Class Segments: Agrarian Property and Political Leadership in the Capitalist Class of Chile.' *American Sociological Review* 41 (December): 1006–29.

5

Who owns America? the same old gang

Do you remember those full-page newspaper ads that showed a little old lady stroking *her* locomotive, supposedly owned by millions of ordinary Americans just like her? Or Standard Oil's gushing claim, 'Yes, the people own the tools of production. . . . How odd to find that it is here, in the capitalism [Karl Marx] reviled, that the promise of the tool has been fulfilled.' How about the Texaco television commercial that has Bob Hope asking us to 'take a look at the owners of America's oil companies,' with Hope then leading us on a tour of a typical community made up of just plain folks like you and me?

A best-selling book, received with much fanfare in the press, repeats the refrain. Its author, long-time management consultant and publicist Peter Drucker, tells us that an 'unseen revolution' has wrought 'a more radical shift in ownership than Soviet communism.' Even more amazing, 'the socialism of Marxist theory has been realized for the first time on American soil.'

Not only are the means of production now in everyone's hands, but the US Chamber of Commerce confides that the United States has become a 'post-industrial society.' College textbooks inform us that a 'dramatic shift from blue collar to white collar, from brawn to brain [has] occurred,' and the best-seller *Future Shock* rhapsodizes that 'for the first time in human history,' a society – our society – has 'managed within a few short decades to throw off the yoke of manual labor.' A book on 'power in America' celebrates the passing of classes and suggests that we organize popular visits to 'Newport, and bus tours through Grosse Pointe, for purely educational purposes – like seeing Carlsbad Caverns once.' It is time, the author

---

This article was first published in 1978. So, in square brackets, I have updated crucial figures wherever possible, based on the most recent first-rate studies by specialists or the latest US government figures available.

advises us, to shout, 'The Working Class is dead. Long live the memory of the Working Class.' And, summing it all up, a popular book on how to be a politician announces that 'the economic class system is disappearing. . . . Redistribution of wealth and income . . . has ended economic inequality's political significance.'

So, what *has* happened to classes? Who *does* own America, and how has it all been changing? Has the capitalist class really been 'lopped off' at the top, as Harvard's Talcott Parsons once pithily put it? Has the ownership of American corporations become so dispersed that control has shifted to 'professional managers' who are merely the 'trustees' for all of us – 'stockholders, employees, suppliers, consumers, and the public' – as Donald S. McNaughton, then chairman of Prudential Life, announced in a speech? Has the yoke of manual labor really been lifted? Is the working class now a mere memory? Or are the claims that prompt these questions really *pseudofacts* that are as plausible and persuasive as they are deceptive? The answer, I think, is clear: economic inequality weighs as heavily and cuts as deeply as ever, and neither capitalists nor workers have vanished from American life.

Who Owns What?

Let's look first at who owns what. It's certainly hard enough to find out, even if, like US government economists, you have access to Internal Revenue Service (IRS) data. No law requires Americans to report their net worth, and besides, wealth is deliberately hidden, whether out of modesty or to avoid taxes. Still, an ingenious method of estimating wealth has been devised, to make the dead disclose what the living conceal. It is called the 'estate multiplier technique,' and it uses IRS data on estate tax returns. This technique treats persons who die in any year as a 'stratified sample' of the living on whose estates tax returns would have to be filed if they died during the year. . . . [It reveals that] a minute number of Americans make up the real owners of America.

The Rose Bowl's 104,696 seats would still be half empty if only every adult American who owns $1 million or more in corporate stock came to cheer, and it would be even emptier if only those who have $100,000 in state and local bonds got a seat. If you counted all state, local, and federal bonds (except US Savings Bonds), and added Treasury bills, certificates, notes, and mortgages – and even foreign bonds – held by Americans in amounts of at least $200,000, you would still find well over a quarter of the Rose Bowl seats not taken. Only 55,400 adults have $1 million or more in corporate stock. A mere 40,000 have $100,000 or more in state and local bonds (all federal tax exempt), and 73,500 adults have $200,000 or more if we count all bonds and debt-holdings.

This tiny owning class at the tip of the top, represented by barely more than one-twentieth of 1 percent of American adults, has a fifth of all the corporate stock, nearly two-thirds of the worth of all state and local bonds, and two-fifths of all bonds and notes. No wonder it took five years of trying by an outstanding economist, James D. Smith, to get the IRS to allow him to study its information – and by then some of the data had been destroyed. [According to the latest IRS data on estate tax returns, for 1982, 32,000 adults way up at the tip of the top – that's much less than one-*fiftieth* of 1 percent of all adults – own assets whose net worth is $5,000,000 or more. But the IRS gives no breakdown of what share of the various kinds of wealth – stocks and bonds, etc. – this fraction of Americans owns.]

Contrast what this propertied class owns to what the rest of us have. . . . The bottom half of all American families combined have [as of 1970] only three cents of every dollar's worth of all the wealth in the country. [Three cents out of every dollar's worth of net family wealth is still roughly the share held by the bottom half of all families. In dollars, even with others in the household working besides dad, a third of all *households*, as of 1984, have total net assets of less than $10,000, counting everything they own (and subtracting what they owe); nearly half (45.1 percent) have a net worth of under $25,000.]

Back at the top, if we count up what the richest 1 percent of the population own, we find that they have a seventh of all the real estate in the country, more than half the corporate stock, and almost all the trust assets. They even have a seventh of all the cash in every checking and savings account and pocket and purse in America.

Summed up, that is a quarter of the net worth of the entire adult population held by the top 1 percent. . . . [The figures for the richest 1 percent here refer to wealth held by *individuals*. But the family is the real unit of ownership and control of wealth; especially among the richest families, aside from a variety of legal devices (e.g. bank and brokerage holdings, trusts, and estates) that formalize the family's community property, individuals often 'own' real property and capital only as members of a particular family. Even in the unusual case where a rich family's wealth isn't held in trusts or estates but is legally spread out among its individual members, if they're in 'good standing' they benefit from the family fortune as a whole, get income from it, and are the potential heirs of one another's holdings, each of which is a slice from the same source. The boundary of the 'family' among the wealthy stretches well beyond the immediate family, and sometimes even its own members don't know exactly where it is. You can see this from the care taken to define and codify inheritance rights with precision; the members of the 'family' among the richest Americans typically include relatives by blood and marriage out to the fifth degree. No one has tried to get at the distribution of wealth taking these wider kinship nets into account.

The most accurate survey to date of the assets owned by American *families* was carried out by the Joint Economic Committee of Congress. It uses data compiled for the Federal Reserve Board, based on a random sample of US households and a special sample of the immediate families of the richest taxpayers in the top 1 percent of the income pyramid. To assure the cooperation of the rich, they got iron-clad guarantees of confidentiality and anonymity from the Fed. This survey reveals that, as of 1983, the richest 0.5 percent of all families, or the 'super rich,' own 15.3 percent of the net value of *all* real estate (and 35.6 percent of the commercial real estate), 46.5 percent of the value of all corporate stock, and 77.0 percent of the value of the trust assets owned by all families; the second half of the richest 1 percent, the 'very rich,' own another 4.2 percent of all the real estate (and 6.5 percent of the commercial real estate), 13.5 percent of the corporate stock, and 5.0 percent of the trust assets. So, the richest 1 percent of the families in our country own a fifth of all the real estate (and over twice that much of the commercial real estate), three fifths of the corporate stock, and over four fifths of all the trust assets owned by all of us. Summed up, the super rich have 35.1 percent and the very rich another 6.7 percent of the net worth of everything owned by all American families: together, the richest 1 percent of families own over two-fifths of the net wealth owned by every family in America.

For most of us who own anything at all, our house ('personal residence') is the biggest asset we own, and it's usually worth most of what we own altogether. Barely two out of three households own their own home, and the median value of the 'equity' in it (what you can sell it for versus what you owe on it) is $40,597, as of 1984. Few Americans own anything else that's worth much. Only 19 percent of all families have a member who owns any corporate stock at all; and half of these families own stock, as of 1984, worth less than $3,892. Among ordinary workers ('operatives, laborers, service'), 92 percent don't own a single share of stock. So, if you don't count the 'equity' in the houses Americans own and live in, the wealth is even more concentrated: the super rich's share of the net wealth minus home equity comes to 45.4 percent, and the share of the very rich comes to another 7.8 percent. Summed up, almost half the wealth owned by all of us – not counting what we could make if we sold our houses – is in the hands of the super rich alone; and something over half of it is in the hands of the super rich and very rich (the richest 1 percent) combined. Taking a slice off the top as big as the richest tenth of all families, their combined net wealth (including their homes), as of 1983, is some $7.6 trillion – more than enough for them to buy the entire national product of the United States that year and still have plenty left over to pick up the combined output of a few Western European countries besides.]

So it's clear who owns America – but has this propertied class been slipping in its hold on the nation's wealth? Maybe, but if it slipped at all, it was not because of any egalitarian tendencies in American capitalism. It took the country's worst crash, the Great Depression, when many fortunes (and even a few of the fortune-holders) took the plunge from the pinnacle, to make a dent on what they own. Even the modest shrinkage that supposedly took place then is probably more apparent than real, because just before the crash there was a phenomenal rise in the price of stock, the biggest asset in the portfolios of the rich.

But since the end of World War II, there has been little change in their share of the nation's wealth; it has been more or less constant in every year studied, at roughly five-year intervals, since 1945. The richest 1 percent of individuals own a quarter, and the top half of 1 percent a fifth, of the combined market worth of everything owned by every American. Remarkably, economic historians who have culled manuscript census reports on the past century report that on the eve of the Civil War the rich had the same cut of the total: the top 1 percent owned 24 percent in 1860 and 24.9 percent a century later, in 1969. Through all the tumultuous changes since then – the Civil War and the emancipation of the slaves, the Populist and Progressive movements, the Great

Depression, the New Deal, progressive taxation, the mass organiz-ation of industrial workers, and World Wars I and II – this class has held on to everything it had. They owned America then and they own it now.

[Indeed, they own a whole lot more of it today. The two broadest and most accurate surveys ever taken of the assets owned by American *families*, using data compiled for the Federal Reserve Board, show that the share of the wealth held by the super rich (the richest 0.5 percent) went up drastically (by nearly two fifths) between 1963 and 1983, at the expense of the rest of us; even the shares of the very rich (second 0.5 percent) and of the 'rich' (next 9 percent) dropped somewhat (by a bit less than a twelfth). Meanwhile, the share of the wealth held by everyone else (the bottom 90 percent) dropped by a fifth. Here are the precise percentages of all US family wealth owned by the rich and the rest of us, in 1963 and 1983: the families of the super rich in 1963, 25.4, and in 1983, 35.1; of the very rich in 1963, 7.4, and in 1983, 6.7; of the rich in 1963, 32.0, and in 1983, 29.9; everyone else in 1963, 35.0, and in 1983, 28.2.]

Income Inequality

Any notion that income has been redistributed, even though property is intact, is also illusory: the higher the income bracket, the higher the percentage in it that derives its income from the ownership of property. At the top, almost all income is in dividends, capital gains, rents, royalties, and interest. . . . [So, for instance, 1980 IRS returns show that, of the taxpayers with the more or less 'average' adjusted gross income (AGI), in 1979, of $20,000–$25,000, a little over 90 cents of every dollar they receive comes in wages or salary; barely a nickel comes from 'unearned' or property income (dividends, capital gains, interest, rent, etc.). For those with an AGI of $50,000–$100,000, income from wages and salary account for 67 cents and unearned income for about 17 cents of every dollar they get. But for individuals with an AGI of $1 million or more, barely 14 cents of every dollar they get is earned income, while 77 cents is unearned. (Spread between these earned and unearned figures are income from 'businesses and partnerships'; moving from the top income level down, these figures are, respectively, 9 cents, 14 cents, and less than 3 cents of every dollar of income received. The rest is from pensions and other sources.)]

The 5 percent of Americans with the highest incomes take in almost half of all the income from property in the country. These individuals get 64 cents out of every dollar in dividends earned on publicly traded stock and 93 cents of the dividends on stock owned in 'closely held corporations' (those having just a few owners). What's more, they take in 30 cents of every dollar earned in interest, 37 cents in rents and royalties, and 64 cents of every dollar in America coming from trusts and estates.

If we divide Americans into five brackets with the same number of people in each, ranging from low to high, and count all known income, the top fifth gets about 40 cents of every dollar of personal income. The bottom fifth gets just one nickel. That is a ratio of eight to one, and that ratio has remained roughly the same in every year since World War II ended.

[But with the Reagan crowd just saying no to the rest of us (but yes to the rich), inequality in income shares slid backwards to about where it was in the late 1940s: during Reagan's first term, the share of all personal income going to the top fifth of Americans became the biggest since 1950, and that going to the second fifth, the biggest since 1947, while the bottom two-fifths of the income pyramid saw the slight gains they'd made over the previous quarter of a century wiped out. The poorest fifth of the population lost 8 percent and the top fifth gained 9 percent in their share of all personal income – amounting to a $25 billion transfer from the bottom to the top of the income pyramid. But the shift of income to the tip of the top in the past decade has been even more dramatic, less visibly maybe in California and elsewhere on the West Coast or in the Washington metropolitan area than in the Midwest and New York, where you can almost see the gap between ordinary people and the rich growing even bigger. In just 10 years, the richest 1 percent's share of all pretax income went up, according to the Congressional Budget Office (CBO), by well over one-third, at the expense of the rest of us: in 1977 they took in 9.2 percent of all pretax personal income, but by 1988 they were taking in 12.5 percent. Their average real annual pretax income rose even more sharply in that same period, by half: leaping from $301,000 in 1977 (in constant 1988 dollars) to $452,000.

This happened not only because Reagan and his allies in Congress slashed the social programs that benefit lower income families while cutting taxes for the rich; it also happened because the giant leap in military spending at the same time that taxes on the rich were cut sharply quickly drove the federal deficit way up. But the big banks and other financial institutions and the rich are the main buyers of the Treasury bills that fund the erupting federal debt. Only 1.4 percent of all households, as of 1984, own any government securities, but most of the rich own them. So what it amounts to is that to fund the federal deficit, which is now mainly the result of tax-giveaways to the rich, our government turns around and borrows money from them and, of course, pays them at a rate of interest that makes it worth their while. Just the rise in interest payments on the debt under Reagan comes to more than all the supposed savings made by cutting spending for health, education, welfare, and social service programs. Federal interest payments jumped two-and-a-quarter times, as a share of gross national product, from 1.5 percent in the 1970s to 3.4 percent by the Spring of 1988 – and they're still compounding daily.

Maybe, because the economy was in rough straits when Reagan came in, some of the income gap would have widened anyway, no matter who was president. But his policies helped the rich sail safely through these troubled waters – at the expense of the rest of us in the middle and at the bottom of the income pyramid. The combined impact of the deteriorating economy and regressive tax cuts, according to the CBO, is that the average after-tax real incomes of the bottom two income-fifths of American families are today, in 1988, lower than in 1977; the incomes of the families in the middle income ranges barely changed in that decade; but the incomes of the richest 1 percent of families soared by three-quarters.] (Here, in the capitalism celebrated by the Advertising Council and Bob Hope, the gap between the top and bottom income-fifths is wider than in Britain, Holland, West Germany, or even Japan. Among the dozen leading industrial countries, only France has a wider gap.)

All the 'redistributive efforts' and wars on poverty . . . made no dent in income distribution. One reason is that the overall tax burden (local, state, federal) probably became more regressive in the decades after World War II – taxes were taking an increasingly bigger bite of the incomes of people in the lower rather than in the higher brackets. . . . So, taking into account the impact of all taxes and all government spending – even though there was a sizeable increase in government 'benefits' to low income Americans – the level of income inequality ('post-fiscal') didn't change from 1950 on [– not, that is, until the advent of Reaganomics].

Tax Injustice

[With Reagan in the White House, the progressive income tax, the last rampart of fairness in America's tax system, fell to the attack of a coalition of the Right, the rich, and organized big business. The federal individual income tax – until the Reagan era – had stood almost alone as a progressive tax. Of all taxes, it was meant to impose equality of sacrifice on all citizens, by taxing according to ability to pay. The income tax was won originally, in 1894, by a coalition of farmers and workers demanding tax justice. A constitutional amendment was necessary to sustain its passage. And only the demands of the working class in the 1930s and the New Deal reforms of 1935 made the income tax really progressive, by levying far higher rates on the rich.

The rich did pay higher – much higher – personal income taxes than most Americans. And they should have, and should again. If Americans at different income levels pay the same share of their income in taxes, they're paying an unfair share. Only a bigger share of a bigger income is a fair tax share. Of course, there were plenty of special provisions, loopholes, and tax shelters to comfort the rich. A lot of their nominal tax load was lifted by taxing capital gains (profits from the sale of assets) at a far lower rate than that for income from work. And what they couldn't legally avoid, many evaded. Of every dollar of capital gains made in the stock market, the best estimate is that about 37 cents goes unreported. Of all income from capital ownership (dividends, interest, rent, royalties, and capital gains), the IRS estimates that 20 percent is hidden from it, compared with barely 3 percent of all income from wages and salaries. But, despite tax avoidance and evasion at the top, federal personal income taxes – until the Reagan 'tax reform' – used to take a bigger slice of the yearly incomes of the rich than of everybody else.

Figuring out the real tax load carried at various income levels – the 'effective rate' – is a rough science. Income that is legally deducted (or indirectly shifted to others) and special tax credits have to be carefully estimated and taken into account. In 1979, two years before the first of Reagan's tax cuts went into effect, taxpayers with annual incomes of $1 million or more paid an average effective individual income tax rate of 34 percent; on $50,000 to 100,000 a year, the effective rate was 23 percent; on $20,000 to $25,000, 13 percent, and on $5,000 to $10,000, 4 percent. These rising effective rates didn't distribute the income tax burden as fairly as possible, but at least they tended to put it where it belonged: on those who have the most and can thus afford to pay the most. But other taxes tend to be regressive: their effective rates fall as income rises.

Social Security taxes weigh most heavily on workers and middle income families. Taxes on corporate profits even before Reagan mainly have been 'flat.' Corporations of almost all sizes, except for the smallest, were paying about the same effective rates. In 1978, on the eve of the Reagan ascendancy, companies ranging from the biggest, with $100 million or more in assets, down to those with $1 million paid the same percentage – 32 percent – though smaller firms paid less. Combined state and local taxes (coming mainly from sales and property taxes) are entirely regressive. But since the federal income tax was bringing in almost half of all federal receipts and accounted for one-third of all taxes levied in this country, it counterbalanced the regressiveness of other taxes, making our overall tax system quite flat: families at virtually all income levels paid about the same effective overall rates. The richest 1 percent paid combined taxes, just as the Reagan era was dawning, averaging 29 cents on each dollar of their yearly incomes; almost every income percentile below them was paying an average of a quarter.

The overall tax burden used to be progressive. It was progressive in 1950, less progressive in 1960, and flat or even slightly regressive by 1970. It regressed, for one reason, long before Reagan, because the share of federal receipts coming from Social Security taxes leaped from 1950 on (from 10 percent then to about 30 percent in the early 1980s), while the corporate tax share was plummeting in the same period (from 28 percent to 11 percent). The corporate share hit this level even before Reagan's first tax bill gave the corporations a host of new tax breaks.

The giant corporations shift part of their tax burden to the rest of us by charging higher prices, but their shrinking share of federal taxes still saves them plenty. It shrank mainly because of the growing tax write-offs (accelerated depreciation allowances and investment tax credits) bestowed on them by Congress. In 1965, these write-offs drained the US Treasury of 50 cents for each tax dollar that the corporations really paid. By 1976, the drain was already 90 cents – and it's undoubtedly worse since Reagan's 'supply side' economics cut the corporation's taxes even more.

The federal income tax itself had also become less progressive over the years. The rich had a lighter income tax load in 1950 than in 1939, according to a Federal Reserve Board study, and it was lighter still by 1976, even by the roughest measure: comparing the yearly share of all taxes paid to the share of all adjusted gross income received by Americans at various income levels. The higher the ratio of taxes to income, the heavier the tax burden. From 1950 on, the federal individual income tax burden for people in middle-income levels became slightly heavier, while for the rich it dropped sharply. In 1950, taxpayers with yearly incomes of $1 million or more paid in income taxes 5.9 times their share of the nation's gross income; by 1979, that ratio had slid to 3.2. So the flood of tax benefits that the rich got in Reagan's first term hit a progressive income tax already badly eroded by earlier legislation.

But the Reagan presidency has bequeathed to American families an all but unprecedented level of tax injustice. The tax bills passed in 1982, 1984, and, especially, 1986, slightly cut back the worst excesses of Reagan's original tax redistribution to the rich; the 1986 Tax Reform Act itself, according to the CBO, took back about a quarter of the tax cuts that the top 5 percent of the population got in the earlier tax cuts. Despite the latter tax 'reforms,' 95 percent of American families are paying a bigger share of their income today, in 1988, in total federal taxes – income, payroll, estate, excise, and corporate (the latter attributed to owners of capital) – than they were paying 10 years ago. The result, surely, is that counting all taxes – local, state, and federal – the rest of us now pay a bigger share of our income in total taxes than the rich pay.]

Vanishing Working Class?

The notion that classes are withering away in America rests not only on the mistaken assumption that the propertied have been lopped off at the top, but on the equally unfounded notion that the working class itself has been vanishing and the 'white-collar' strata of the so-called middle class have been multiplying. So renowned a pundit as Harvard's John Kenneth Galbraith, among many others, believes the class struggle is a 'dwindling phenomenon' because 'the number of white-collar workers in the United States . . . overtook the number in the blue-collar working force [by the mid–1950s] and is, of course, now greater.'

Of course? The sort of counting done here misses and distorts what has really happened; it confuses occupational composition with class lines. Since the 1900s, especially during World War II, and in quickening pace in recent years, women – and increasingly married women – have been moving into the labor force. About four out of 10 people in the labor force are now women, and almost half of all women now have paying jobs or are looking for them. It is this influx of women into paying jobs that accounts for the growing number of 'white-collar' jobs – mainly in 'clerical or sales' work – in the past few decades. Of all working women, not even one in 10 was a 'clerical or sales' worker in 1900. By 1940, on the eve of World War II, the figure jumped to almost three in 10, and it climbed until it reached more than four in 10 in 1970.

At the same time, the proportion of women working in crafts or as 'operatives and laborers' (except on the farm) dropped. It also dropped in so-called 'service' occupations which, for women, are typically dirty and menial jobs as domestics or 'food service' workers. Some 'white-collar' jobs are now almost entirely filled by women – and 10 occupations alone, among them waitress, typist, cashier, hairdresser and beautician, nurse and dietician, sales clerk, and teacher, account for more than two out of five employed women. Of all clerical and sales jobs, two out of three, and the same ratio in service jobs (except private household), are filled by women. In contrast, of all those working in crafts or as operatives and laborers (off the farm), only one in six is a woman.

Among men, meanwhile, the portion with clerical and sales jobs has not risen for decades. Only seven in a hundred men at work had clerical or sales jobs in 1900, and it rose to just 12 in a hundred by 1940. In the following three decades, the ratio did not grow at all: it stayed about 12 in a hundred. The same years, though, saw a significant rise in the proportion of men classified as 'professionals and technicians' by the US Census – from three, to six, to 14 in a hundred. But many such 'professionals' are vocational school products, and about four out of 10 in the rapidly growing category of 'technicians' are not college graduates. This, of course, is scarcely the image evoked by the terms 'professional' or 'technician.' Many are really highly skilled workers; advanced education or certification is not required to fill their jobs, nor does their work differ much in independence and control from the work done by those classified as 'craftsmen.'

The plain fact is that the category of 'manual workers' has not shrunk at all in this century. Fewer than 40 in a hundred men worked in 1900 as a 'craftsman, operative, or nonfarm laborer.' In 1920, the figure rose to 45 in a hundred, and it has barely changed since: in 1970, 47 out of every hundred men in the labor force were classified as manual workers. But to this figure we must add many if not most of the men who are called 'service workers' – a US Census category that hides a host of blue-collar jobs within its semantic recesses: janitors, housemen, porters, waiters, dishwashers, and laundry workers. How many of the seven in a hundred men in such service jobs in 1970 should be identified as 'real workers' is anybody's guess – and mine is that it is most. We must also add an uncounted number of jobs that strangely get catalogued in the Census as 'white collar' – among them stock clerks, baggagemen, newspaper carriers ('sales'), and even mailmen. Their work is certainly – and often heavily – 'manual labor.'

A safe estimate, then, is that more than five of every 10 men who work in this country are manual workers, maybe as many as six in 10 – and this does not count the three out of a hundred who work as agricultural laborers.

[As of 1985, 44 percent of the labor force are women, and well over half (55 percent) of all women (and the same proportion of married women) have paid jobs or are looking for them. A bit over four in 10 of employed women are still in clerical or sales work, while there's been a slight rise – to nearly 18 percent – in the portion employed in crafts or as operatives and nonfarm laborers. Of all clerical and sales jobs, two out of three are still filled by women (eight out of 10 clerical, nearly half of sales). Among men, though, the portion working in clerical or sales jobs has risen to about one in six. My guess is that much if not all of this increase is the result of the epidemic of plant closings and the spreading disintegration of our industrial base since the mid-1970s which forced permanently laid-off industrial workers as well as men going to work for the first time into less well-paid clerical, sales, and service jobs. It's also not possible from the official published statistics to be sure how much of this apparent change in men's work is real, or the result of the new occupational classification system used in the 1980 Census; its occupational data are not comparable with the data in the 1970 Census.] Perhaps the only real difference in the working class today compared with past decades is that many working men now count on their wives' (or daughters') earnings to make the family's ends meet.

In fact, the wives of working men are typically manual workers themselves, for among employed women the division is sharp between those whose husbands are workers and those who are married to 'professionals' or 'managers.' Among the latter's working wives, only one in six is in manual (or service) jobs. But among the working wives of craftsmen, two in five have such jobs; among the working wives of operatives, almost one out of two; and among the wives of laborers, about two out of three. They certainly are not smuggling any middle-class values, loyalties, or way of life into the working class based on their own experience at work. For them, on the contrary, as for most men in America, the 'yoke of manual labor' is yet to be lifted.

Besides, whatever the social images 'manual labor' evokes or whatever pain it involves, in getting at the realities of class the distinction between it and 'nonmanual' or 'white-collar' employment is, at best, misleading. How does wearing a white collar lift you into another class? Perhaps there is more prestige attached, though even this is doubtful, particularly among workers themselves. Some 'white-collar' workers may have more security, but how many cashiers, typists, or beauticians get 'salaries' rather than hourly wages, or are less subject to layoffs than highly organized manual workers?

Since most 'white-collar' employees are women, and don't wear collars, white or otherwise, anyway, the name itself surely fools us about what it represents. The vast majority of the clerical and sales workers of today are, in any event, not the respectable clerks of yesteryear. Their work is not only routinized and standardized, but they often work in offices that are larger than (and even as noisy as) small manufacturing shops – tending steno machines, typewriters, accounting machines, data processors, or keypunch equipment. [And, of course, today, women also sit long hours before word processors and PCs.] They work in supermarkets and department stores with hundreds of others who punch in and punch out and wait to be relieved before they take a break. They are as bereft of control over their work and the products of their work as 'manual' workers – in fact, they have less independence and control than such workers as crane operators and longshoremen. Beneath their nice clean collars (if they wear them at all), they are propertyless workers, entirely dependent for their livelihoods on the sale of their capacity to work. And this is the essence of working-class reality.

Where Have All the Capitalists Gone?

So, neither the working class nor the propertied class has yet departed our fair land. But do the propertied really make up a *capitalist* class? Haven't they, because ownership of the large corporations has become so dispersed, lost control of these decisive units of production in America? Of all the pseudofacts behind the notion that classes have withered away in America, none is as persistent as the doctrine of the 'managerial revolution' or 'unseen revolution' implied by these questions.

The claim is that there has been a 'separation of ownership and control' in large corporations – that as the corporations have grown immense, as the original founders have died off or their fortunes have supposedly dwindled, as their kids have taken to mere coupon-clipping and jet-setting, and as stock ownership has spread out widely, the capitalists have lost control of the means of production. The result, we are told, is that not capital but bureaucracy, not capitalists but 'anonymous administrators,' now control large corporations and hold decisive power in contemporary America. The 'managers' have usurped their capitalist predecessors.

With the capitalists gone and the managers no longer their mere agents, the inherent conflict that used to exist between labor and capital also supposedly becomes a relic of the past. Instead, America now has not a system of class domination but an occupational order based on merit: 'rewards' get distributed according to ability ('functional importance'). What's more, with capital dissolved and new managers motivated by other urges and the pride of professionalism in control, pumping out profit is no longer what drives the corporations in the new 'post-capitalist society' we are alleged to be living in. Instead, they have become the 'trustees,' as Prudential's chairman said – and he was just paraphrasing Harvard economist Carl Kaysen's words spoken in the late 1950s – for all of us in the 'new industrial state.'

The intent of such notions is clear: we are to believe that 'labor' and 'management' are just parts of the same team, doing different tasks. It is a theoretical shell game that tries to hide the hard realities of class domination – of the ownership and control of the big companies by a class whose lives are certainly made easier if we don't know they're there, right behind the 'anonymous bureaucrats.'

It hides the simple but profound fact that they live on what the rest of us produce.

One reason that the illusion of managerialism persists is that it is incredibly difficult to figure out who does control a large corporation. [Another reason for the illusion's persistence is that widely used college textbooks still purvey it to unsuspecting students. The best-selling introductory sociology textbook, for instance, teaches the silliest of all managerial pseudofacts: 'Those who control the corporation – the managers and to a lesser extent the directors – are for most purposes *responsible to nobody but themselves*' (my emphasis).] And the illusion is nurtured, as the late Senator Lee Metcalf put it bluntly and accurately, by a 'massive cover-up' of the principal owners. There are several closely related ways that capital really controls the corporations. First, the real owners do not actually have to manage the corporation, or hang around the executive suite with its top officers or directors, or even be formally represented on the board, in order to have their objectives realized – i.e. to exert control. They just hire them or let them know their wishes.

And how much stock it takes to control a corporation is neither fixed nor standard. The few recent studies that claim to find 'management control' in most large corporations simply assume that it always takes at least 10 percent of the stock in one pair of hands in order to assure control, but it does not work that way. If you own 10 percent of the stock in a corporation, you are supposed to report it to the Securities and Exchange Commission (SEC), but if the same percentage is split among several of your close associates, without any formal ties between you, or with a bunch of your relatives, you don't have to report it – and even if you are required to report, who is to know if you don't? At the time of his death, Senator Lee Metcalf had been trying for years to get at such information, but his staff had to rely on its own investigations and on volunteered data.

How much stock is needed to control a corporation depends on how big the other stockowners are – and who they are, and how they are connected – and how dispersed the rest of the stock is; it also depends on how deeply the firm is indebted to the same few big banks or other creditors. What sorts of ties the corporation has to others, and especially to big banks and other 'financial institutions' allied with it, is also crucial. The ability to exert control over a corporation grows with the number of other major firms in which any family, individual, or group of associates has an interest or actual control.

What a particular large holding of stock implies for any attempt at control depends to an unknown extent on who holds it. If it is held, say, by a leading capitalist family like the Mellons – who control at least four firms in the top 500 nonfinancials (Gulf, Alcoa, Koppers Company, Carborundum Company) as well as the First Boston Corporation, the General Reinsurance Corporation, and Mellon National Bank and Trust (the fifteenth largest bank in the country, measured by deposits), and perhaps also, through the Mellon Bank's 7 percent shareholding, Jones and Laughlin Steel – the meaning is just not the same as if some otherwise unconnected shareowner held it.

Even in corporations that a family like Mellon does not control, the presence of its representative among the principal shareowners, or on the board, can be critical. So the late Richard King Mellon as one of the principal shareowners in General Motors carried a rather different clout in its corporate policy than, say, songwriter Billy Rose did in AT&T, though he was reputed to be one of its biggest shareowners. Precisely because the number of shareowners is so large and their holdings typically so minute compared with the few biggest shareowners in a large corporation, it may not take more than 1 or 2 percent of a company's stock to control it.

The critical holdings and connections that make control possible are invisible to the uninformed eye, and often even to the seasoned investigator. Senator Metcalf's staff found, for instance, that Laurance S. Rockefeller owns a controlling block of almost 5 percent of the voting stock in Eastern Airlines, but his name does not appear on the required listing of its 30 top stockholders for the Civil Aeronautics Board. Neither the SEC nor the Civil Aeronautics Board nor Eastern itself could find all the accounts in which Rockefeller's shares were held and aggregate them until they asked him to do it for them – in reponse to Metcalf's prodding.

This helps explain why even the 'insiders' who work as financial analysts at *Fortune*, *Forbes*, or *Business Week*, with their immense research resources and excellent files, have to rely heavily on gossip to estimate the holdings of even the leading families in corporations they have long controlled. These holdings are hidden in a welter of accounts held by brokers, dealers, foundations, holding companies, other corporations, associates, intermediaries, and 'street names' (as the fictitious firms that just hold stock for someone are called on Wall Street), or other 'nominees.'

The extent of a leading capitalist family's holdings is also concealed by a finely woven though tangled web of kinship relations. Apparently unrelated persons with entirely different surnames can be part of a single cohesive set of kindred united to control a corporation. In Dow Chemical Company, for instance, in the mid-1960s, 78 dependents (plus spouses) of H. W. Dow owned a total of 12.6 percent of Dow's stock. So, without research aimed at penetrating the web of kinship, any effort to find out who really controls a large corporation is hobbled at the outset.

In an outstanding recent study, Philip Burch, Jr., mined the 'inside information' presented over the years in the financial press and found that at least 60 percent of the 500 top industrial corporations are 'probably' (236) or 'possibly' (64) under the control of an identifiable family or group of associates. Even these estimates are probably short of the mark because, in Ralph Nader's words, 'no one really knows who owns the giant corporations that dominate our economic life.' My own guess is that behind the thick veil of nominees there are real controlling owners in most if not all of the large corporations that now appear to be under so-called management control.

Even if some large corporations were not really controlled by particular owning interests, this would not mean power had passed to the 'new princes' from the old economic royalists. The higher executives might have limited independence of particular owners in their activities but they still would be bound by the general interests of capital. The heads of the large corporations are the main formal agents or functionaries of capital. Their personal careers, interests, and commitments are closely tied to the expansion of corporate capital. Some are among the principal shareholders of the companies they run, and most own stock that not only provides much of their income but ranks them among the population's large stockowners – and puts them in the propertied few.

Typically, the managers also move in the same intimate circles as the very rich. You'll find them together at debutante balls, select clubs, summer resorts and winter retreats, and other assorted watering places; and their kids attend the same private schools and rush the same fraternities and sororities – and then marry each other. Scratch a top executive and the chances are he will prove to be related to a principal shareowner. Intimate social ties and entangling kinship relations, common interests, and overriding commitments unify the families of the heads of the largest corporations and their principal owners into the same cohesive, dominant class in America.

Finally, even if 'managers' alone had full control of every corporation, they would still have to try to pump the highest possible profits out of the workers and make the most of the corporation's investments. Management's conduct is shaped above all by the imperatives of capital accumulation – the competitive struggle among the giants (now global rather than national), the types of investments they make and markets they penetrate, and the relations they have with their workers. High managerial income and status depend, directly and indirectly, on high corporate profits. 'Stock options' and bonuses and other forms of executive 'compensation' aside from salaries are closely tied to corporate profit rates. Whatever their so-called professional motivations or power urges, their technocratic teamwork, and bureaucratic mentality, managers' decisions on how to organize production and sales have to be measured against the bottom line: they dare not imperil corporate profitability.

The spate of articles in the financial press on 'how to fire a top executive' – you have them 'take early retirement' – and the new placement services now catering to them are rather pointed indicators of what happens to supposed 'management control' in times of receding profit margins. In 1974, a year of severe economic crisis around the world, about half of all the chief executives in the nation's top 500 firms were expected to be replaced – in what a weekly newsletter to corporate heads called 'a wave of executive ousters' that would 'cause the greatest disruption in the business community since the 1929 depression.'

Any obvious lowering in profit rates is also reflected in a drop in the price of the corporation's stock; this squeezes its capital base and makes it an attractive – and vulnerable – target for takeover. And this, in turn, leads to executive ousters. In addition, with the marked centralization of huge shareholdings in the trust departments of a few of the biggest banks that administer the investment portfolios of the very rich – typically, they will not take a trust of under $200,000 – the tremors would be deep and the impact rather painful for any managers who turned out a below-average rate of return. The banks must unflinchingly act as 'trustees' only for the top investors and real owners who control the large corporations.

Any political strategy that ignores or distorts these realities or is blind to the deep class divisions in our country cannot meet the common needs of the majority of Americans. So long as the illusion persists that our economic life has been 'democratized' or that a 'silent revolution' has already interred capital, emancipated labor, and redistributed wealth and income, we can be sure that a real effort to achieve those aims will be slated for yet another postponement.

Part II

The Working Class in the United States and Other Places

6

Death in Vietnam: class, poverty, and the risks of war

Has every young American man had an equal chance of getting killed in the war in Vietnam, whatever his social origins? This is the leading empirical question of this article. Socially relevant and politically significant, this question is also important from a sociological standpoint. Ample evidence shows that the 'life chances' of the poor and of workers in general suffer by comparison with those of more privileged strata in the United States. This is true not only of such diverse 'opportunities' or 'rewards' as formal education, access to health and medical care, decent housing, and humane working conditions, but of mortality rates themselves. Analysis of more than 30 studies – many of them in the United States – of 'social class, life expectancy, and overall mortality,' shows, according to Aaron Antonovsky (1967), that 'despite the variegated populations surveyed, the inescapable conclusion is that class influences one's chances of staying alive. Almost without exception, the evidence shows that classes differ in mortality rates. . . . What seems to be beyond question is that, whatever the index used and whatever the number of classes considered, almost always a lowest class appears with substantially higher mortality rates. Moreover, the differential between it and other classes evidently has not diminished over recent decades.' Most relevant here is Antonovsky's conclusion that 'when men are quite helpless before the threat of death, life chances will tend to be equitably distributed.' The risks of death in war would seem to fit that category all too well, placing all fighting men on a par in their relative helplessness before the threat of death in combat.

Thus, our leading empirical question also has a special – and poignant – theoretical relevance: does war equalize the threat of death? To what extent does the civilian class situation of the American fighting man determine his life chances in the armed forces, and the likelihood of his death on remote battlefields? Despite its importance, the question is all but unresearched. A study by Albert J. Mayer and Thomas F. Hoult (1955) of casualties in the Korean war did find that, in Detroit, '. . . the lower the relative economic standing of a man's home area, or the greater the number of nonwhites in his area, the more likely it was that he would be a war casualty.' Aside from this important study, based on ecological analysis (i.e. comparing the death rates in various areas of the city), no others even focus on this question. But our study uses personal income and occupational data on the individual servicemen themselves, and differentiates them by their branch of service and rank; it is thus the most accurate US study to date of the social correlates of death in combat.

Methods and Data

This study is based on data gathered systematically on every serviceman from the state of Wisconsin killed in the war in Vietnam through December 31, 1967. The names, rank, branch of service, date and cause of death, and nearest of kin of all but one of the 380 Vietnam dead from Wisconsin were obtained from the State of Wisconsin Department of Veterans Affairs. Data on the occupations and income of the parents of the servicemen were obtained through the cooperation of the Wisconsin Department of Taxation. The parental income of 71 servicemen and the father's occupation of 78 servicemen could not be ascertained, and they were excluded from the relevant quantitative analyses, as is indicated in the specific tables in this study. We adjusted gross family income, with some slight modification, in accordance with the Office of Economic Opportunity's scale of poverty thresholds by size of family for 1959 (US Office of Economic Opportunity 1966). Thus, the number of 'poor' in this study is a minimum estimate, by official standards.

The occupational and income distributions of the casualties' parents were compared with the distributions of these attributes in a one-third random sample of the parents of male seniors in all the public, private, and parochial schools in 1957 in Wisconsin. We believe that this matching cohort is much more adequate for the purposes of our analysis than any available from Census data. The 1957 sample provides a reasonably accurate estimate of the social characteristics of the parents of sons close to the age of draft liability, which the Census cannot provide. The high school cohort presents one important problem though: 11 percent of the school population has dropped out before reaching the senior year of high school. This cohort, therefore, probably *understates* the proportion of poor and manual workers among all age-peers of the 1957 seniors in the high school cohort. But school dropouts are quite likely to be very under-represented in the pool of inductees also, so this is probably not a major drawback of these data for present purposes. The vast majority (80 percent) of the 'young men rejected for military service between 1958 and 1960 . . . because they could not pass the Army's examination in basic scholastic skills . . . were school dropouts.'[1]

Findings

What, then, do we find concerning the relative representation of young men from different social origins among the servicemen who were killed in Vietnam? Our evidence clearly shows that the poor are highly over-represented among the dead: whereas only 14.9 percent of the high school cohort come from poor families, nearly twice that proportion, or 27.2 percent, are poor among the casualties of war.[2] The disproportion is especially striking among army privates, i.e. the men most likely to have been draftees. There, 35.2 percent are from poor families. But, in contrast with the situation among privates and noncoms, the poor are *under-represented* among the commissioned *officers* killed in Vietnam (table 6.1).[3]

What about workers' sons? Have they, too, borne a heavier burden of the casualties in Vietnam? Yes, they have, although by no means as great as that borne by the undifferentiated poor. In the high school cohort, 51.9 percent are workers' sons compared with 60.3 percent of the war dead. That is, workers' sons are over-represented by roughly a sixth (1.162 times their proportionate share); and the over-representation is not much different for the sons of the skilled as contrasted to the semi-skilled and unskilled. The sons of fathers in no other occupational group are over-represented among the casualties as a whole. Once again, however, it is striking that whereas skilled workers' sons are more or less proportionately represented among dead officers, and the sons of the less skilled are under-represented among dead officers, the sons of professionals and technicians are highly over-represented among the officers, as are (although to a lesser extent) the sons of managers,

Table 6.1 *Percent 'poor' among the parents of Wisconsin servicemen killed in Vietnam through December 31, 1967, classified by branch of service and rank, compared with the parents of male seniors in the Wisconsin High School Class of 1957*[a]

	High school cohort (%)	Privates (%)	NCOs (%)	Officers[b] (%)	All ranks (%)
Army					
Poor	14.9	35.2	28.0	9.5	28.7
Others	85.1	64.8	72.0	90.5	71.3
	100	100	100	100	100
	(N=4080)	(N=71)	(N=82)	(N=21)	(N=174)
Marines, Navy, Air Force					
Poor	14.9	26.8	26.6	14.3	25.2
Others	85.1	73.2	73.4	85.7	74.8
	100	100	100	100	100
	(N=4080)	(N=41)	(N=79)	(N=14)	(N=135)
All branches					
Poor	14.9	32.1	27.3	11.4	27.2
Others	85.1	67.9	72.7	88.6	72.8
	100	100	100	100	100
	(N=4080)	(N=112)	(N=161)	(N=35)	(N=309)

[a] Excluding those whose parental income could not be ascertained.
[b] The 'Officers' category includes two army warrant officers.
The rank of one serviceman whose parents were not poor could not be ascertained.

In his Master's thesis, James W. Russell (1968) also examines the relationships of career-status – i.e. whether servicemen were professional soldiers or draftees – with servicemen's deaths in Vietnam. This is clearly a distinction relevant to battle survival. He finds the same essential relationships between class, poverty, and mortality rates among noncareer and career men, although these relationships, as we might expect, were strongest among noncareer men. Increased experience, training, and commitment would diminish the effects of one's civilian background on one's life's chances in combat.

officials, and proprietors (table 6.2).

Given that poverty cuts across the occupational strata, although it is greatest among semi-skilled and unskilled workers and small farm proprietors in Wisconsin,[4] the question is how poverty affects the life chances of individuals within the different occupational groups; were poor men more likely than others to be killed in Vietnam, whatever their class? The answer is clear: the poor in every occupational group are over-represented among the war dead (table 6.3). Looking at the casualties among men of all ranks combined, we observe that the poor are over-represented by at least twice their share in all occupational groups, excepting among the semi–skilled and unskilled, perhaps because the latter form a more homogeneous stratum than the other occupational groups. The sons of poor farmers were particularly hard hit, constituting nearly two and a half times what their proportionate share of the casualties would have been. It is also interesting to note that whereas the sons of poor semi–skilled and unskilled workers and of poor farmers are most over-represented among the privates, the sons of skilled workers and of the middle strata are most over-represented among the noncoms killed in Vietnam – an unfortunate and unforeseen consequence, perhaps, of their 'social mobility' in the armed forces.

An equally important question concerning the relationship between class and poverty is whether the sons of workers, farmers, or middle strata families are proportionately represented among the casualties, once we take poverty level into account. For example, were even the sons of well-off (nonpoor) workers killed disproportionately in the war compared with well-off servicemen from other social origins? Or does taking poverty level into account eliminate the class differences in casualty rates? The answer is, poverty wipes out class differences in mortality, i.e. among the poor the differences between the casualty rates of the various classes virtually disappear. Their relative proportions in the matching high school cohort and among the casualties in Vietnam are roughly identical. Workers' sons, for example, constitute 47.1 percent of the men from poor families in the cohort and 48.8 percent of the men from poor families among the casualties.

Among those who were not poor, however, men from farm-owner and middle-strata families are quite *under*-represented among the well-off servicemen killed in Vietnam, but, in contrast, even well-off workers' sons are *over*-represented. This is true of both skill groups among the workers, as well as of the workers as a whole:

Table 6.2 *Percentage distribution of occupations of fathers of Wisconsin servicemen killed in Vietnam through December 31, 1967, classified by rank and branch of service, compared with the occupations of fathers of male seniors in the Wisconsin High School Class of 1957*[a]

Occupational groups	High school cohort[b] (%)	Privates (%)	NCOs (%)	Officers (%)	All ranks (%)
Army					
Professional, technical, and kindred	7.5	1.4	2.5	23.8	4.6
Managers, officials, and proprietors (nonfarm)	11.9	9.7	12.5	23.8	12.7
Clerical, sales and kindred	10.8	6.9	6.3	14.3	7.5
Skilled workers	14.6	15.3	22.5	14.3	18.5
Semi-skilled and unskilled workers	37.3	47.2	40.0	19.0	40.5
Farm owners	17.8	19.4	16.3	4.8	16.2
	100 (N=4846)	100 (N=72)	100 (N=80)	100 (N=21)	100 (N=173)
Marines, Navy, Air Force[c]					
Professional, technical, and kindred	7.5	10.0	5.3	23.1	8.5
Managers, officials, and proprietors (nonfarm)	11.9	10.0	6.7	15.4	9.3
Clerical, sales and kindred	10.8	–	13.3	7.7	8.5

Table 6.2 *Continued*

Occupational groups	High school cohorts (%)	Privates (%)	NCOs (%)	Officers (%)	All ranks (%)
Skilled workers	14.6	20.0	12.0	15.4	14.7
Semi-skilled and unskilled workers	37.3	42.5	53.3	30.8	47.3
Farm owners	17.8	17.5	9.3	7.7	11.6
	100 (N=4846)	100 (N=40)	100 (N=75)	100 (N=13)	100 (N=129)
All branches[c]					
Professional, technical, and kindred	7.5	4.5	3.9	23.5	6.3
Managers, officials, and proprietors (nonfarm)	11.9	9.8	9.7	20.6	11.3
Clerical, sales and kindred	10.8	4.5	9.7	11.8	7.9
Skilled workers	14.6	17.0	17.4	14.7	16.9
Semi-skilled and unskilled workers	37.3	45.5	46.5	23.5	43.4
Farm owners	17.8	18.8	12.9	5.9	14.2
	100 (N=4846)	100 (N=112)	100 (N=115)	100 (N=34)	100 (N=302)

[a] Excluding those whose father's occupation could not be ascertained.
[b] Technically, the distribution in the cohort is of the occupations of heads of households, though the overwhelming majority were fathers.
[c] The rank of one serviceman whose father was a 'manager' could not be ascertained.

Table 6.3 Percent 'poor', by father's occupation, among Wisconsin servicemen killed in Vietnam through December 31, 1967, classified by rank, compared with the male seniors in the Wisconsin High School Class of 1957[a]

	All branches									
Occupational groups	High school cohort (%)	(N)	Privates (%)	(N)	NCOs (%)	(N)	Officers (%)	(N)	All ranks (%)	(N)
Workers										
Skilled	7.6	(675)	11.1	(18)	22.2	(27)	0	(5)	16.0	(50)
Semi-skilled and unskilled	17.5	(1341)	29.4	(51)	21.4	(70)	12.5	(8)	24.0	(129)
(Workers combined)	14.2		24.6		21.6		7.7		21.8	
Farm owners	23.6	(839)	65.0	(20)	50.0	(20)		(1/2)	57.1	(42)
Middle strata[b]	10.1	(1225)	20.0	(20)	30.6	(36)	10.5	(19)	22.4	(76)[c]
Total	14.9	(4080)	31.2	(109)	27.5	(153)	11.8	(34)	26.9	(297)

[a] Excluding those whose paternal income and father's occupation could not be ascertained.
[b] Professionals, technicians, etc.; managers, officials, etc.; clerical, sales, etc. The number of poor in each of these occupational groups is too small to calculate percentages for meaningful comparisons.
[c] The rank of one serviceman whose father was a 'manager' could not be ascertained.

Table 6.4 *Percentage distribution of occupations of fathers of Wisconsin servicemen killed in Vietnam through December 31, 1967, all branches, compared with the occupations of fathers of male seniors in the Wisconsin High School Class of 1957, classified by poverty level[a]*

Occupational groups	High school cohort				Servicemen			
		Poor (%)	Others (%)			Poor (%)	Others (%)	
Professional, technical, etc.		2.6 ⌐	7.6 ⌐			6.3 ⌐	6.5 ⌐	
Managers, officials, proprietors (nonfarm)	20.4 ⟨	10.7	14.2	⟩ 31.7 21.4 ⟨		3.8	13.8	⟩ 27.2
Clerical, sales, etc.		7.1 ⌊	9.9 ⌊			11.3 ⌊	6.9 ⌊	
Skilled workers		8.4 ⌐	18.0 ⌐			10.0 ⌐	19.4 ⌐	
Semi-skilled and unskilled workers	47.1 ⟨	38.7 ⌊	31.9 ⌊	⟩ 49.9 48.8 ⟨		38.8 ⌊	45.2 ⌊	⟩ 64.6
Farm owners		32.6	18.5			30.0	8.3	
		100 (N=608)	100 (N=3472)			100 (N=80)	100 (N=217)	

[a] Excluding those whose parental income and father's occupation could not be ascertained.

among the nonpoor men in the high school cohort, 49.9 percent are from workers' families, but among the nonpoor casualties, 64.6 percent are from workers' families, i.e. roughly one and one-third times their proportionate share of the dead in Vietnam (table 6.4). That even well-off workers suffer a heavier burden of Vietnam deaths underscores the pervasive and profound effect of the class structure on the individual's life chances. Here, then, is further evidence that the workers' location in the class structure of the United States, be their income sufficient to keep them above the poverty level or not, imposes unequal and cumulative disadvantages on them that severely restrict their relative life chances – even, indeed, their very survival in a foreign war – compared with men drawn from more privileged classes.

Interpretation

The question is, what explains this? What processes lead to the higher mortality rates for the poor and for workers (whether or not they are from poor families)? The most plausible explanation is that they are over-represented among the dead because they are over-represented in the pool of draftees in the first place. That this country's system of military recruitment is, indeed, a 'selective service' has been widely accepted; Senator Edward Kennedy, for example, charges that the Vietnam war draft, because it virtually exempts college students, bears 'down most heavily on the lower income brackets.' Republican Congressman Alvin O'Konski of Wisconsin exclaimed, long before this study of the death rates of servicemen from his state: 'They say the poor are always with you. . . . If the draft goes on as it has, they may not be with us much longer.'[5] Steward Alsop, not usually given to radical pronouncements, says bluntly that the Selective Service System 'is quite clearly based on class discrimination.'[6] But others have made the equally plausible opposite argument, that the mental, 'moral,' and physical disqualification rates tend in reality to disproportionately *exempt* poor men from military service, so that they are probably *not* over-represented in the armed forces. In short, 'the "disadvantaged" do have an advantage in escaping the draft' (Chapman 1967, pp. 81–6).

The evidence, however, does not support this view. A systematic ecological analysis of differential induction rates in Wisconsin, by James W. Davis and Kenneth M. Dolbeare, shows that 'the income-related bias in present deferment policies is sufficiently great to overcome the countervailing effects of higher proportions of unfitness in the lower income areas and to establish an income-based pattern of military service. . . . The induction rate is higher in the low income areas and lower in the high income areas. This suggests,' these researchers also point out, 'that the higher service experience of registrants in low income areas is *not* due to enlistments, but quite the opposite, to *inductions*' (1968, pp. 145–6, italics added). So, even though poor men tend to be exempted from induction for *unfitness* more often than the nonpoor, they are still more likely than the nonpoor to be drafted because they hardly benefit from the student deferment policy. The sons of the poor and of manual workers are far less likely than other men to go to college, or to graduate; consequently, 'college deferments' actually tend in practice to defer the draft of men from the more privileged strata of American society.

In addition, more subtle processes may be involved than the mere enforcement of existing draft regulations. Draft board members are empowered to some extent to decide on deferments, to decide 'who serves when not all serve.' Few draft board members are workers or poor. Among local board members during the years of this study in the metropolitan areas of the United States, only 6.6 percent were from manual occupations; outside of metropolitan areas, the figure was 7.3 percent. In the state of Wisconsin, the figure was 8.3 percent (National Advisory Commission on Selective Service 1967, pp. 75, 79). Not much is known about how the social composition of the draft boards affects who gets exempted or drafted. A study of local boards in an urban area by a participant-observer reveals that board members tend when deciding on hardship or occupational deferments – the types of deferments most needed by, and the only ones available for, the sons of workers and the poor – to rely on their evaluations of the registrant's personal appearance or even his choice of words in a letter. Board members' judgments, according to this study, are based on such values as 'thrift, education, morality, nativism, etc.'[7]

The operation of the Selective Service System, whatever its peculiarities, is thus exemplary of the various built-in structural biases involved in the relationship between the 'state' and the class structure. The Selective Service System operates so that – whatever the intentions of those who established, direct, and staff it – it shields the sons of privileged families from the ravages of the very wars fought to protect their interests, by giving *de facto* legal and institutional support to the cumulative social disadvantage already weighing on workers and the poor under capitalism.

These cumulative social disadvantages also are probably recapitulated in the 'universalistic' armed forces themselves. Even when they end up in uniform, men coming from managerial, professional, technical, and kindred families may be less likely to see combat than men from workers' or poor families. Subtly or explicitly, 'well-qualified and intelligent young men' are probably encouraged to take administrative or noncombat posts – something that would not, in the first place, seem to require much encouragement. In general, the military occupational speciality (MOS) or job assignment of a recruit is probably influenced considerably by his social origins, and, perhaps, especially by the formal education and skills (verbal and mechanical) he brings with him from civilian life. Radar operatives or artillerymen, for instance, usually have less frequent direct contact with the enemy or enemy action that subjects them to concentrated small arms fire than riflemen or infantrymen. Similarly, men in supply service battalions or administrative MOS classifications are probably less subject to risk from enemy action.

But a war against a popularly based guerrilla movement, like that in Vietnam, may reduce such differential risks. In wars with more or less clear 'rear' and 'forward' positions, where the 'front' is identifiable and where the terrain is relatively open, the differences between 'safe' and 'hazardous' assignments are likely to be greater than in an expeditionary war against a movement for national independence and radical change. Here, the 'enemy' is everywhere; fixed positions are few; women and children can be 'enemy troops'; hidden snipers and 'fighters by night and workers by day' abound in the fight 'against U.S. and allied forces in Vietnam.'[8] When National Liberation Front troops are able to penetrate even the heavily defended American Embassy in Saigon, a 'safe' MOS does little to protect its possessor.

The question, then, is, do class origins affect men's chances of getting killed in combat? Once drafted into the armed forces, do all men, whatever their social origins, here at last find equality? Are they equally 'helpless before the threat of death'? The Defense Department distinguishes in its casualty lists between 'deaths resulting from hostile action' and 'deaths resulting from other causes,' such as the same sort of accidents or diseases that might kill in civilian life. If a man's social origins affect his chances of death in combat, we should find measurable differences between the proportions of poor versus nonpoor sons, and of workers' versus non-workers' sons, killed in 'hostile action' in Vietnam. For this type of internal analysis, no external cohort is necessary or relevant.

The data reveal only a very slight but systematic pattern of

Table 6.5 *Percent killed in 'hostile action' among 'poor' and other Wisconsin servicemen killed in Vietnam through December 31, 1967, classified by rank and branch of service*[a]

	Privates (%) (N)	NCOs (%) (N)	Officers (%) (N)	All ranks (%) (N)
Army				
Poor	92 (25)	87 (23)	(1/2)	88 (50)
Others	89 (46)	78 (59)	74 (19)	81 (124)
Marines, Navy, Air Force				
Poor	75 (11)	91 (21)	(2/2)	86 (34)
Others	80 (30)	79 (58)	75 (12)	78 (101)[b]
All branches				
Poor	87 (36)	89 (44)	(3/4)	87 (84)
Others	85 (76)	79 (117)	74 (31)	80 (225)[b]

[a] Excluding those whose parental income could not be ascertained.
[b] Including one serviceman killed in hostile action, whose rank could not be ascertained.

differences beween the combat death rates of the poor and the non-poor (table 6.5). In all ranks combined, in the army and other services, men from poor families are somewhat more likely than their nonpoor comrades-in-arms to be killed in hostile action. This holds true for privates and noncoms in the army, but not for privates in the other services. The difference in combat death rates between the poor and the nonpoor is greatest among the noncoms in both the army and the other services. Indeed, among the privates of all the armed services combined, the death-rate difference between poor and nonpoor is negligible. This suggests, perhaps, that the MOS assignments of privates carry fewer intrinsic differences in the risk of death in combat than the MOS assignments of noncoms.

Whatever the case, when we look at the relationship between class, poverty, and the rate of death in hostile action, a pattern does emerge (despite the paucity of cases in some categories): the sons of poor worker, farmer, and white-collar families, combining all ranks and branches of the armed forces, are more likely to be killed in hostile action than their fellow fighting men from more well-off families. But the differences among these classes, holding poverty level constant, are not systematic – although, again, one finding stands out: of all groups, poor workers' sons suffer the highest

Table 6.6 *Percent killed in 'hostile action' among poor and other Wisconsin servicemen killed in Vietnam through December 31, 1967, classified by rank and by class*[a]

	All branches			
	Privates (%) (N)	NCOs (%) (N)	Officers (%) (N)	All ranks (%) (N)
Workers[c]				
Poor	88 (17)	95 (21)	(1/1)	92 (39)
Others	85 (52)	79 (76)	75 (12)	81 (140)
Farm owners				
Poor	92 (13)	80 (10)	(0/1)	83 (24)
Others	(6/7)	70 (10)	(1/1)	78 (18)
Middle strata				
Poor	(4/4)	82 (11)	(2/2)	88 (17)
Others	87 (16)	84 (25)	59 (17)	78 (59)[b]
Poor semi-skilled and unskilled	93 (15)	93 (15)	(1/1)	93 (31)
Other semi-skilled and unskilled	83 (36)	82 (55)	(5/7)	82 (98)

[a] Excluding those whose parental income and father's occupation could not be ascertained.
[b] The rank of one serviceman whose father was a 'manager' could not be ascertained.
[c] We have sufficient numbers of sons of semi-skilled and unskilled workers to view the relationship in this group alone: see the last two lines of the table.

proportion of combat deaths (Table 6.6).

The cumulative evidence presented here thus reveals that the sons of the poor and of the workers of America have borne by far the greatest burden of the war in Vietnam, in the measured but immeasurable precision of death.[9]

Notes

1 Tannenbaum 1966, p. 32. The 1957 cohort sample was gathered under the supervision of K. G. Lutterman and William H. Sewell, for a study of the 'effects of family background and ability on earnings'; we are grateful to

them for making it available for this study. The parents of the high school cohort are likely to be slightly older on the average than the parents of those who died in Vietnam from 1962 through 1967. But the parents of both groups are at the age of their prime earnings, so this slight age difference is probably irrelevant to our analysis. It should be noted also that the present analysis was limited to casualties incurred through 1967 because a closely comparable civilian cohort was needed for comparison with the draftees.

2 We do not think that this over-representation of the poor among the dead in Vietnam is the result of any disproportionate numbers of poor black servicemen. We tried to identify black servicemen from the photos accompanying the obituaries of the men who died in Vietnam. To the extent to which this provided us with valid information, only nine blacks (2.4 percent) were identified among the 380 dead servicemen. As it happens, we could not obtain data on the parental income or father's occupation of these nine men, so they were not included in our tables. It is therefore likely that our population of casualties is all white.

3 Given the structure of the conscription army until now, it seems plausible that sons from poor families would be less likely to acquire the education, skills, and motivations required to rise into the officers' ranks. What is known of the social composition of armed forces officers at this time supports this supposition: unskilled and service workers' sons, according to the one relevant study which has come to our attention, constituted 5.3 percent of the officers in the army. Among Regular Army enlisted men, i.e. excluding draftees, they constituted 14.1 percent. These findings are from an unpublished study by Rufus Browning, cited by Charles H. Coates and Roland J. Pellegrin (1965, pp. 267–73).

4 The distribution of poverty in the 1957 male cohort among the specific occupational groups constituting the 'middle strata' is as follows: 5.7 percent of the professionals and technicians, 11.7 percent of the managers, proprietors, and officials, and 11.1 percent of the clerical and sales group fell below the poverty line.

5 Quoted in Jacquin Sanders (1966, p. 13), which was originally a *Newsweek* cover story on the draft; and in Bruce K. Chapman (1967, p. 86).

6 Alsop 1970. Alsop reports also that 'Yale, Harvard and Princeton, to cite three obvious examples, together have graduated precisely two – repeat, two – young men, in the whole course of the war, who were drafted and killed in action in Vietnam.' He adds, however, that they had, respectively, 34, 13, and 13 young men who volunteered and were killed in Vietnam.

7 The data are from an unpublished dissertation by Gary Wamsley, cited by Davis and Dolbeare (1968, pp. 81–2).

8 Paraphrases and quotes from Col. Robert B. Riggs (1968).

9 We should point out here that this distinction between deaths in hostile action and from other causes does not affect the findings presented in

Tables 6.1–6.4. When we examine the same relationships among class, poverty, and death rates among only men killed in hostile action, our findings do not differ significantly.

References

Alsop, Steward. 1970. 'The American Class System.' *Newsweek*, June 29: 88.

Antonovsky, Aaron. 1967. *Milbank Memorial Fund Quarterly* 65 (2) (April). Reprinted in *Structured Social Inequality*, edited by Celia S. Heller. New York: Macmillan, 1969.

Chapman, Bruce K. 1967. *The Wrong Man in Uniform.* New York: Trident Press.

Coates, Charles H., and Roland J. Pellegrin. 1965. *Military Sociology.* University Park, Md.: The Social Science Press.

Davis, James W., and and Kenneth M. Dolbeare. 1968. *Little Groups of Neighbors: The Selective Service System.* Chicago, Ill.: Markham.

Mayer, Albert J., and Thomas F. Hoult. 1955. 'Social Stratification and Combat Survival.' *Social Forces* 34 (December): 155–9.

National Advisory Commission on Selective Service. 1967. *In Pursuit of Equity: Who Serves When Not All Serve?* Washington, D.C.: Government Printing Office.

Riggs, Col. Robert B. 1968. 'Made in USA.' *Army*, January: 24–31. Reprinted in *American Society, Inc.*, edited by Maurice Zeitlin. Chicago, Ill.: Markham, 1970.

Russell, James W. 1968. 'Who Dies in Vietnam?' Master's thesis, University of Wisconsin.

Sanders, Jacquin. 1966. *The Draft and the Vietnam War.* New York: Walker & Co.

Tannenbaum, Abraham, J. 1966. *Dropout or Diploma.* New York: Teacher's College Press, Columbia University.

US Office of Economic Opportunity. 1966. *Dimensions of Poverty*, Supplement I. Washington, D.C.: Government Printing Office, June 5.

7

How mighty a force? The internal differentiation and relative organization of the American working class

Is the American labor movement now in its 'last days' (von Hoffman 1978)? Are the unions doomed, in *Fortune*'s words, to survive as mere 'encrustations' in our society (Ruskin 1979, p. 40)? Surely many of the country's toughest and biggest unions, faced with the disintegration of their industrial bases in the present economic crisis, 'appear to be in open retreat, creating the impression that union strength has deteriorated badly' (Bernstein 1982, p. 1)? But the critical question is whether this 'open retreat' is a momentary, and reversible, tactic or symptomatic of the unions' underlying long-term decline in organizational size and strength. For most observers, apparently, the answer is not in doubt.

A remarkable consensus, cutting across left–right political lines and contending theoretical perspectives, holds that there has been a long-term '. . . decline of trade unionism as a political as well as an economic influence in the country as a whole' (Aronowitz 1979, p. 18). This consensus is based on two assumptions. The first is that 'union members make up a *steadily declining* percentage' of the labor force in the United States (Kotz 1977, p. 11, italics added) and 'that few, if any, dips in union membership have been as precipitous as in recent years' (*Nation's Business* 1978, p. 44). Today, we are told, 'only a minority of workers, and a small minority at that, belong to unions' (McDermott 1980, p. 4). amounting to roughly 'one worker out of every five' (Raskin 1979, p. 33). Second, this supposedly steady membership shrinkage not only has led to 'the waning power of organized labor' but, indeed, has resulted in 'the trade unions . . . no longer [having] any decisive economic power.'[1] In short, *Fortune* tells us that the union movement has been reduced to 'seething impotence' (Raskin 1978, p. 82). Or in Nicholas von

Hoffman's satirical imagery, incorporating both assumptions: 'Big Labor isn't big anymore. On the teeter-totter with Big Business, the unions find themselves high in the sky with legs flailing.' So organized labor, 'this once mighty force in society, has shrunk to the status of just another special-interest group' (1978, p. 22).

What do the statistics show on trends in union membership since the late 1930s? As is often noted, union membership is now at a post-World War II low: by 1978, the nearest year for which published Bureau of Labor Statistics estimates are available, 19.7 percent of the entire labor force belonged to unions. In 1945, that figure stood at 21.9 percent. So what has been repeatedly described as a 'continual' and 'steady' – if not 'precipitous' – drop in union membership since the end of the war turns out to amount to a dip of 2 percent in nearly four decades. A post-war high in union membership was reached in 1953 when the unionized proportion of the labor force rose to an estimated 25.5 percent. But, if the decline in union membership since then is surely significant, it scarcely attests to the deterioration of the 'once mighty force' of American unionism as a counterweight to big business. In fact, the mid-1950s stand out as an exceptional period: that decade aside, the percentage of the labor force in unions has remained more or less stable since the end of World War II, at between 22 and 23 percent (table 7.1).[2]

Of course, although the 'decline' has been neither as linear nor as deep as is usually claimed, there has, in fact, been stagnation and some drop in union membership as a percentage of the labor force. What explains it? No doubt the changing composition of the labor force has slowed the momentum of industrial union growth. Marked increases in labor productivity and labor displacement have occurred in many industries – from textiles to steel – during the postwar era. Over the past few decades there has been a significant and widely noted shift of employment from the goods-producing to the so-called service sector. In that period, the proportion of the nonfarm labor force employed in manufacturing has fallen from one out of three to one out of four (Samuelson 1981, p. 11) And in the past few years, in particular, this process seems to have accelerated quickly – so much so, in fact, as Emma Rothschild observes, that 'the increase in employment in eating and drinking places since 1973 is greater than the total employment in the automobile and steel industries combined.' The total employment in eating and drinking places, health services, and business services is, according

Table 7.1 *Union membership, 1940–1978*

Year	Total union members (×1000)	Percent total labor force	
1940	8,717	15.5	
1941	10,201	17.7	
1942	10,380	17.2	
1943	13,213	20.5	
1944	14,146	21.4	
1945	14,322	21.9	
1946	14,385	23.6	
1947	14,787	23.9	$\bar{x} = 23.0$
1948	14,300	23.1	
1949	14,300	22.7	
1950	14,300	22.3	
1951	15,900	24.5	
1952	15,900	24.2	$\bar{x} = 24.4$
1953	16,948	25.5	
1954	17,022	25.4	
1955	16,802	24.7	
1956	17,490	25.2	
1957	17,369	24.9	$\bar{x} = 24.6$
1958	17,029	24.2	
1959	17,117	24.1	
1960	17,049	23.6	
1961	16,303	22.3	
1962	16,586	22.6	$\bar{x} = 22.6$
1963	16,524	22.2	
1964	16,841	22.2	
1965	17,299	22.4	
1966	17,940	22.7	
1967	18,367	22.7	$\bar{x} = 22.7$
1968	18,916	23.0	
1969	19,036	22.6	
1970	19,381	22.6	
1971	19,211	22.1	
1972	19,435	21.8	$\bar{x} = 22.0$
1973	19,851	21.8	
1974	20,199	21.7	
1975	19,553	20.6	
1976	19,634	20.3	
1977	19,902	20.0	$\bar{x} = 20.1$
1978	20,246	19.7	

Sources: US Bureau of the Census 1975, p. 178; Bureau of Labor Statistics 1980, p. 59

to Rothschild, 'greater than the total employment in the entire range of basic productive industries: construction, all machinery, all electric and electronics equipment, motor vehicles, aircraft, ship building, all chemicals and products, and all scientific and other instruments' (1981, p. 12).

But there is still a real question as to how much this shift in labor force composition itself explains the stagnation of overall union growth. Stanley Aronowitz, among many others, argues, for instance, that with the growth of 'the unproductive sector' of the economy, 'the size of the labor force employed in activities of coordination approximates those who are being coordinated . . . ,' and that this is the underlying cause of the ostensible 'decline of trade unionism' (1979, p. 18). Women, professionals and technicians and other white-collar employees are, it is assumed, the most difficult to organize, both because of their own supposed hostility to unions and the objective circumstances that make it hard for organizers to reach them effectively.[3] Analysis of National Labor Relations Board (NLRB) certification elections, however, renders suspect this widely held assumption that the slowdown in union growth is attributable to white-collar resistance to unionization. Michael Goldfield analyzes the success rates of union certification elections from 1973 to 1979 in various types of 'work units,' as classified by the NLRB, and finds that 'taken as a whole, non-industrial workers . . . showed a slight *increase* in their success rates during this period,' while the comparable success rates for craft and industrial workers went down. What's more, the certification success rates for unions organizing professional and technical workers and office, clerical, and other kindred white-collar workers during this recent period (1973–9) has generally been higher than among blue-collar workers. Over this whole period, Goldfield found, the certification success rates for unions among industrial workers averaged 44.5 percent, compared with 58.9 percent for union elections among professional and technical workers (which constituted 5 percent of all certification elections) and 49.2 percent in elections for office, clerical, and other white-collar employees (constituting 10 percent of the election total).

Of course, the percentage of all bargaining elections among the latter is much smaller than their percentage of the labor force; this suggests the possibility that 'the victory rate mght be lower if more elections were held. . . . Even with higher victory rates, it is still possible, and quite likely, that workers in the nonproduction sectors are increasing at a far greater rate than they are being unionized.

Thus, the higher victory rates are not inconsistent with a lowering percentage of unionization in these sectors.' These results suggest that, while they may still be less unionized than industrial workers, the rapid growth of service, professional and technical, and office and clerical workers in the labor force is not itself 'an obvious hindrance to unionization drives. Moreover, it is clearly false to attribute the decline in union victory rates to losses among more highly trained and educated workers' (Goldfield 1982, pp. 188–90).

Survey research data, which will be analyzed in detail below, also cast doubt on this assumption that 'the better educated' workers resist unionization. Aside from the implication that you have to be dumb to join a union, this amounts to the claim that professionals and technicians are intrinsically anti-union, although one would have thought that the rapid unionization of teachers, college professors, and airline pilots in recent years had already dispelled that illusion. Take women professionals in the nonproduction sectors of the economy (finance, trade, services, and government), for example. They are the consummate embodiment of three prevalent assumptions about the 'decline' of unions: the more women and better educated nonproduction employees there are in the labor force, the more the unions decline. We find, however, that nearly four out of 10 of these women professionals are organized (35.6 percent; $N = 87$). Or take 'quasi-professional technicians.' Von Hoffman argues, for example, that 'the unions' . . . main strength in the past has been the highly skilled craft unions, whose members' services were essential to their employers. They have been displaced in no small measure by nonunion, quasi-professional technicians.'[4] Presumably, if these technicians have 'displaced' unionized skilled craftsmen, then von Hoffman is thinking of the likes of electrical and industrial engineering technicians, draftsmen, chemical technicians, and surveyors rather than those who clean teeth, take X–rays, or embalm the dead. If so, the fact is that the considerable number of nearly four out of 10 technicians in the nonfarm 'production sector' (manufacturing, mining, construction, forestry and fishing, transportation, communications, and utilities) are organized.

The attempt to understand the labor movement's relative strength can well do without such unexamined assumptions, vague generalities, and mere reiterations of aggregate membership figures. To discover whether the unions still hold 'decisive economic power,' despite the overall stagnation of union membership, we have to analyze their structural location in the economy. The capacity of the working class to realize its immediate – if not 'historical' – interests is closely related to and limited by its level of organization within the various realms of the production process, especially those that are decisive in shaping our entire economic life.

Class Segments and Class Organization

Put differently, the 'working class' is itself constituted of various internal segments that have been differentially shaped by (and have participated in shaping) the development of American capitalism. These class segments have been formed in specific historical circumstances and by concrete struggles, as well as by their structural location in the productive process as a whole. How much the various 'intraclass situations' occupied by different workers turn into durable internal cleavages, even political divisions, within the working class is a historical and essentially political question, depending on how the class organizes itself. In the United States, where no working-class-based Left or socialist party has yet emerged, the unions constitute *the* form of conscious self-organization of the working class, the only organizational means for overcoming its internal divisions and allowing it to act as a more or less unified class against capital. How decisive a social force the 'working class' can be thus depends on how well organized its internal segments are, particularly the segments whose history-making potential is greatest because of their crucial structural locations.[5] The critical empirical question, in short, is the extent to which the different segments of the working class, occupying more or less distinct intraclass locations, are relatively organized – and, in this sense, as Erik O. Wright puts it, thus vary in their 'capacity for the struggle over class objectives' (1978, p. 99). What follows, then, is a preliminary empirical attempt to answer this question.

The Data

Our secondary analysis is based on survey data gathered for a Quality of Employment Survey (QES) in a national probability sample of 1,515 individuals 16 years of age and older who were, at the time of their interview in 1977, working for pay 20 or more hours a week. Households were sampled at a constant rate, but, as the principal investigators note, 'designated respondents had variable selection rates according to the number of eligible persons within a household. Therefore, each respondent was weighted by the number of persons in the household.'[6]

Unlike most previous estimates of labor organization by industry and occupation, the present analysis of the relative organization of different types of workers and, in particular, of workers in different structural locations is based on a single data source. Most previous estimates of labor organization have been based on a mix of numbers from different surveys, involving a variety of 'guesstimates' and assumptions about the allocation of workers to various industrial categories. Also, in contrast to the excellent recent analysis of unionization rates in detailed industries by Richard B. Freeman and James L. Medoff (1979), the data in the QES study are not confined to workers in the 'private sector.' Most important, unlike the Freeman–Medoff analysis, ours is a multivariate analysis of the relative organization of various types of workers, showing contingent interrelationships, wherever the data allow, among several independent variables and the dependent variable, i.e. the percentage organized.[7]

The Current Population Survey (CPS) and QES estimates of membership in labor organizations among employed wage and salary workers in 1977 differ somewhat: overall, the CPS estimate is that 23.8 percent of them belonged to labor organizations compared with the QES estimate of 28.5 percent. The difference in estimates may result from what Freeman and Medoff correctly call a 'principal drawback' of the CPS household survey. As they point out, the CPS asks 'one member of the family to respond for all, possibly leading to inaccurate knowledge (of membership status, occupation, and industry)' (1979, pp. 44–5). Nonetheless, while there are slight differences, the detailed estimates for membership in labor organizations are in general quite closely correlated in the various occupational categories (table 7.2).

The Organization of the 'Working Class'

It is hardly surprising that discussions of the supposed decline, if not 'seething impotence,' of the labor movement in the United States appearing in the pages of such business magazines as *Fortune*, *Forbes*, or *U.S. News* should speak in vague terms about the 'work

Table 7.2 *Percentage of employed wage and salary workers organized[a] by occupation, comparing Current Population Survey and Quality of Employment Survey, 1977*

	CPS[b]			QES[c] (N)
Professional, technical, and kindred workers	20.8			26.8 (239)
Managers and administrators, except farm	9.0	14.8	18.6	12.6 (127)
Clerical and kindred workers	16.2			16.1 (218)
Sale workers	4.5			8.1 (62)
Craft and kindred workers	40.4			40.0 (200)
Operatives, except transport	42.3	40.3	45.3	47.2 (180)
Transport equipment operatives	42.9			51.7 (58)
Nonfarm laborers	33.3			52.0 (50)
Service workers, including private household	16.7			18.9 (164)
All occupations	23.8			28.5 (1298)

[a] In unions or similar employee associations.
[b] Estimates of the CPS (Bureau of Labor Statistics 1979, table 2, pp. 9–11).
[c] Estimates from the QES 1977 as calculated by the authors. See the text for a description of the data base.

force' but ignore the working class itself. They have, after all, long celebrated the alleged passing away of classes in America. But the same, remarkably, is also typical of such discussions on the Left, even when the real issue supposedly under discussion is meant to be 'the crisis in the working class.' The closest, for instance, that John McDermott, who laments that unions 'no longer have any decisive economic power . . . [and have] been economically out-flanked by capital,' comes to delineating the organization of the working class itself is the following: 'If we leave out the Vice Presidents of big corporations and their straw bosses, we find that about 29 percent of workers belong to trade unions' (1980, p. 4).

Admittedly not an easy analytical task, some attempt has to be made to conceptualize the working class, since the real issue underlying most claims about the alleged impotence of the unions is the alleged impotence, even disappearance, of the working class itself as a crucial – if not history-making – force. Mainstream sociologists ordinarily simply distinguish between 'manual' and 'nonmanual' or 'blue-collar' and 'white-collar' workers. Although this does not fully grasp working-class reality, it probably comes close to deeply held popular images of what the working class is. 'The manual laborer is still the best authority on where the shoe of management pinches and the heel of capital treads.'[8] If, as an initial approximation, we say that manual workers constitute the working class, it is heavily organized; 45.3 percent of manual workers (craftworkers, operatives, and laborers) belong to unions or other labor organizations compared with less than one in five of the white-collar and service employees (or even less in the CPS estimates) (see table 7.2). In fact, by this definition, not only is the American working class highly organized, but its level of organization is on a par with that of the working classes of Germany, France, and Great Britain.[9]

But the US Census category of 'service workers' also hides a host of manual jobs within its semantic recesses: janitors and charwomen, laundry workers and porters, waiters, busboys, and dishwashers. Although notoriously hard to organize because of their casual employment and relatively small-scale and scattered work places, they are surely manual workers. With all service workers included, then, the proportion of the 'working class' (manual and service workers) that is organized drops to 39.1 percent.

But whatever the social images 'manual labor' evokes and whatever the pain it involves, in real class terms the distinction between it and nonmanual or white-collar employment is now probably, at best, misleading. The question is, what are the substantive class relations in which men and women at work in these various 'white collar' jobs are really involved? How does wearing a white collar lift someone into another class?

Perhaps there is more prestige attached, although this is doubtful – why should a tool and dye maker accord more social honor to a file clerk? Some white-collar employees may have more security, but how many cashiers or typists get 'salaries' rather than hourly wages, or are less subject to layoffs than industrial workers? The vast majority of the clerical and sales workers of today are, in any event, not the respectable clerks of yesteryear. Their work is not only routinized and standardized, but they often work in offices that are larger than (and even as noisy as) small manufacturing shops – tending steno machines, mail sorters, typewriters, billing machines, data processors, or keypunch equipment; or they tend stock in a grocery store and hand out equipment to 'manual' workers from behind their steel-mesh cages on the shop floor. Many work in supermarkets and department stores with hundreds of others who punch in and punch out and wait to be relieved before they take a break. They are as bereft of control over their work and the products of their work as 'manual' workers – in fact, they have even less immediate independence and control over their work than, for instance, crane operators or longshoremen. Beneath their nice clean white collars, if they wear them at all, they are propertyless workers, entirely dependent for their livelihoods on the sale of their capacity to work. And this is the essence of working-class reality.[10]

Similarly, while there has been a rise in the past few decades in the proportion of the labor force classified by the US Census as 'technicians,' many of them are vocational school products; few are college graduates. This, of course, is scarcely the social image evoked by the term 'technician' or 'engineer.' Advanced education or certification is not required to fill many technical jobs, nor, most important, does the work done by many technicians differ much in independence and control from the work of those that the US Census classifies as 'craft and kindred workers.' Capital has penetrated and now determines their immediate labor process, much as it does for other 'skilled' members of the working class. So if, in accordance with this logic, we include not only manual and service workers, but clerks, sales employees, and technicians in the working class, the proportion organized falls to 31.3 percent.

Some Marxists object to this expansive conception of the working class. They restrict it, instead, to manual workers engaged in the production of physical commodities and, perhaps, engineers and technicians, whom they also consider 'productive' workers. Other wage and salary earners, employed in the 'sphere of circulation' (finance, trade, and business services) or in the 'state' sector (government employees) are 'unproductive' workers, paid out of 'revenue' rather than producing 'surplus value,' and thus constitute either new 'intermediate strata' or a 'new petite bourgeoisie.'[11] By this restricted definition, the working class shrinks even as its organization grows. Taking only manual workers in what we will be calling the nonfarm 'production sector' (forestry and fishing, mining, manufacturing, construction, transportation, communication, and utilities) – who are, conceptually, surely 'productive workers' – over half of the 'working class,' 52.1 percent, is organized.

To sum up, then, the percentages of the 'working class' organized by the various conceptual criteria discussed here are as follows: manual workers (craftworkers, operatives, and nonfarm laborers), 45.3 percent ($N = 488$); manual and service workers (except private household), 39.1 percent ($N = 644$); manual, service, clerical, and sales workers, 31.6 percent ($N = 924$); manual, service, clerical, sales, and technical workers (see table 7.3, note d (later), for the definition of technical workers), 31.3 percent ($N = 954$); and only manual workers in the 'production sector,' 52.1 percent ($N = 386$).

Why we reject the latter, narrow conception of the 'working class' (only manual production-sector workers) should already be clear from our previous discussion. But, without fully entering into this recondite Marxian theoretical debate, it might be worth remarking why this is an erroneous conception of the working class, in Marx's own terms. If his conception of 'productive labor' is not consistent, and is sometimes obscure, he nonetheless is quite explicit in saying that manual industrial workers are not the sum and substance of the working class. 'As the cooperative character of the labor process becomes more and more marked,' Marx writes, 'so, as a necessary consequence, does our notion of productive labor, and of its agent the productive laborer, become extended. In order to labor productively, it is no longer necessary for you to do manual work yourself; enough, if you are an organ of the collective laborer, and perform one of its subordinate functions.' Marx is also explicit in identifying a variety of workers, 'some working more with the hand and some more with the brain,' including quality control experts, engineers, and technicians, as 'productive laborers, directly exploited by capital and subordinated to its process of production and surplus value creation.'[12]

As to the workers employed in the 'commercial sector,' this does not render them *ipso facto* unproductive. If it is true that 'the only capital that produces surplus value is productive capital,' it does not follow, as Nicos Poulantzas argues, for instance, that workers employed by 'commercial capital' are unproductive workers. On the contrary, many workers in the commercial sector surely perform 'real functions' and not merely formal ones involved in exchange. The cashier, for instance, packages your groceries and, in so doing, completes their production, aside from ringing up your sale. Or take workers in the so-called 'service' industries. Why is the auto mechanic you pay out of your pocket ('revenue') any the less productive than an auto assembly line worker? Or the man who fixes, rather than originally assembles, your stereo? As far as their employers are concerned, they produce 'surplus value,' and are paid out of previously produced 'variable capital,' even if their products are 'services.' The same even applies to the copy writer on Madison Avenue. The ad company has to produce its ads before it can sell them, and these ads must, if they are to provide a profit, embody the surplus labor of their producers, i.e., writers, graphic artists, composers, and printers, or sound engineers.[13]

None of this implies that we should ignore the very real differences in the place of the various strata and segments of the working class in the immediate production process under capitalism. On the contrary, as we have emphasized, the working class is scarcely homogeneous. It is internally differentiated, not only by the various occupational strata already described, but by the distinctive historical experiences and structural locations of its various segments within the entire productive process; these segments cut, so to speak, 'horizontally' across the class's internal social layers. The question, then, is not merely quantitative (To what extent is the working class organized?) but qualitative: What segments of the working class are organized, to what extent? Which class segments, as the result of their structural location, distinctive historical experiences, and relative organization, have the capacity to fight effectively, not only to realize their own immediate economic interests, but also to influence the life and struggles of other workers, and even of their class as a whole?

The Production, Circulation, and State Sectors of the Economy

Whether or not the activities of finance, trade, and such 'business services' as advertising and public relations primarily involve 'unproductive labor' in Marx's terms, or employ labor mainly in what Thorstein Veblen calls the 'wasteful occupations,' the economic centrality of the 'production sector' appears to be unquestionable.

It is the productivity of labor in the production sector, in which the basic commodities that are productively consumed are produced, and the struggles and accommodations between capital and labor there, that constitutes the inherent limit on the magnitude of profits and the potential rate of capital accumulation – and is the crucial internal variable in the development of capitalism itself. In particular, the percentage of all social labor that can be devoted to finance and commerce, and to health, education, and recreation 'services,' as well as to government and public administration, depends on the productivity of labor in the production of commodities that are productively consumed. Only on the basis of the increasing surplus produced by the workers in the production sector has the continued growth and recent vast expansion of the circulation and state sectors been possible (cf. Magdoff 1982, p. 360). Even if the workers in the latter sectors are not employed in 'wasteful occupations' or 'unproductive labor,' thereby indirectly sharing in the former's exploitation by private capital, their immediate interests have tended, for historical reasons, to be contradictory.[14] The latter's relative lack of organization probably has tended to depress not only their own but the overall level of wages and working conditions as well. The way to resolve this contradiction, of course, is for the labor movement to organize the unorganized in trade, finance, and services (the circulation sector), and government (state sector) (where it is already doing so with considerable success).

The 'Sexual Division of Labor'

The vast growth in the circulation and state sectors of the economy and of white-collar jobs in the labor force has coincided with the massive influx of women into the labor force in recent years. But if this influx has tended to break down the historical differentiation between women's 'household labor' and men's labor outside the household, it has also reproduced a new sexual division of labor within the labor force itself.

In the last decade, women accounted for 60 percent of the growth in the labor force. Some four out of 10 employed wage and salary earners are now women, and almost half of all women have paying jobs or are looking for them. For married women, the increased labor force participation in recent decades has been particularly dramatic. By March 1980, 51 percent of all married women were in the labor force, contrasted with 41 percent in 1970 and 24 percent in 1950.[15] But women are employed overwhelmingly in white-collar jobs, mainly in clerical and sales, and outside the production sector. Barely a fourth of women wage and salary workers are employed in the production sector compared with slightly more than half of all men.[16] Of employed women nearly two out of three are in white-collar jobs; one out of three are in clerical work alone. Among men, in contrast, some four out of 10 are white-collar workers, and just six in a hundred are clerks. Conversely, of all white-collar workers, over half are now women; and of clerical workers, in particular, eight out of 10 are women. Of all blue-collar workers, however, more than eight out of 10 are men.[17]

In the late 1930s and early 1940s, women played a crucial role, both in the 'women's auxiliaries' and as industrial workers themselves, in the struggles to organize the unorganized. During World War II, the proportion of women in the labor force rose by 142 percent, but the proportion organized leaped 232 percent from the full prewar year of 1940 to the height of the war in 1944; that year, over a fifth of all union members were women compared with less than a tenth four years earlier. But once the men were mustered out, and reclaimed their jobs from their wives, daughters, and sisters, much of the newfound strength of women in the labor movement disappeared.[18]

Not until the rapid growth of white-collar unions among teachers and other public employees in recent years did women once again take on a potent presence in organized labor. Of course, it is often alleged that a major reason for the slowdown or stagnation in union organizing is the huge flow of women into the labor force. 'Women,' so we are told, '. . . traditionally have been more difficult to organize' (Roomkin and Juris 1979, p. 38). That women are much less organized than men is correct.[19] But that they are harder to organize is not at all certain when we compare their rates of union and other labor organization membership with men's, within the same strata and segments of the working class.

First, it is precisely the workers in the fundamental production sector of the economy, as would be expected from the history of the struggles of the labor movement since the 1930s, who are the most highly organized. The entire production segment of the working class is heavily organized, both in absolute terms and as compared, in particular, with the circulation segment. Even the manual workers employed in finance, trade, and service industries are far less organized than their compeers in the production segment. Although the numbers in the relevant sample categories are small, the pattern in the state sector is also clear: public employees in each of the occupational strata and in the state-employed segment as a whole are far more organized than the workers in the circulation segment. Over half (52 percent) of the manual workers in the production sector are in labor organizations and over four in 10 of their public employee (state sector) counterparts are organized, compared with only about one in six (17 percent) of the manual workers employed in trade, finance, and services (circulation sector).

Second, our analysis also reveals that women in the production sector are far more organized than women employed in the circulation sector; in fact, the disparity between the levels of labor organization in these two sectors is considerably greater for women than it is for men. Nearly four and a half times as many women in the production segment of the working class are organized as in the circulation segment, compared with a ratio of three and a half times for the men. But what is most important, as can be seen from the comparisons possible in table 7.3, is that the disparity in the levels of organization of men and women workers is least precisely where the unions have penetrated most, i.e. in the production sector. Where the unions have been able to successfully organize the workers, they have also been able to organize women workers, to almost the same extent as they have organized men, and both among manual and clerical workers. In fact, among clerical workers in the production sector, the level of organization of men and women scarcely differs and, if anything, women production clerks are somewhat more organized (25 percent) than their men co–workers (23 percent).

It is also quite likely, we suspect, that the conditions under which men and women work in the production sector are typically far more homogeneous than they are in the activities of the nonproduction sectors. So it may be put as a general hypothesis that, the more similar the working conditions of men and women, the less of a difference there will be in their levels of organization. What this implies is that women are no more resistant to unionization than men, and that the disparity in their overall levels of labor organization is the result, not of women's greater hostility to unions or submissiveness to their bosses, but of the still substantial differences in the sorts of work they do and the places they do it. This, in turn, may make women harder to organize, but only because

Table 7.3 *Percentage of the working class organized, by occupational stratum, sex, and economic sector*[a]

Occupational stratum	Women	(N)	Men	(N)	Total	(N)
Production sector[b]						
Manual	45	(76)	54	(310)	52	(386)
Service[c]	–	(4)	44	(9)	54	(13)
Clerical	25	(32)	23	(22)	24	(54)
Sales	–	(0)	–	(6)	–	(6)
Technical[d]	–	(1)	31	(13)	36	(14)
Entire segment	41	(113)	50	(360)	48	(473)
Circulation sector[e]						
Manual	17	(12)	17	(80)	17	(92)
Service[c]	13	(85)	10	(31)	12	(116)
Clerical	6	(114)	15	(20)	7	(134)
Sales	5	(22)	12	(34)	9	(56)
Technical[d]	–	(6)	–	(7)	15	(13)
Entire segment	9	(239)	15	(172)	11	(411)
State sector[f]						
Manual	–	(0)	44	(9)	44	(9)
Service[c]	–	(3)	42	(24)	37	(27)
Clerical	38	(21)	–	(8)	41	(29)
Sales	–	(0)	–	(0)	–	(0)
Technical[d]	–	(0)	–	(3)	–	(3)
Entire segment	33	(24)	41	(44)	38	(68)

[a] Nonfarm employed wage and salary workers only.
[b] Forestry and fishing, manufacturing, mining, construction, transportation, and public utilities.
[c] Except private household workers such as cleaners, maids, and servants.
[d] The technical workers here are those classified in the standard occupational classification system as 'health technologists and technicians,' 'engineering and science technicians,' and 'technicians except health, engineering, and science,' for instance, air traffic controllers and radio operators.
[e] Finance, trade, and business and professional services.
[f] Government (state, local, federal) employees.

they are employed in situations in which it is difficult to reach, persuade, and organize them.

Regional Class Differentiation

The development of capitalism in the United States, as elsewhere, has penetrated its various regions unevenly, creating, as a consequence, considerable regional variation in the distribution of various strata and segments of the working class, particularly manual workers employed in heavy or mass production industries. The vast industrial belt stretching throughout the northeast and the north-central states has constituted the historical heartland of the country's industrial working class. In the south, in contrast, even after its defeat in a bloody civil war and the abolition of its peculiar institution of black slavery, the region retained what emerged as an almost *sui generis* class structure for generations afterwards, in which a planter aristocracy dominated a rural society of poor whites in the hill country and sharecroppers in the black belt of the delta.[20] The growth of southern industry, mainly textile manufacturing, tended to replicate the planters' authoritarian regime within the company milltowns, where unionism, despite many heroic battles, has yet to become a potent presence among the workers. Only in the region's hard rock and coal mining communities and in the steel mills and some other heavy industry have unions established lasting beachheads (see Regensburger 1987).

So it comes as no surprise that the relative organization of the southern working-class segment is retarded in comparison with its northern and western counterparts, even in its manual stratum (see table 7.5 later). To the extent that unionism has penetrated the south, it is almost entirely located in the production sector. The size of our sample precludes separate analysis of the circulation and state sectors; combining them tends to inflate unionization there, since public employees are relatively more organized. Still, few southern workers in these combined nonproduction sectors are organized. Only one in 20 manual workers in the nonproduction segment of their class are organized compared with nearly four out of 10 of their peers in the production segment. But while the disparities in other regions are not as extreme as in the south, they do exist in every one of the four main regions of the country. In each region, the production segment of the working class is far more organized than its nonproduction opposite, and this is so even in the most heavily, and overwhelmingly, unionized region of the country, the north-central, with its industrial belt stretching across Detroit, Toledo, Cleveland, Chicago and the Gary–Hammond–East Chicago metropolitan areas and their environs.[21] Even in this bastion of industrial unionism, i.e. the north-central, where two out of three manual workers in the production sector are organized, just half that proportion of manual workers, or one in three, are organized in the combined circulation and state sectors (table 7.4).

In the north and west combined (henceforth called the 'north' for short), the level of organization of women in the production segment is on a par with the men's: 50 percent of the women ($N = 76$) and 56 percent of the men ($N = 237$) in the entire production segment (i.e. all manual, service, clerical, sales, and technical workers in the production sector) are organized. Among production-sector manual workers only, the same is true; indeed, slightly more of the women, proportionately, than of the men are organized: 63 percent ($N = 46$) versus 60 percent ($N = 203$). Again, we see that where union penetration is deepest, both by region and economic sector, women as well as men tend to be highly organized. In the south, however, although men are highly organized, women are not. Southern women are far less organized than men, even in the production sector; in the entire southern production segment, 22 percent of the women ($N = 37$) but 39 percent of the men ($N = 123$) are organized. Among production-sector southern manual workers only, the comparable figures are 17 percent of the women ($N=30$) but 43 percent of the men ($N = 107$). Possibly men and women workers tend to be employed in different industries or to be job-segregated within the same industries far more in the south than in the rest of the country; this would account for the disparities in their levels of organization. We return to this point in our analysis of unionization in manufacturing.

Where data allow comparisons among working-class occupational strata in the nonproduction sectors, the rates of organization of men and women are much less, across the board, in both regions, than among their counterparts in the production sector. Also, in both north and south, in the nonproduction sectors, fewer women than men, proportionately, are organized in each stratum. In the north, 15 percent of the women ($N = 148$) and 25 percent of the men ($N = 138$) in the entire nonproduction segment are organized; in

Table 7.4 *Percentage of the working class organized, by occupational stratum, region, and economic sector*

Occupational stratum	North-east	(N)	North-central	(N)	South	(N)	West	(N)
Entire economy								
Manual	43	(94)	62	(143)	31	(173)	51	(77)
Service	32	(25)	26	(42)	9	(63)	23	(26)
Clerical	12	(41)	15	(55)	13	(85)	31	(36)
Sales	18	(17)	8	(12)	5	(19)	–	(14)
Technical	–	(7)	–	(6)	8	(13)	–	(4)
Entire segment	32	(184)	43	(258)	20	(353)	37	(157)
Production sector								
Manual	46	(72)	68	(119)	37	(137)	62	(58)
Service	–	(5)	–	(4)	–	(3)	–	(1)
Clerical	8	(12)	27	(15)	20	(15)	42	(12)
Sales	–	(2)	–	(2)	–	(1)	–	(1)
Technical	–	(4)	–	(4)	–	(4)	–	(1)
Entire segment	41	(95)	61	(144)	35	(160)	58	(74)
Nonproduction sectors								
Manual	32	(22)	33	(24)	6	(36)	16	(19)
Service	30	(20)	21	(38)	8	(60)	20	(25)
Clerical	14	(29)	10	(40)	11	(70)	25	(24)
Sales	21	(15)	10	(10)	6	(18)	–	(13)
Technical	–	(3)	–	(2)	–	(9)	–	(1)
Entire segment	23	(89)	19	(114)	8	(193)	18	(83)

the south, the comparable percentages are a mere 7 percent of the women ($N = 115$) and 10 percent of the men ($N = 78$). (No comparison is possible between women and men in the manual stratum alone, in either region, because so few women in the nonproduction sectors are manual workers.)

'Race'

Whatever the legacy of racism in the working class, manifested in the practice of some craft unions, especially in the building trades, the Congress of Industrial Organizations (CIO), with its clarion call of mass industrial unionism, organized from the start every worker who wanted to join the union, black or white; and its unions openly committed themselves, particularly those under Left leadership, to racial equality. The CIO unions became the only mass organizations in which black and white Americans regularly participated side by side in struggles to protect and advance their common class interests. With the upsurge of 'black consciousness' in the 1960s, black workers (in such organizations as the Dodge Revolutionary Union Movement among Detroit's auto workers) were especially active in pushing the most militant union demands, and, in recent years, they have also proven to be more class conscious than their fellow white workers.[22] The flow of blacks into the north over the past half-century not only transformed them into an overwhelmingly urban working-class population, but also made them even more urban and big city, proportionately, than white workers.

Nationwide, the level of organization among blacks is also slightly higher than among whites.[23] This is so in the entire working class, and in both the production and nonproduction sectors: 36 percent of the blacks ($N = 117$) versus 31 percent of the whites ($N = 821$) in the class as a whole; 57 percent ($N = 53$) versus 47 percent ($N = 417$) in the production segment; 19 percent ($N = 64$) versus 14 percent ($N = 404$) in the nonproduction segment. The small sample size among some categories of workers allows only the following comparisons within strata of these major segments. Black manual workers are more organized than their white peers in the production segment, but they are less organized in the nonproduction segment: 51 percent of the white production-segment manual workers ($N = 338$) versus 61 percent of their black counterparts ($N = 46$) are organized; among the manual workers in the nonproduction sectors, however, the level of organization is slightly reversed: 19 percent of the white workers ($N = 84$) but 14 percent of the black workers ($N = 14$) are organized. The level of organization among the black and white service workers in the nonproduction sectors is identical: one in six. No comparison is possible between black and white clerical workers in the production sector but, in the nonproduction sectors, the level of organization among white clerical workers is about half that among black clerical workers: 12 percent of the white clerks versus 24 percent of the black clerks are organized.

The pattern also holds in the two major regions of the country. As expected, northern workers, black or white, are far more organized than their southern counterparts, in both sectors. But what is striking is that not only in the north but also in the south the level of organization of black workers is substantially higher than that of white workers – a pattern which is consistent with the historical fact that, from the early 1930s on, blacks joined unions earlier and in far higher percentages than whites in southern heavy industry, especially in steel, auto, and coal and iron mining. Also, in both north and south alike, blacks and whites in the production segment are far more organized than in the nonproduction segment. The numbers in most categories are too small for systematic comparisons. But we can see one sharply instructive contrast: not one southern black manual worker in the nonproduction sectors and barely one in a dozen of their white counterparts is in a union. In contrast, in the northern black production segment, whose level of organization is the highest of all segments, over three out of four manual workers are organized (table 7.5).

Size of Work Place

Any technical operation places the workers into definite relations not only with the machinery and equipment involved but with each other and with the surveillance, administrative, and managerial staff. So every work place has its characteristic 'paratechnical relations.'[24] If the routinized coordination of masses of laborers and machinery is the essence of factory production, the fragmentation, standardization, and mechanization of the labor process has long since been extended, under the incessant demand of capital for increasing productivity, beyond the walls of the factory itself; it now characterizes much of the work done, especially in big work units, not only in the production sector as a whole but in the circulation and state sectors as well. The big modern office, for instance, subdivided into specialized clerical units designed to fulfill standardized tasks carried out by less and less skilled 'clerks' tending a host of business machines, subject to several layers of supervisors who are themselves subject to the dictates of the 'front office,' tends

Table 7.5 *Percentage of the working class organized, among manual workers and in the entire segment, by race, region, and economic sector*

	North and west				South			
	White	(N)	Black	(N)	White	(N)	Black	(N)
Production sector								
Manual workers	58	(225)	77	(22)	35	(113)	46	(24)
Entire segment	53	(281)	65	(29)	33	(136)	46	(24)
Nonproduction sectors								
Manual workers	24	(58)	–	(5)	8	(26)	–	(9)
Entire segment	19	(246)	26	(31)	8	(158)	12	(33)

increasingly to take on the appearance and rhythm, if not the danger, dirt, and sound, of the factory.

Aside from the 'depersonalization' of relations between workers and bosses and the fragmentation and placing of the work itself that may make these workers prone to join unions, workers in the bigger units also tend to be singled out as union-organizing targets because it takes far fewer organizers to reach far more potential union members than it does to penetrate dozens of small and scattered shops, where organizers are also easier to spot and stop. The question, then, is how the scale of the work unit, with its characteristic paratechnical relations, is related to the extent of labor organization in the production and nonproduction sectors, and in the economy as a whole.

Among manual workers, the bigger the plant (or work place) they work in, the higher the level of organization, in the economy as a whole and in the production sector in particular. In fact, only in the smallest shops of under 50 workers are fewer than half the manual workers unionized; in the bigger plants, the vast majority are organized, rising to three out of four workers in the plants numbering 2,000 or more. Among service workers, the relationship between the size of the work unit and labor organization is also marked and direct, in the economy as a whole and in the nonproduction sectors (our sample of service workers in the production sector is too small for analysis). But no such relationship, however routinized and fragmented their labor might be, appears between the size of the office and the unionization of clerical workers; roughly the same proportions, varying from a fifth to a fourth of clerical employees, are organized in all sizes of work places in the production sector, and no pattern at all shows up in the nonproduction sectors. For the other occupational strata, the numbers in the relevant categories in our sample are too small for analysis. But what is clear is that the biggest plants in the economy are the heartland of a union majority in the working class (table 7.6).

The Industrial Nucleus

The hub of the production sector, of course, is manufacturing; it draws on the raw materials extracted in mining and forestry and transforms them into the products utilized in all other industries and transported to the nation's markets. Within manufacturing itself, however, a division has long been recognized, not only between capital goods and consumer goods production, but between 'light' and 'heavy' or 'basic' industry. In fact, these distinctions also cut across one another; the mass production of certain consumer goods, for instance, most notably automobiles, has been, if not 'basic,' undoubtedly critical to much of the rest of American manufacturing, in steel, glass, rubber, oil, and gasoline, etc. The critical, basic, or 'key' industries, as Robert Averitt dubs them, constitute the industrial nucleus of all manufacturing, because of both their close technical and their market interdependence. They consist of the manufacturing industries that produce the most important capital goods, that are characterized by considerable 'technological convergence' (e.g. machine tools, chemicals, and electronics), that have high 'backward and forward linkages' to other industries (i.e. account for a high proportion of the output and input of other industries) or that have a high price–cost effect on them, or that constitute leading 'growth' or innovative industries. These basic or key industries are the following: machinery (including electrical), steel, nonferrous metals, transportation equipment (other than aircraft and auto), aircraft, auto, chemicals (especially industrial chemicals), rubber products, petroleum refining, electronics, and scientific and other instruments (Averitt 1968, pp. 38–44).

Given the close technical interdependence and overall industrial

Table 7.6 *Percentage of the working class organized, by occupational stratum, size of work place, and economic sector*

Occupational stratum	Size of work place							
	1–49	(N)	50–499	(N)	500–1999	(N)	2000+	(N)
Entire economy								
Manual	28	(188)	47	(167)	65	(51)	72	(71)
Service	15	(76)	21	(48)	33	(21)	37	(8)[a]
Clerical	12	(103)	21	(56)	14	(35)	19	(16)
Sales	5	(42)	19	(16)	–	(3)	–	(2)
Technical	17	(12)	–	(6)	–	(6)	–	(5)
Entire segment	21	(421)	36	(293)	41	(116)	58	(102)
Production sector								
Manual	35	(124)	51	(140)	69	(48)	75	(67)
Service	–	(2)	–	(5)	–	(4)	–	(2)
Clerical	20	(20)	25	(12)	27	(11)	22	(9)[a]
Sales	–	(3)	–	(4)	–	(0)	–	(1)
Technical	–	(5)	–	(2)	–	(4)	–	(3)
Entire segment	25	(154)	5	(163)	61	(67)	65	(82)
Nonproduction sectors								
Manual	16	(64)	30	(27)	–	(3)	–	(4)
Service	13	(74)	19	(43)	23	(17)	33	(6)[a]
Clerical	10	(83)	21	(44)	8	(24)	–	(7)
Sales	5	(39)	17	(12)	–	(3)	–	(1)
Technical	–	(7)	–	(4)	–	(2)	–	(2)
Entire segment	11	(267)	21	(130)	12	(49)	30	(20)

[a] These percentages are given to show the consistency of the pattern, despite the small percentage basis.

centrality of the key or basic industries, how well organized their workers are tends to weigh far more heavily in the balance with capital, in any measure of organized labor's relative strength, than the organization of other workers. The initiatives, strikes, demands, and militance of workers in any of the basic industries are crucial not only for other workers in the 'key nexus' but also for the workers in other manufacturing industries. Averitt suggests, in this connection, that the 'key industry unions' typically have 'provided the first wedge to industrial wage pressures throughout the economy' (1968, p. 142). It was, of course, in several of the basic industries – steel, auto, rubber, electrical machinery – that some of the most important CIO industrial unions were organized during the insurgent years of the 1930s. In recent years, however, some of the newer key industries, such as electronics, have resisted unionization. The empirical question, then, is how well the basic industries as a whole are organized and how their organizational level compares with that of other manufacturing.

First, most industrial workers, in the key industries and other manufacturing industries alike, are organized. And though the proportion of unionists is higher among men, women, too, are heavily organized: over four out of 10 women manual workers in manufacturing belong to unions compared with nearly six out of 10 men. Second, the key industries are significantly more unionized overall than other manufacturing, and the gap between levels of organization is widest among women: well over half of all women manual workers in the key industries but fewer than four out of 10 in other manufacturing are unionized (table 7.7, part C).

When we examine the levels of unionization in the basic industries and the rest of manufacturing by region, however, the differences between them disappear in the north but are magnified in the south. Although women manual workers in the key industries located in the north are somewhat more highly organized than their sisters in the rest of northern manufacturing, the opposite holds among men. But for both men and women, the differences in the extent of unionization between the industrial nucleus and the rest of manufacturing in the north are modest. Most important, the vast majority of industrial workers in the north in the key and other manufacturing industries alike, over six out of 10 among both men and women, are organized. In the south, however, the key industries are by far more organized than the rest of manufacturing; here, too, over six out of 10 manual working men in the basic industries –

Table 7.7 Percentage of industrial workers organized, among manual workers and the entire segment, by region and sex, in 'key' and other industries

	'Key' industries						Other industries						All manufacturing					
	Women	(N)	Men	(N)	Total	(N)	Women	(N)	Men	(N)	Total	(N)	Women	(N)	Men	(N)	Total	(N)
Part A North and west																		
Manual workers	67	(15)	59	(74)	61	(89)	61	(26)	65	(52)	64	(78)	63	(41)	62	(126)	62	(167)
Entire segment	43	(23)	56	(88)	53	(111)	53	(36)	58	(60)	56	(96)	49	(59)	57	(148)	55	(207)
Part B South																		
Manual workers	34	(9)	63	(32)	56	(41)	9	(21)	25	(20)	17	(41)	17	(30)	48	(52)	37	(82)
Entire segment	36	(11)	53	(38)	49	(49)	9	(22)	25	(24)	17	(46)	18	(33)	42	(62)	34	(95)
Part C All regions																		
Manual workers	54	(24)	60	(106)	59	(130)	39	(47)	54	(72)	48	(119)	44	(71)	58	(178)	54	(249)
Entire segment	41	(34)	55	(126)	52	(160)	36	(58)	49	(84)	43	(142)	38	(92)	52	(210)	48	(302)

steel, machinery, motor vehicles, chemicals – are union members, as are a third of their fellow women workers. But the workers elsewhere in southern manufacturing are largely unorganized, although men fare much better than women: among women, barely one-tenth are in a union, while one-fourth of all men are (see table 7.7, parts A and B).

The pattern is similar when the levels of unionization of black and white workers in the basic industries and other manufacturing are compared in the major regions of the country. The proportions of both white and black manual workers organized in the key industries are significantly higher than in other manufacturing, but the disparity is especially sharp between black workers in the key industries and in other manufacturing; a ratio of roughly 8 to 5 holds in the proportions belonging to unions in the former compared with the latter. (table 7.8, part C). Black manual workers are far more organized than white workers in both the basic industries and the rest of manufacturing, and in both the north and south; the numbers in each cell are quite small, but the pattern is sharp and consistent. Even in the south, seven out of 10 black workers in basic industries are union members, compared with some five out of 10 white workers. Both black and white workers in the basic industries located in the south are far more unionized than in the rest of southern manufacturing: a ratio of over 3 to 1 among white workers and approaching that among blacks (see table 7.8, parts A and B). Throughout the country, then, among black and white workers alike, and including the otherwise 'union-free environment' of the south, the key industries critical to all of manufacturing are heavily organized, constituting the base of the union majority among America's industrial workers.

The distinction between basic or key industries and other manufacturing industries rests mainly on technical criteria. But the technical differences between them tend to coincide also with differences in the actual social organization of the immediate process of production in these industries. The key industries generally tend to operate on a large scale, involving as they do routinized forms of coordination of masses of labor and machinery within the factory. Their paratechnical relations thus tend to differ from manufacturing carried out on a small-scale or craft basis; and the latter are far more characteristic of manufacturing outside the basic industrial nucleus.

In a word, the basic industries tend to be characterized overall by production in large plants while the rest of manufacturing tends,

Table 7.8 *Percentage of industrial workers organized, among manual workers and the entire segment, by region and race, in 'key' and other manufacturing industries*

	'Key' industries				Other industries				All manufacturing			
	White	(N)	Black	(N)	White	(N)	Black	(N)	White	(N)	Black	(N)
Part A North and west												
Manual workers	57	(80)	89	(9)	61	(67)	78	(9)	59	(147)	83	(18)
Entire segment	49	(101)	90	(10)	54	(83)	64	(11)	52	(184)	76	(21)
Part B South												
Manual workers	52	(31)	70	(10)	15	(33)	25	(8)	33	(64)	50	(18)
Entire segment	44	(39)	70	(10)	16	(38)	25	(8)	30	(77)	50	(18)
Part C All regions												
Manual workers	56	(111)	79	(19)	46	(100)	53	(17)	51	(211)	67	(36)
Entire segment	48	(140)	80	(20)	42	(121)	47	(19)	45	(261)	64	(39)

instead, to be carried out in comparatively small and medium-sized shops. Thus, four out of 10 manual workers in the basic industries in our sample work in manufacturing plants having 2,000 or more employees compared with only one out of a dozen manual workers in the rest of manufacturing. That is, proportionately almost five times as many manual workers in the key industries as in other industries work in the largest plants. At the other end of the scale, over three-quarters of the manufacturing workers outside the basic industrial nucleus are employed in plants of under 500 workers compared with only four out of 10 of the basic industrial workers. (The distribution is similar, if even more skewed in the same direction, when workers in other occupational strata are also counted.)[25]

Overall, counting the plants in all regions of the country, the relationship between plant size and unionization is strong and direct: the bigger the plant, the more organized it is. In the smallest manufacturing shops, numbering under 50 workers, roughly one out of three manual workers belongs to unions compared with three out of four in the biggest plants of 2,000 workers or more. But even in plants of from 500 to 2,000 workers, nearly two out of three manual workers are organized. Counting all workers in a given segment, the relationship between unionization and size of plant is also the same, though, unfortunately, the data do not allow us to compare the various strata individually (table 7.9, part C).

The regional pattern is much the same: the bigger the manufacturing plant, the more organized are its workers (although, in the north, there is a slight drop rather than an increase in the biggest plants). But it is in the south that the difference between the levels of unionization in the smallest shops and largest plants is sharpest: nearly three out of four manual workers in the southern plants numbering 2,000 or more workers are organized compared with a mere one out of 10 in shops of under 50 workers (see table 7.9, parts A and B.)

If the biggest manufacturing plants are far more organized than the smallest and the key industries tend to have the biggest plants, we might ask: is the overall difference between the levels of organization in the key industries and the rest of manufacturing an effect of their characteristic plant sizes? The answer is a complicated no. Within both the key industries and the rest of manufacturing, the bigger the plant, the more organized it is; this also holds in both the north and the south (table 7.10). But, as we already know,

Table 7.9 *Percentage of industrial workers organized, among manual workers and the entire segment, by plant size and region*

	1–49	(N)	50–499	(N)	500–1999	(N)	2000+	(N)
				Plant size				
Part A North and west								
Manual workers	47	(30)	55	(62)	78	(27)	74	(43)
Entire segment	35	(40)	52	(71)	69	(35)	64	(55)
Part B South								
Manual workers	10	(20)	28	(29)	43	(14)	74	(19)
Entire segment	15	(26)	25	(32)	35	(17)	70	(20)
Part C All regions								
Manual workers	32	(50)	46	(91)	66	(41)	75	(62)
Entire segment	27	(66)	44	(103)	58	(52)	65	(75)

in the north the industries in the key nexus and in the rest of manufacturing have similar levels of unionization. This is what we would expect, given the specific history of the growth and consolidation of America's industrial unions (and of 'industrial unionism' as a cause and a battle cry). Clothing workers and furriers, for instance, were among the most radical and combative unions, and their leaders – most prominently Sidney Hillman and Ben Gold – were socialists and Communists who, along with John L. Lewis, that peculiar Republican, broke with the conservative American Federation of Labor (AFL) leadership to set up the CIO. Thus industrial unionism came to the country's basic industries after it had already become a potent organizational presence elsewhere in manufacturing. Compelled to compete with the breakaway CIO and pressed by insurgent workers, the AFL itself also organized the equivalent of industrial unions in many prior craft jurisdictions and other such settings.

What is surprising, however, is that, with the size of plant held constant, it turns out that in all size categories, from the smallest to the biggest plants of the north, the vast majority of workers outside the basic industrial nucleus are organized, whereas, in contrast, in the industrial nucleus itself the smallest shops (of under 50 workers) are proportionately not half as unionized as their

Table 7.10 Percentage of industrial workers organized, among manual workers and the entire segment, by region and plant size, in 'key' and other manufacturing industries

	Plant size in 'key' industries								Plant size in other industries							
	1–49	(N)	50–499	(N)	500–1999	(N)	2000+	(N)	1–49	(N)	50–499	(N)	500–1999	(N)	2000+	(N)
Part A North and west																
Manual workers	27	(11)	48	(21)	77	(17)	70	(37)	58	(19)	59	(41)	80	(10)	100	(6)[a]
Entire segment	19	(16)	45	(20)	67	(21)	64	(45)	46	(24)	57	(46)	71	(14)	60	(10)
Part B South																
Manual workers	25	(8)[a]	55	(11)	43	(7)[a]	80	(15)	–	(12)	11	(18)	43	(7)[a]	50	(4)[a]
Entire segment	25	(12)	50	(12)	33	(9)	75	(16)	7	(14)	10	(20)	37	(8)[a]	50	(4)[a]
Part C All regions																
Manual workers	26	(19)	50	(32)	67	(24)	73	(52)	35	(31)	44	(59)	65	(17)	80	(10)
Entire segment	21	(28)	46	(37)	57	(30)	67	(61)	32	(38)	42	(66)	59	(22)	57	(14)

[a] These percentages are given to show the consistency of the pattern, despite the small percentage bases.

counterparts in the rest of manufacturing (see table 7.10, part A). Unfortunately, whether this finding is an artifact of an unreliably small number in that category or is descriptively reliable is a moot question (at least for this analysis). Whatever the case, this finding makes little sociological sense. The small shops in the south, for instance, are not less organized than their counterparts in the north.

The smaller shops in the key industries are probably satellites of major plants, located near them or in the environs of the industrial workers' community. There is, then, no reason, on the face of it, why they should be any less (let alone so much less) organized than small shops in other manufacturing industries in the north. In fact (and, we suspect, precisely for this reason), small shops in the basic industries located in the south are far more organized than small shops in the rest of southern manufacturing. In other words, the difference between the levels of unionization in the key industries and in other manufacturing in the south shrinks considerably when the size of plant is considered. More precisely, the gap between the levels of unionization among southern manual workers in the basic industries and elsewhere in manufacturing is far narrower in the bigger plants than it is in the smallest shops, in which the gap is wide indeed.

In plants of under 500 workers in the south, the ratio of organized manual workers in the key industries to those in the rest of manufacturing is well over 6 to 1, but in the plants of 500 workers or more, the comparable ratio is only $1\frac{1}{2}$ to 1 (see table 7.10, part B). Unlike the anomalous finding for the smallest northern plants in basic industry, this finding is intuitively sensible and expected. If their sizes (and intraplant paratechnical relationships) are alike, the social milieus outside the small plants in the basic industries and other manufacturing probably differ substantially. The typical southern manufacturing plant (i.e. not in the basic industries) is a textile mill or factory located in a company town, relatively inaccessible to union organizers (NLRB or not), whose workers are more easily subject to surveillance and are isolated from other workers in other southern mills and factories. In contrast, the location of the small key industrial shops of the south near the major key plants and within the urban working-class communities surrounding them makes an organizing drive there harder to break than one in an isolated company town.

Conclusion: Giant Corporations, the Unions, and the Working Class

America's giant corporations – owned and controlled by a minute propertied class – dispose of most of the productive assets, take in most of the profits, and employ most of the industrial workers in the country. The 200 largest manufacturing corporations, for instance, control close to 60 cents of every dollar of assets owned and of profits made in manufacturing, and they employ 60 out of every 100 industrial workers in the country.[26] These 'economic giants,' as Averitt puts it, 'form an economy apart, creating and reacting to economic forces differing in substance from those impinging on their smaller rivals.' This, in other terms, is the 'monopoly sector' of the economy where, in contrast to the relatively 'competitive sector,' the scale of production and of the business firm is immense, 'market forces' are manipulated, and wages and prices are, as economists politely put it, 'administered.'

In this 'center economy' of the giant corporations, as Averitt terms it, 'center business and center labor act as central bargainers for the entire manufacturing economy, with ramifications that extend ultimately into the most remote periphery corner' (1968, pp. 56, 142). And 'center labor' is, as our analysis suggests, organized labor.

This is because the basic industries and the biggest mines, mills, and factories are, of course, controlled by the giant corporations. They are also, as our analysis has shown, the heartland of a union majority among America's workers. As *Fortune* magazine correctly noted 30 years ago, in words as applicable today as they were then, 'Big business is organized – by labor.'[27] It is here, in the relationship between workers and giant companies in the 'center economy', that the allocation of resources, the wage structure, the organization of production and the long-run tendencies of the entire economy are decisively shaped (cf. O'Connor 1973, pp. 15–16, 21–2). And the workers here are mainly organized workers; they are certainly not – let alone seethingly – impotent. On the contrary, they wield 'decisive economic power,' and the real question is how, and in whose interests, they will wield it in the future.

Notes

1 Lens 1978. McDermott (1980, p. 17) adds that '. . . the trade union as we know it has been economically outflanked by capital and made more or less obsolete in its present form.'

2 The phrase 'steady' or 'continuous drop' in union membership appears in, at least, Aronowitz (1979, p. 18), Kotz (1977, p. 11), von Hoffman (1978), Lens (1978, p. 12), Raskin (1979, p. 33), and Ferguson and Rogers (1979). Goldfield analyzes aggregate union membership figures since 1936 and, after plotting several graphs, concludes that, first, 'the percentage of union members in the total labor force has remained relatively stable since the late 1950s,' and, second, the decline during 1972–8 was probably 'no more drastic than that of other periods.' He also examined union victory rates (in National Labor Relations Board (NLRB) certification elections), as we discuss briefly below, and found, by formulating a linear model using generalized least squares estimators, that 'the thesis that unions have been suffering a greater degree of decline than previously is suspect on the basis both of NLRB certification results and of unionization figures' (1982, pp. 170, 174).

3 Roomkin and Juris (1979, p. 38) make this assumption and cite various references supposedly substantiating it.

4 von Hoffman 1978, p. 26. Bell (1972, pp. 174, 179) has also argued that the unions are 'incapable of organizing . . . technical workers . . . [who are] replacing the skilled workers as the crucial group in the industrial process.'

5 See Zeitlin et al. (1976) for an explication of the concept of 'class segments' within the dominant class.

6 Quinn and Staines 1979. (The QES was sponsored by the Employee Standards Administration of the US Department of Labor and was directed by Robert Quinn and Graham Staines. The data were made available for our analysis of relative labor organization through the Inter-university Consortium for Political and Social Research; we are grateful both to the original principal investigators, Quinn and Staines, and to the Consortium.)

7 The QES, following the new practice of the Current Population Survey of the US Census, asked respondents not whether they belonged to a union but 'to a union or employee association similar to a union.'

8 Hodges 1962, p. 29. See Giddens (1973, especially pp. 179–86) on the manual/nonmanual 'class differentiation,' and the studies cited therein.

9 Unfortunately, we have found no systematic comparative data on working-class unionization, but Bain et al. (1973, p. 1) provide estimates of 42 percent of manual workers organized in Germany and 53 percent in Britain, as of 1966 and 1972, respectively. No estimate is available of manual worker unionization in France, but 28 percent of all French

employees, roughly the same as in the United States, are in unions (Eurostat 1980).

10 There is a voluminous literature on 'white-collar workers,' of course, but Mills (1951) is probably unsurpassed in insight, except perhaps by Braverman (1974). On white-collar 'proletarianization,' see Glenn and Feldberg (1977).

11 The Communist parties of France and Italy include engineers and technicians in their conceptions of the working class but exclude the 'intermediate strata' of white-collar 'unproductive' workers. Poulantzas (1975, pp. 216, 221), restricts the working class to 'productive wage earners,' by whom he means only those 'directly involved in material production . . . producing use-values that increase material wealth,' and excludes all other 'unproductive salaried workers.' He thus relegates engineers and technicians, as well as the latter, to the 'new petty bourgeoisie.' Also see Poulantzas (1977).

12 Marx 1967, vol. 1, pp. 508–9; Marx 1976, p. 1040. See, in this connection, Wright (1978), Carchedi (1977, pp. 56–7), and A. Hunt (1977, pp. 87–94).

13 See, aside from the works cited in the previous footnote, E. K. Hunt (1979, especially pp. 320–3), and the references cited therein, for the theoretical debate about 'productive and unproductive labor.' Note also Marx's formulation that there are 'processes of production which are only continued in circulation, the productive character of which hence is merely *concealed by the circulation form*. . . . They may be, from the standpoint of society, mere costs, unproductive expenditure of living or materialized labor, but for that very reason they may become productive of value for the individual capitalist.' This formulation and his remark that storage, transportation, and communication represent, in part, '*a continuation of a process of production within the process of circulation*' (Marx 1967, vol. 2, pp. 126, 152, italics added) seem to us to apply as well to the processes of production within the process of circulation represented by service industries and even advertising, as discussed in the text. Also see Rubin (1972, ch. 19), whose discussion of the problem of productive versus unproductive labor has not been surpassed since he wrote over 50 years ago.

14 Marx wrote that as the result of the growth of the worker's 'net product, more spheres are opened up for unproductive workers, who live on his product and whose interest in his exploitation coincides more or less with that of the directly exploiting classes' (1967, vol. 2, p. 571).

15 US Census news release, reported in the *Los Angeles Times*, August 16, 1982.

16 According to our calculations from the data presented in the Bureau of Labor Statistics (1979, table 5), 23.4 percent of the women and 51.4 percent of the men among wage and salary workers are employed in the industries comprising the production sector by our definition.

17 Calculated from data presented in *Employment and Earnings* 26, June 1979, pp. 35–6; 64.3 percent of employed women and 41.3 percent of employed men are white-collar workers, and 34.9 percent of the women versus 6.0 percent of the men are clerical workers; of all white-collar workers, 51.5 percent are women, and of all blue-collar workers, 18.3 percent are women. Of clerical workers, in particular, 80.4 percent are women. The distribution in our QES data is almost identical: of all clerical workers in our sample, 77.0 percent are women; of manual workers, 18.1 percent are women. It is also worth noting that the proportion of women among clerical workers in the circulation sector is far higher than in the production sector, with the state sector ranged between them: 59.3 percent of the clerks in the production sector, but 85.1 percent in the circulation sector and 72.4 percent in the state sector are women. (See the numbers in table 7.4, later, from which these percentages are calculated.) Aside from this marked concentration of women in the clerical stratum of the working class, there is also – to coin a phrase – a sexual division of labor within the sexual division of labor; as Glenn and Feldberg (1977, p. 54) observe, historically, 'a new, male managerial stratum took over the quasi–managerial activities of the clerks, leaving the detail work to the now predominantly female office staffs.' Also see Gardiner (1977, especially pp. 159–61).

18 See Bartle 1983; we calculated the increases in women's labor force participation and union membership during World War II from the figures given by Bartle (1983, tables 1 and 2).

19 Official CPS estimates for 1977 are that only 15.7 percent of the female wage and salary workers but 29.6 percent of their male peers are in labor organizations (Bureau of Labor Statistics 1979, table 2). The QES estimates are that such organizations embrace 21.7 percent of the women and 33.3 percent of the men among wage and salary workers. So the QES estimates a far higher proportion of women organized and less of a gap between the levels of organization of men and women workers. Yet the CPS and QES estimates of the overall participation of men and women in the wage and salary work force are quite close: the CPS estimates that 58.2 percent of all wage and salary workers are men compared with the QES figure of 61.6 percent. Since respondents in the CPS household interviews reported on the union membership of others in the household who were not personally interviewed, this may have resulted in a CPS underestimate of the labor organization membership of women workers.

20 See Wiener (1978) for an analysis of the transformation of class relations in the post-civil war south. Also see Wiener (1979).

21 The QES contains no data on unionization by city. Freeman and Medoff (1979, table 5) found the following proportions of 'production workers' (non-office employees) in unions in these Standard Metropolitan

Statistical Areas (SMSAs): in Chicago, 48 percent; in Detroit, 51 percent; in St. Louis, 52 percent; in Cleveland, 52 percent; in Toledo, 58 percent; and in Gary–Hammond–East Chicago, 69 percent. Of the 16 SMSAs having half or more of their production workers unionized, 15 are in the northeast or north-central regions; only San Francisco–Oakland, with 54 percent organized, falls outside these areas. Of the 19 more SMSAs that are 40–49 percent organized, only five are outside these same regions: Seattle, Birmingham, Ala, Honolulu, Tulsa, and Beaumont–Port Arthur–Orange, Tex.

22 See Geschwender (1977), and Leggett (1964, p. 230) in which it is reported that unionized black workers are far more likely than other black workers to 'use a class frame of reference to appraise their circumstances.'

23 The CPS estimates that 29 percent of all black wage and salaried workers (including professionals) compared with 23 percent of all whites in that category are in labor organizations (Bureau of Labor Statistics 1979, table 2). Our QES estimates are that 33 percent of the black versus 28 percent of the white wage and salaried workers are organized. The ratios of black to white workers organized are thus almost identical in the two surveys, although the QES estimates of the overall proportions organized are, again, higher.

24 'Paratechnical relations' is the term coined by Giddens (1973, p. 86) to refer to what Marx considered the aspect of the 'relations of production,' expressed in the 'immediate process of production.' Burawoy (1979, p. 15) calls these 'relations on the shop floor into which workers enter, both with one another and with management,' 'relations in production.'

25 Computed from the numbers in each category given in table 7.9, part C.

26 US Bureau of the Census (1980, table 953, p. 568) for manufacturing corporation assets, 1977, and calculated from table 955, p. 569, for profits 1978 as compared with assets 1978 (none available for 1977), given in table 953; calculated for employment 1977 from US Bureau of the Census 1978 (table 939, p. 573). I used the 1977–8 data on assets, profits, and employment to be consistent with the date of the QES data base.

27 *Fortune*, no author given, 1952, p. 74. Daniel Bell, then *Fortune*'s labor editor, probably wrote this fine report.

References

Aronowitz, Stanley. 1979. 'The Labor Movement and the Left in the United States.' *Socialist Review* 9 (March–April): 9–61.

Averitt, Robert T. 1968. *The Dual Economy: The Dynamics of American Industry Structure*. New York: Norton.

Bain, George S., David Coates, and Valerie Ellis. 1973. *Social Stratification and Trade Unionism: A Critique*. London: Heinemann.

Bartle, Kathleen. 1983. 'Short Term Employment: Women and Unions in World War II.' Pp. 128–97 in *How Mighty A Force? Studies of Workers' Consciousness and Organization in the United States*, edited by Maurice Zeitlin. Los Angeles, Calif.: Institute of Industrial Relations, University of California.

Bell, Daniel. 1972. 'Labor in the Post-industrial Society.' *Dissent* 19 (Winter): 163–89.

Bernstein, Harry. 1982. "Pension Power": Unions See Strength in Cooperation.' *Los Angeles Times*, July 11: 1, 24–8.

Braverman, Harry. 1974. *Labor and Monopoly Capital: The Degradation of Work in the Twentieth Century*. New York: Monthly Review Press.

Burawoy, Michael. 1979. *Manufacturing Consent: Changes in the Labor Process Under Monopoly Capitalism*. Chicago, Ill.: University of Chicago Press.

Bureau of Labor Statistics. 1979. *Earnings and Other Characteristics of Organized Workers*, May 1977. Report 556. Washington, D.C.: US Department of Labor.

—— 1980. *Directory of National Unions and Employee Associations, 1979*. Bulletin 2079. Washington, D.C.: US Department of Labor.

Carchedi, Guglielmo. 1977. *On the Economic Identification of Social Classes*. London: Routledge & Kegan Paul.

Eurostat. 1980. *Social Indicators for the European Community, 1960–1978*. Luxembourg: European Communities Statistical Office.

Ferguson, Thomas, and Joel Rogers, 1979. 'Labor Law Reform and Its Enemies.' *The Nation*, January 6: 1, 17–20.

Fortune Magazine. 1952. 'Big Business is Organized – by Labor.' June: 74.

Freeman, Richard B., and James L. Medoff. 1979. 'New Estimates of Private Sector Unionism in the United States.' *Industrial and Labor Relations Review* 32 (January): 143–74.

Gardiner, Jean. 1977. 'Women in the Labor Process and Class Structure.' Pp. 155–63 in *Class and Class Structure*, edited by Alan Hunt. London: Lawrence and Wishart.

Geschwender, James A. 1977. *Class, Race and Worker Insurgency: The League of Revolutionary Black Workers*. New York: Cambridge University Press.

Giddens, Anthony. 1973. *The Class Structure of the Advanced Societies*. New York: Harper & Row.

Glenn, Evelyn Nakano, and Roslyn L. Feldberg. 1977. 'Degraded and Deskilled: the Proletarianization of Clerical Work.' *Social Problems* 25 (October): 52–64.

Goldfield, Michael. 1982. 'The Decline of Organized Labor: NLRB Union Certification Election Results.' *Politics & Society* 11 (2): 167–209.

Hodges, Donald C. 1962. 'Cynicism in the Labor Movement.' *American Journal of Economics and Sociology* 21 (January): 29–36. (Reprinted in *American Society, Inc.*, edited by Maurice Zeitlin. Chicago, Ill.: Rand McNally, 1977.)

von Hoffman, Nicholas. 1978. 'The Last Days of the Labor Movement.' *Harper's*, December: 22ff.

Hunt, Alan. 1977. 'Theory and Politics in the Identification of the Working Class.' Pp. 81–111 in *Class and Class Structure*, edited by Alan Hunt. London: Lawrence and Wishart.

Hunt, E. K. 1979. 'The Categories of Productive and Unproductive Labor in Marxist Economic Theory.' *Science & Society* 43 (Fall): 303–25.

Kotz, Nick. 1977. 'Can Labor's Tired Leaders Deal with a Troubled Movement?' *New York Times Magazine*, September 4: 8ff.

Leggett, John. 1964. 'Economic Insecurity and Working Class Consciousness.' *American Sociological Review* 29 (April): 226–234.

Lens, Sidney. 1978. 'On the Waning Power of Organized Labor.' *The Progressive*, March: 12–13.

Magdoff, Harry. 1982. 'Measuring Productivity: the Economists' New Clothes.' *The Nation*, March 27: 359–61.

Marx, Karl. 1967. *Capital*, vols 1–3. New York: International.

—— 1976 'The Results of the Immediate Process of Production.' Appendix to *Capital*, vol. 1 (trans., ed. Ben Fowkes). New York and London: Penguin.

McDermott, John. 1980. *The Crisis in the Working Class and Some Arguments for a New Labor Movement*. Boston, Mass.: South End.

Mills, C. Wright. 1951. *White Collar*. New York: Oxford University Press.

Nation's Business. 1978. 'Why Labor Unions are Worried.' March: 42–5.

O'Connor, James. 1973. *The Fiscal Crisis of the State*. New York: St. Martin's.

Poulantzas, Nicos. 1975. *Classes in Contemporary Capitalism*. London: New Left Books.

—— 1977. 'The New Petty Bourgeoisie.' Pp. 113–24 in *Class and Class Structure*, edited by Alan Hunt. London: Lawrence and Wishart.

Quinn, Robert, and Graham Staines. 1979. *Quality of Employment Survey, 1977: Cross Section*. Ann Arbor, Mich.: Inter–university Consortium for Political and Social Research.

Raskin, A. H. 1978. 'Seething Impotence in the Labor Camp.' *Fortune*, July 31: 82.

—— 1979. 'Big Labor Strives to Break Out of Its Rut.' *Fortune*, August 27: 32–40.

Regensburger, William. 1987. 'Worker Insurgency and Southern working-class Combativeness.' Pp. 71–159 in *Insurgent Workers: Studies of the Origins of Industrial Unionism*, edited by Maurice Zeitlin. Los Angeles, Calif.: Institute of Industrial Relations, University of California.

Roomkin, Myron, and Hervey A. Juris. 1979. 'The Changing Character of Unionism in Traditionally Organized Sectors.' *Monthly Labor Review* February: 36–8.

Rothschild, Emma. 1981. 'Reagan and the Real America.' *New York Review of Books* 28 February: 12–18.

Rubin, Isaak Ilich. 1972. *Essays on Marx's Theory of Value* (trans., Milos Samardzija and Fredy Perlman). Detroit, Mich.: Black and Red (originally published in Moscow and Leningrad in 1928).

Samuelson, Robert J. 1981. 'Big Industries of Yesterday Face a Sobering Tomorrow.' *Los Angeles Times*, December 9: part 2: 11.

US Bureau of the Census. 1975. *Historical Statistics of the United States: Colonial Times to 1970*, part 1. Washington, D.C.: US Government Printing Office.

—— 1978. *Statistical Abstract of the United States: 1978*. Washington, D.C.: US Government Printing Office.

—— 1980. *Statistical Abstract of the United States: 1980*. Washington, D.C.: US Government Printing Office.

Wiener, Jonathan M. 1978. *Social Origins of the New South*. Baton Rouge, Lo., and London: Louisiana State University Press.

—— 1979. 'Class Structure and Economic Development in the American South.' *American Historical Review* 84 (October): 970–92, plus commentaries and reply, 993–1006.

Wright, Erik O. 1978. *Class, Crisis and the State*. London: New Left Books.

Zeitlin, Maurice, W. Lawrence Neuman, and Richard E. Ratcliff. 1976. 'Class Segments: Agrarian Property and Political Leadership in the Capitalist Class of Chile.' *American Sociological Review* 41 (December): 1006–29.

8

Political generations in the Cuban working class

The concept of political generation focuses on the intersection of biography, history, and social structure. It thus compels us to pay attention to variables of explanatory value that we might otherwise overlook. However, despite the wide interpretive use to which some variant of the concept of generation has been put (whether, for example, in creative literature, literary criticism, or qualitative political analysis), its use has been infrequent in the sociological analysis of politics, and especially so in the analysis of data gathered through survey research methods.[1] The most significant lack in this area is of studies of the formation of political generations elsewhere than in the advanced industrial societies of the West.[2]

This study is about the formation of political generations in the Cuban working class and the relevance of these generations for the recent social revolution. Its thesis is (a) that different political generations were formed among the Cuban workers as a result of the impact on them of distinctive historical experiences and (b) that the differential response of the generations to the revolution is understandable in terms of these experiences.

My approach to the specific problem of generations in Cuba is based on Karl Mannheim's general formulation of the problem. He suggests that common experiences during their youth might create a common world view or frame of reference from which individuals of the same age group would tend to view their subsequent political

A brief portion of this article appeared in 'Political Attitudes of Cuban Workers,' a paper delivered at the meeting of the American Sociological Association, August, 1963. I am indebted to the Center of International Studies, Princeton University, for a grant that made my research for this study possible and to its director, Klaus Knorr, for his encouragement. I should also like to acknowledge the theoretical stimulation provided by Norman Ryder's unpublished paper, 'The Cohort as a Concept in the Study of Social Change,' (Ryder 1959) and the helpful suggestions of my colleagues Michael T. Aiken, Jerald Hague, and Gerald Marwell.

experiences. Sharing the same year of birth, they 'are endowed, to that extent, with a common location in the historical dimension of the social process.' Much like the effect of class on its members, the generation also limits its members 'to a specific range of potential experience, predisposing them for a certain characteristic mode of thought and experience, and *a characteristic type of historically relevant action*'(Mannheim 1952, p. 286, italics added).

From the standpoint of our analysis, it is particularly significant that the Cubans themselves see their history to a great extent in generational terms, a fact that is not at all surprising given the dramatic and profoundly traumatic nature of the events that formed several Cuban generations. Cuban literature – political, historical, fictional – is replete with references to the 'generation of '68' or the 'generation of '95' or the 'generation of the thirties,' generations formed during singularly significant historical epochs in Cuba: respectively, the Ten Years' War against Spain (1868–78), the War of Independence (1895–8), and the abortive revolution 1933–5. It is especially significant that the movement led by Fidel Castro, in common with other revolutionary nationalist and anticolonial movements, placed special emphasis on its being a new generation, shorn of the cynicism and the betrayal of revolutionary ideals typical of its elders. The movement's cadre consisted predominantly of young people in their late teens and early twenties and, to this extent, shared with other revolutionary youth movements an identification of the general social movement with their particular generation (see Eisenstadt 1956, p. 311).

The very first lines of the manifesto of the 26th of July movement, which stated its general aims in the anti-Batista struggle, were: 'The 26th of July Movement is resolved to take up the unfulfilled ideals of the Cuban nation and to realize them, . . . [counting] on the contribution and the presence of the reserves of *youth* who are anxious for new horizons in the chronic frustration of the Republic. *That is its credential and its distinctive feature.*' The manifesto condemned 'the colonial mentality, foreign economic domination, [and] political corruption' of the republic, and the regime of exploitation and oppression installed by Batista, and implicitly repudiated the older generation, saying that only the youth of the country had resisted this 'storm of horror and shame' without bowing. The movement traced its roots directly to the revolutionary students and workers of the 'generation of the thirties,' who also had fought against 'the intact chains of the past' and who, 'in the "hundred days" that the revolutionary forces held power . . . did more in the defense of the interests of the nation and of the people than all the governments of the preceding thirty years' (Pedrero 1959, pp. 89–91, 97–9, 103–5, and 125, italics added).

On the one hand, the young rebels of the 26th of July movement identified with the generation of the thirties, its accomplishments, and aspirations; on the other, they condemned that generation for its failure to fulfill the ideals of its youth and for its capitulation to reaction – a capitulation that led, they believed, to the need for the revolutionary movement of their own generation.

Not only did this generational animus characterize a good deal of the rebel movement before the conquest of power but also it apparently has continued as one significant source of self-identification since the revolution. In one of his first public speeches (on January 8, 1959) after the fall of Batista's regime, Castro again identified the youth of his generation as one of the decisive social bases of the revolution: 'When the 26th of July Movement organized itself and initiated the war, it . . . was evident that the . . . Movement had the sympathy of the people, and . . . that it had *the nearly unanimous support of the youth of Cuba*' (Castro 1959, p. 44, italics added).

This generation of '53, the generation of Castro and his fellow rebels, is held up as a model of sacrifice and heroism on the nation's behalf. Its special quality has been reiterated in many speeches by Castro. 'Ours is the generation for which no one set a good example . . . but it drew upon itself for the idealism, virtue, and courage necessary to save the country. . . . *It is the best generation that the nation has had*. It grew up in the midst of negation and bad examples. But the coming generation will be better than ours. It will be inspired not only by the generations of [18]68 and [18]95 but also *by the generation of 1953* (Castro 1959, italics added).

Thus, as a result of having lived through a history of rather abrupt social and political transitions and clearly demarcated political intervals, Cubans apparently have developed a relatively high level of generational self-consciousness. Stated formally, the major hypothesis of this paper is that the specific historical period in which succeeding generations of workers first became involved in the labor movement had significant consequences for the formation of their political outlooks. Shaped by the early experiences of their youth in the labor movement – that movement's conflicts, organization, tactics and strategy, ideology, and leadership –

working-class political generations emerged in Cuba with measurably different attitudes toward the *Fidelista* revolution.

For our purposes, the concept of political generation will be defined, as Rudolf Heberle has put it, as 'those individuals of approximately the same age who have shared, at the same age, certain politically relevant experiences (1951, pp. 119–20). The concept leaves open to empirical investigation the decision as to (a) which age groups to isolate for analysis and (b) which experiences to delineate as of decisive political relevance for that age group.[3]

Thus, in the analysis of political generations in the Cuban working class and their contemporary relevance in the context of the revolution, two strategic methodological decisions were necessary: (a) which age category or categories to locate in time and (b) in which historical periods, depending on which experiences were hypothesized to be politically relevant.

1 Normative expectations of political involvement in Cuba were established and perpetuated by the political activities of students, whose agitation and action since the foundation of the republic were often decisively bound up with the politics of the working class – whether, for instance, in the anti-Spanish colonial struggle for independence or in the abortive revolution of the 1930s. The late teens and early twenties have been viewed in Cuba as a period in life demanding political commitment and involvement – the period of coming to manhood politically. In two of Cuba's most significant political periods, the political cadre that predominated in the movement consisted of young men and women; the short-lived government of Ramon Grau San Martín during the revolution of the thirties rested to a considerable extent on the support of the youth. Raul Roa, a student leader at that time, and now foreign minister of Cuba, dubbed that regime 'the ephebocracy,' or teenage government.[4] And in the guerrilla struggle and urban *resistencia* against Batista, men and women in their late teens and early twenties apparently formed the majority of the movement's leaders and cadre, whatever their class of origin.[5] On these grounds, I chose the age category of 18–25 to locate the generations temporally.

In addition, I chose this age category on more general sociological grounds. First, the meaning of age varies in accordance with social norms governing specific activities and their relationship to age; it is precisely at the age at which coming to manhood is normatively defined that men and women become more responsive to the impact of social change, since they are relatively less subject to parental influence in their new role. That is, it is likely that individuals who have come of age are more 'responsive to the impact of social change' than children who are still 'insulated from it by [their] home environment, (Hyman 1959, p. 131). It is therefore reasonable to assume that the experiences of workers in the period after they enter the labor force, assume their own support, and are no longer under parental supervision would be particularly significant to them, especially if this occurs in a period of social upheaval.

Second, it is a central assumption here that the social pressures arising out of the work situation are fundamental in determining the worker's political outlook. The work place is probably the most important source of the worker's political socialization, more so than for non-workers. A recent study found, for example, that French workers were more likely than other Frenchmen to discuss politics at work (Hamilton, 1967, ch. iv). Much of the most significant political socialization of workers – in so far as that involves assimilation of the political orientations current in their class – occurs after they go to work to support themselves. This being so, crucial historical events impinging on workers are more likely to affect their personal politics if they have been working for a few years than if they have just begun. These are additional reasons why I chose to focus on historical events when workers were in their late teens and early twenties rather than when they were younger.

2 From the standpoint of our analysis of political generations, five critical periods in Cuban political history of the past several decades can be distinguished. Their general social conditions, political issues, and 'concrete internal political and social struggles' (Herberle 1951, pp. 122–3) constitute the decisive politically relevant experiences of succeeding Cuban generations – i.e. of those who were 18–25 years old when each of these critical periods began. In table 8.1, I have briefly indicated the decisive events of each political generation analyzed in this study and the predicted political consequences of those events.

The Decisive Events of the Political Generations

Sugar speculation in the aftermath of World War I ended abruptly with Cuba's economic collapse in the early 1930s (partly as a

Table 8.1 *Temporal location and decisive political events of political generations, and predicted political consequences*

Age category at time of study (1962)	Period that began when workers were 18–25	Decisive politically relevant events	Predicted rank of generation's support for	
			Communists	Revolution
21–27	1959 on	Establishment of the revolutionary government and ensuing revolutionary changes, including nationalization of industry and declaration of 'socialist' regime	[a]	4
28–35	1952/3–8	Batista's coup; guerilla war and urban resistance led by Castro; agitation and organization in working class; rebirth of working-class economic struggle; abortive national general strike; fall of Batista	3	1
36–43	1944–51	Relative political democracy and economic stability; alliance of government and anti-Communist labor officials; purge of Communists from CTC[b] leadership	4	5
44–51	1936/7–43	Suppression of insurrection; re-emergence of Communist leadership of labor movement; collaboration with Batista; achievement of tangible socioeconomic benefits for organized workers	2	2
52–59	1928–35	Mass working-class and student insurrection; 'dual power' of 'Soviets' under Communist leadership; establishment of radical nationalist regime	1	2

[a] The youngest generation's response to the Communists before the revolution is excluded here and in the following tables, since the question refers to an attitude held before they were adults.

consequence of the Great Depression in the United States), provoking a period of social upheaval. Working-class and student political strikes throughout the country resulted not only in the overthrow of the repressive Machado regime but also in increasingly more militant political initiatives. These included the students' taking control of the University of Havana and demanding its 'autonomy' from government interference and the workers' occupation of several railroad terminals, public utilities, ports, 36 sugar centrals, and a number of adjoining towns, in many of which they established 'soviets' (councils) of workers, peasants, and soldiers. Students, young intellectuals, and workers, aside from taking independent political action, were in liaison with each other, with the former acting in many instances as workers' delegates to the short-lived radical nationalist Grau regime. The young Communist party was dominant in the leadership of the workers, and, despite the equivocal role of the Communists in the final overthrow of the Machado regime, they maintained and increased their influence among the workers throughout the revolutionary period. Fulgencio Batista, who had led a revolt of the enlisted men and noncommissioned officers and gained leadership of the army, repressed the revolutionary movement and consolidated his power in late 1936 and early 1937.

Suppression of the revolution, forceful dissolution of working-class organizations, and the advent on the international Communist scene of the Popular Front period resulted in the transformation of the radical and independent workers' movement into a reformist movement under Communist leadership, which inaugurated an era of government–labor collaboration. The relative stability and economic security in Cuba during World War II accentuated even further the reformism of the workers' movement, as well as its growing bureaucratization. Under Communist leadership, the organized workers were able to gain certain tangible economic and social benefits.

Batista relinquished power in 1944, and a period of relative political democracy began – a period, however, that also included an alliance of the government and anti-Communist labor officials which increasingly used extra-legal and violent methods to harass the Communist leadership of the labor movement. The Communists were thus finally ousted in 1947 from official leadership of the Confederación de Trabajadores de Cuba (CTC), the national labor organization that the Communists themselves had formed in 1938 under Batista's aegis. The growing bureaucratization of the unions, their loss of contact with the mass of the workers, and their collaboration with the government was heightened during this period of comparative internal economic stability and 'prosperity.'

CTC officials, under the leadership of Eusebio Mujal (whence comes the derogatory term *mujalista*), did not resist Batista's coup d'etat of March, 1952, in which he regained power. In the years following, and throughout the guerrilla war and *resistencia*, the CTC was largely an appendage of the regime and was often used as a weapon against the workers themselves; and the already significant union corruption of prior years became increasingly supplemented by gangsterism and intimidation of the workers. The Communists, having lost the government's tutelage and having been outlawed by Batista, retained a measure of grass-roots influence among the workers and led some important victorious strikes, especially in the sugar industry. But the regime fell not as the result of a working-class insurrection, which never materialized on a mass level, but as the result of conflict with the guerrilla forces and urban *resistencia* under the leadership of Castro's 26th of July movement, whose cadre consisted predominantly of young men and women. Until the final demise of the Batista regime in 1959, their age peers, whether active in the anti-Batista movement or not, and whatever their class, were both more suspect to the police and the military and more likely than Cubans of other ages to suffer arbitrarily at the hands of the regime.[6]

The relatively passive role of the workers in the anti-Batista struggle contrasts strikingly with their decisive insurrectionary role against the Machado regime. Nonetheless, the years of the Batista regime had seen a reinvigoration of the Cuban tradition of independent working-class economic struggle – under the leadership of Communists and non-Communists alike. The apparent political quiescence of the workers should not be exaggerated. For instance, during the 1955 strike in the sugar industry, several militant political actions also took place; the sugar workers were joined by other workers in cities such as Santa Clara and some sugar towns of Camaguey and Havana provinces, and their economic demands became coupled with such political slogans as 'Down with the criminal government!'

In eastern Cuba and in Santiago, Cuba's second largest city, there were especially significant instances of working-class political support of the anti-Batista movement. A spontaneous political strike set off by the funeral of two young 26th of July leaders on August 1, 1957, spread from Santiago to other cities in Oriente Province and several towns throughout the country. The strike was complete in Santiago, shutting down the Nicaro nickel plant and shops in the city for five days. In subsequent months 'strike committees' were organized in many plants by 26th of July organizers and other opposition elements, in preparation for a general strike in 1958. The general strike, called for April 9, 1958, collapsed in Havana in several hours, with little mass support; but it completely paralyzed industry and commerce in Santiago, where the workers stayed out despite the regime's threats of arrest and offers of immunity from prosecution to anyone killing an advocate of the strike. Despite their failure to overthrow the regime, then, the actions mentioned here were certainly significant in the movement against Batista's regime and must have affected the workers' political consciousness.[7]

If it is correct that the struggle against Batista and the events flowing from it were of decisive significance in shaping the political consciousness of the workers of this generation of '53, then clearly they should be far more likely than the members of other generations to support the revolution. How correct this inference is, and the evidence regarding it, will be seen below.

Methods

The data for this study are drawn from interviews with industrial workers in Cuba in the summer of 1962. By that time the revolutionary government had clearly consolidated its power (the Bay of Pigs invasion being a year in the past); the original relatively undifferentiated popular euphoria had already been replaced by relatively clear lines of social cleavage generated in response to actions taken by the revolutionary government; it was two years since the nationalization of industry and more than a year since Castro had declared the revolution to be 'socialist.' A study of the differential appeals of the ideology and social content of the revolution to Cuban workers could now be meaningful and valuable.

Interviews were carried out with a randomly selected sample of 202 industrial workers employed in 21 plants widely scattered throughout the island's six provinces. Plants were chosen from a list of all those functioning under the direction of the Ministry of Industries.[8]

The plants were selected by means of a self-weighting random sample in which the probability that a plant would be chosen was directly proportional to the number of workers employed in it. This sampling method tended to exclude the smaller industrial establishments (*chinchales*) that abound in Cuba. In each plant, 10 workers were selected by a method designed to obtain a simple random sample. My wife and I each separately interviewed five workers per plant, in Spanish. All interviewing was done in complete privacy, in a location provided within the work center such as a storage room, office, or classroom. We told each worker interviewed (as well as anyone else concerned) that we were correspondents for *The Nation*; that we had permission from the Ministry of Industries, the plant administration, and the union delegate to interview workers in the plant; that the worker was chosen by a scientific method of randomization; that he would not be identified personally in any way; and that his answers would be entirely anonymous; we simply wanted to know his opinions about some things at work and in Cuba in general, so as to be able to write an objective report about the condition of the Cuban working class.[9]

It might be objected, of course, that such survey research could not obtain meaningful results because Cuba was already a police state in the summer of 1962. This obviously pertinent question cannot be discussed at length here. The reader will have to be content with the elliptical assertion that this objection is without foundation and our observation that Cubans could and did inquire and speak freely about whatever they wished – at that time. There were no formal safeguards of freedom of speech and association, and the potentialities for authoritarian rule were great, but that potential had yet to become a reality. We were able to carry out our interviewing without disturbance or interference of any kind and to obtain, I believe, data quite as valid as those obtained in any competent survey research.[10]

The interview schedule begins with questions which are, on the surface, far removed from political issues of any kind. These questions pertain to length of residence in a particular place, length of time working in the work place, and so on. Questions of more or less obvious political content begin somewhere in the middle of the interview. I combined five of these, which I think together adequately indicate how the workers view the revolution, into an 'index of attitude toward the revolution.' Of these five questions, two are open-ended and three are forced-choice questions.

The open-ended questions are (a) 'Speaking generally, what are the things about this country that you are most proud of as a Cuban?'[11] and (b) 'What sort (*clase*) of people govern this country now?' The answers to the first question given by 115 workers were favorable to the revolution. A response was considered 'favorable' only if it clearly indicated, or explicitly stated, support for the revolution.[12]

The workers could be especially blunt, as was a young worker at a paper milling plant in Cardenas, whose answer was simply, 'Of nothing, *chico*. . . . I don't like Communism,' or a West Indian cement worker (with two teenage daughters in the militia) in Mariel, who explained (in English): 'I stay only because I have two daughters who will not leave – otherwise I'd go away. . . . No one bothers me, I just do not like it. Why? I can't say why. I guess I just prefer the old Cuba.'

In contrast to these clearly hostile remarks were such noncommittal replies as a shoemaker's, 'Of our movies and our athletes,' or a brewery worker's equivocal, 'I am a peaceful worker. I have no passionate interest in anything. After my work, I pass the time in my house in Manacas with my little one and my wife,' or a cigar-maker's witty but equally noncommittal, 'Our women and our cigars.'

Occasionally a revolutionary worker would wax poetic, as did a copper-miner in Matahambre: 'Cuba is a cup of gold to me. It is the only country in the world that is now moving forward.' A sugar-worker's simple statement was more typical, however: 'I earn good money now. I lack nothing. . . . All of the workers are with the revolution.' A Havana brewery worker said: 'I am content with the revolution in general. . . . For the first time one can do what one wants without fear.'

The replies to the second question by 125 workers were favorable to the revolution. Given the double meaning in Spanish of the word *clase*, which can mean 'type,' 'sort,' or 'kind,' as well as 'class,' the workers could, of course, choose to interpret the question's meaning in a number of ways. As with the preceding question, we counted as 'favorable' replies only those that could be clearly regarded as such.[13]

A worker at the nationalized Texaco plant responded that those governing Cuba 'are completely Communists. All of their accomplishments have been through the work of others – including how they think. I have a sister-in-law and a brother-in-law in prison for speaking against the government – [sentenced to] seven years.' Another antirevolutionary worker said: 'Socialists, they say. The kids say Communists. I don't know. Listen, if somebody comes and takes that pen of yours, and you bought it, what are you going to think?'

'Well, I've never been "political,"' a cigarette-machine operator said, 'for me, they are all right.' A brewery worker's reply was equally equivocal: 'My experience so far is good. I don't worry about such things – neither before the revolution nor now.' A skilled electrician in Santiago committed himself only so far as to say that the men in the government are 'persons with socialist ideas, who though they have good intentions have committed many serious administrative errors.'

'The truth is,' a carpenter in a sugar central said, 'that now those who govern here are Cubans. They are honest and hardworking men.' A 67-year-old maintenance man at the Nicaro nickel plant who had been an agricultural worker until recently said: 'Look, before I couldn't look a boss in the eye – I looked at my feet. Not now, now we have liberty and walk where we wish, and nothing is prohibited to us. It is a great joy to be alive now. These men [who govern us] are 100 percent better than before. I have known governments from [Mario Garcia] Menocal [Cuban president, 1913–21] until Batista left three years ago, and I have never seen any like this government.' Equally articulate in his support of the revolution was a 25-year-old bootmaker in a newly established factory in Guanajay: 'We are the government, *we* run things. Go to a factory or *consolidado* [consolidated enterprise] anywhere, *chico*, and see: those who work govern, those who govern work, not like the capitalists who lived without working before the revolution triumphed. Now, the power of the workers and peasants has emerged.'

The workers were also asked the following questions with fixed alternatives: (c) 'Do you believe that the country ought to have elections soon?' (d) 'Do you think that the workers now have more, the same, or less influence on [*en*] the government than they had before the revolution?' (e) 'Do you belong to the militia?'[14]

The index of attitude toward the revolution was constructed by coding favorable responses as +1 and all others as 0 (table 8.2).[15]

Table 8.2 *Index of attitude toward the revolution*

Points	Definition	N
3–5	Favorable	142
2	Indecisive	24
0, 1	Hostile	36
Total		202

Findings

Comparison of the political generations confirms our expectation that members of Castro's rebel generation, or the generation of '53, are most likely to support the revolution (table 8.3). United by the common political frame of reference they developed during the anti-Batista struggle, the generation of '53 stands out as the decisive generational base of the revolution. Further, the two other generations that stand out are precisely those whose members experienced the revolutionary events of the 1930s as young men. It is, of course, possible to argue that, having experienced an abortive rather than a successful revolution, they should be cynical and pessimistic rather than optimistic about the Castro revolution, and this argument does make a good deal of sense. Yet, while the *social* revolution was crushed, the Machado regime *was* overthrown, and thus the political revolution in the narrow sense was a success. Moreover, seen in retrospect, the revolution also yielded significant gains for the

Table 8.3 *Political generation and attitude toward the revolution*

Age category at time of study (1962)[a]	Favorable (%)	Indecisive (%)	Hostile (%)	(N)
21–27	55	19	25	(36)
28–35	90	2	8	(51)
36–43	61	17	21	(51)
44–51	69	15	15	(26)
52–59	70	9	22	(23)

[a] This and the following tables do not include eight workers who were under 21 and seven who were over 59 in 1962.

workers in subsequent years – especially the legitimation of their right to political and economic organization, a right that allowed them to win substantial economic benefits. It is also relevant that the repression of the revolution of the 1930s, which in any case had significant 'anti-imperialist' overtones, was widely believed in Cuba to have been the result of US political intervention.[16] The anti-imperialism of the revolutionary government may therefore be another source of the workers' support. Thus, it is understandable that these generations may view the present revolution as the renascence and continuation of the struggles of their own youth and may be more disposed to support it than the generation who came to manhood during the republican interregnum of relative stability or the present generation for whom prerevolutionary struggles are mere 'history.'

The low proportion of the present generation who support the revolution is unexpected. My own prediction (see table 8.1) was that this generation would be outranked by the generations of '53 and the thirties but would itself outrank the republican generation. The explanation may be that the workers of this generation know little if anything through personal experience about the prerevolutionary situation of the working class. Many of them (55 percent) were not yet working before the revolution and thus could hardly appreciate the positive changes in the situation of the working class wrought by the revolution.

The impact of the anti-Batista struggle on the workers of the generation of '53 has made it the generational base of the revolution. Moreover, in a significant sense it was their generation that brought the revolutionary government to power. The leaders of the revolution itself, it will be remembered, who led the *resistencia* and were the rebel cadres in the hills and in the cities, are members of the generation of '53. In accordance with the hypothesis of political generations, the fact that the members of this generation acquired their political frame of reference in the course of the anti-Batista struggle should have made them more likely than members of other generations to support the revolution now, *regardless of the generation to which the rebel leaders themselves belonged.* But the fact that the rebels were predominantly of their own generation may have been an additional source of their support for and identification with the rebels and their cause. It may be surmised that the rebels became, in a significant sense, collectively the reference group of that entire generation, and the chief rebel leaders its foremost culture heroes or 'reference individuals.'[17] That the rebel leaders couched so much of their program in generational terms also may have considerably increased the likelihood that the members of the generation of '53 would identify with them. In turn, this act of identification may itself have reinforced the attitudes this generation was developing in response to the set of stimuli created by the historical situation.

If this assumption is correct, that identification with the members of their generation who were actively participating in and leading the rebel movement was one more element in the complex of elements comprising the distinct politically relevant experiences of the generation of '53, we should expect a similar identification in the present. Are members of the generation of '53 more likely than others to identify with the leaders of the revolution? Using the question 'Aside from personal friends or relatives – of all the people you hear or read about – could you name three individuals whom you admire very much?' as a rough empirical indicator, we found that the generation of '53 is distinctive in this regard.[18] Its members are more likely than those of other generations to name a revolutionary leader (Fidel Castro, Raul Castro, Ernesto 'Che' Guevara, Juan Almeida, etc.) as at least one of the three individuals whom they admire greatly (table 8.4).

That the political generations vary in their response to the revolution in accordance with their historical location in prerevolutionary Cuba suggests also that they should have varied in their *pre*revolutionary political orientations as well. The political strength of the Communists in the working class, for instance, was significantly different in the critical periods that formed the political generations. We might predict, therefore, that the workers varied in their attitudes toward the Communists before the revolution in accordance with the role of the Communists during the workers' common youthful experience in the labor movement. If the Communists were then a significant independent political force, the workers of that generation should have been more likely to support the Communists before the revolution than workers whose youthful experience in the labor movement came during a period of Communist weakness or irrelevance.

As a rough guide to their prerevolutionary attitude toward the Communists, the workers in our sample were asked: 'How would you describe your attitude toward the Communists before the revolution? Hostile, indifferent, friendly, or supporter?'[19]

As table 8.5 indicates, the political generations do view the

Table 8.4 *Political generation and reference individuals*[a]

Proportion naming at least one reference individual who
is a

Age category at time of study (1962)	Cuban revolutionary leader[b] (%)	Communist political figure[c] (%)	Cuban hero or martyr[d] (%)	Popular celebrity[e] (%)	High culture figure[f] (%)	Anti-Castro political figure[g] (%)	(N)
21–27	55	11	11	17	25	8	(36)
28–35	78	18	12	14	18	2	(51)
36–43	55	14	13	9	22	2	(51)
44–51	54	19	4	23	13	4	(26)
52–59	57	4	9	4	22	13	(23)

[a] Percentages do not total 100 because three responses were required. Categories in which no more than 10 percent of any generation named a reference individual are excluded from this table.
[b] Only *fidelistas* or so-called new Communists.
[c] Cuban Partido Socialista Popular leaders ('old Communists') or international Communist figures, e.g. Mao, Khrushchev, Lenin, Ho.
[d] Historic heroes or martyrs such as José Marti, Máximo Gómez, Antonio Maceo, Antonio Guiteras, or martyrs of the anti-Batista struggle such as Frank Pais, José Antonio Echevaría.
[e] Athletes, movie stars, radio and TV entertainers, etc.
[f] Scientists, novelists, artists, philosophers, poets, etc.
[g] Counter-revolutionary leaders such as Carlos Prio Socarras, José Miró Cardona, Manuel Urrutía, or political figures such as presidents Kennedy or Eisenhower, Allen Dulles, etc.

Communists in expectably different ways. The two generations with the highest proportion of workers sympathetic to the Communists before the revolution are those that were formed, respectively, during the anti-Machado struggles and the abortive revolution of the 1930s, in which the Communists played a leading political role, and during the period when the Communists were dominant in the leadership of the CTC. It is significant, moreover, that although the workers of the revolutionary generation of '53 might be expected to 'recall' favorable attitudes toward the Communists in the prerevolutionary period, their generation does not differ in this respect from the generation of republican stability, although the latter has a higher proportion of workers who were hostile to the

Table 8.5 *Political generation and prerevolutionary attitude toward the Communists*

Age category at time of study (1962)[a]	Friendly and/ or supporter (%)	Indifferent (%)	Hostile (%)	(N)
28–35	29	43	27	(51)
36–43	29	35	35	(51)
44–51	38	38	23	(26)
52–59	39	39	22	(23)

[a] The youngest generation of workers (21–27 in 1962) is excluded from this table since the question refers to an attitude held before they were adults.

Communists. It was during the republican interregnum that the Communists were at their weakest level in the working class. During this period they were purged from official leadership of the CTC, and the workers who entered the labor movement at this time would have been more likely than other workers to assimilate anti-Communist political orientations. As to the attitude of the generation of '53 toward the Communists before the revolution, there are good historical reasons why they should have been, at best, ambivalent about the Communists. Fidel's leadership of the assault on Moncada was denounced by the Communists as a 'bourgeois,' 'romantic,' and 'putschist' adventure (*Daily Worker*, August 10, 1953, p. 2), and throughout the guerrilla war against Batista – until it entered its last months – the Communists' official attitude toward it was at best equivocal. As late as May, 1958, the Communists were still referring to the 26th of July movement as 'those who count on terroristic acts and conspiratorial coups as the chief means of ousting Batista,' although they described the movement as the 'most militant and progressive sector of the non-Communist opposition' (quoted in *Daily Worker*, May 4, 1958, p. 6). In the unsuccessful April 9, 1958, attempt at a general strike, the Communist leadership – though not opposing it – declared that it did not have enough support to succeed, and this statement, circulated by Batista, was construed by the 26th of July movement as detrimental to the strike effort. As late as June 28, 1958, when the guerrilla war had reached a high point, the Communists had not reconciled themselves fully to the necessity for armed struggle, and the party's National Committee called for 'clean, democratic elections' to eliminate Batista.[20] The fact is that the Communists, despite the influence they still retained among the workers, were the tail end of the anti-Batista struggle, with the unquestioned leadership of the struggle residing with the 26th of July movement. Thus, it is understandable that members of this generation of '53 were no more likely than the generation of the republic to view the Communists favorably.

So far, this analysis has treated the political generations in terms of their members' common location in the historical process. The common politically relevant experiences of their members, taken as a whole, have differentiated the political generations from each other. But the generations are themselves internally differentiated structurally; and thus individuals of the same generation in different structural locations will have experienced the politically relevant events of their youth differently. As Bennet Berger puts it: 'The temporal location of a [generational] group must first be kept analytically distinct from its structural location; second, when considering them together, we should be aware that the impact of structural (e.g. occupational) factors on the nature of the temporal location may, under some conditions, be such as to fragment the cultural "unity" of a generation beyond recognition.'[21]

One of the most significant structural determinants of the Cuban workers' response to the revolution, as I have shown elsewhere (Zeitlin 1966), was their prerevolutionary employment status. The workers who were unemployed and underemployed before the revolution were more likely to be pro-Communist before the revolution and are now more likely to support the revolutionary government than those who were employed regularly.

So it is important to consider the impact of their prerevolutionary employment status on the workers of different political generations (table 8.6). Indeed, we find that within every political generation the workers who were unemployed and underemployed are more likely to support the revolution than those who were regularly employed before the revolution. Moreover, among both the unemployed and the regularly employed, the generation of '53 exceeds the other generations in the proportion of workers favoring the revolution. Among the employed workers the generation of the thirties comes second, as we should expect. Among the unemployed workers, however, the generation of the republican interregnum has as great a proportion of workers favoring the revolution as does the generation of the thirties. Here is a particularly instructive

Table 8.6 *Political generation, prerevolutionary employment status, and political attitudes*[a]

Age category at time of study (1962)	Underemployed and unemployed[b] Percentage supporting			Regularly employed Percentage supporting		
	Revolution	Communists	(N)	Revolution	Communists	(N)
21–27	75	[c]	(8)	42	[c]	(12)
28–35	100	31	(22)	85	35	(20)
36–43	81	41	(21)	43	17	(23)
44 plus[d]	82	64	(11)	68	39	(31)

[a] Those who were not workers before the revolution are excluded from this table.
[b] 'Underemployed and unemployed' refers to workers who worked, on the average, nine months or less per year before the revolution, while 'regularly employed' refers to those who worked 10 months or more.
[c] See table 8.5 note a.
[d] This category combines the generations of the second Machado regime and the first Batista regime and is referred to in this study henceforth as the 'generation of the thirties.'

instance of how generational peers, located differently in the social structure, are differently affected by historical events. The relative stability, prosperity, and political democracy of the republican interregnum, having left the problem of unemployment and underemployment untouched, proved from the perspective of the unemployed workers to be irrelevant to their situation and may indeed (as our evidence seems to indicate) have inclined them (even more than their unemployment may otherwise have done) toward radical solutions to their problems.

Among unemployed workers, as table 8.6 indicates, those in the generation of the republican interregnum were second only to the generation of the thirties in prerevolutionary support of the Communists. Also consistent with our findings on aggregate generational differences in prerevolutionary attitudes toward the Communists is the fact that the generation of the thirties, both among the employed and unemployed, had the greatest proportion of prerevolutionary Communist sympathizers.

Looking at the relationships differently, it might be expected that the unemployed, since they were generally more likely to support the Communists before the revolution, would also do so in each political generation. In fact, this is true in every political generation *but one*. In the generation of '53, unemployed workers were *not* more likely than their employed peers to sympathize with the Communists. In view of the experiences of the different political generations with the Communists, as pointed out earlier, this finding makes more sense than if they had been more likely than the employed to support the Communists. The most significant radical movement on the contemporary scene for the generation of '53, which possessed the political initiative and clearly led the anti–Batista struggle of that period, was not the Communist but the 26th of July movement. There is little reason, then, why the unemployed of *this* generation should have been more responsive to the Communists than were their employed peers. Not only were the *fidelistas* leading the anti-Batista struggle, but their agitation among the workers was also radical in social content, and perhaps even more radical than the agitation of the Communists who continued to counsel moderation for so long. Indeed, we already know that the unemployed of the generation of '53 were more likely to support the revolution than the employed workers, though they were not more likely to support the Communists before the revolution.

Finally, it is important to note that it is among the regularly employed workers that the relationships between generations most closely approximate those found when the generations are viewed in the aggregate. This is especially worthy of emphasis, since it is where unemployment (which tended to override the effects of their historical experiences) is absent that the generational relationships we predicted from knowledge of Cuban history are strongest and clearest. Thus, for example, among the employed workers of the generation of the republican interregnum, whose historical experiences were not 'contaminated' by unemployment (which provides one basis for radicalism), the ideology developed under the impact of the republican experience became operative. Our findings suggest, therefore, that participation in historical struggles will have the greatest effect on the ideological development of precisely those economically secure workers to whom revolutionary politics would otherwise appeal least.

Conclusion

In conclusion, then, not only does comparison of the political generations in the aggregate reveal significant political differences in accord with hypotheses based on the concept of political generation, but comparison of *intra*generation subgroups is also in accord with those hypotheses.

The theoretical significance of our findings lies, first, in their demonstration of the analytic utility of formulating specific hypotheses in terms of the concept of political generations. It may indeed be correct, as Herbert Hyman has argued, that the 'generic process of learning of politics' does not include generational influence and that 'susceptibility to this influence may not be universal or may be constrained in many cases by other factors,' but this hardly warrants relegation of the concept to the conceptual dustbin, as is implied in Hyman's otherwise incisive and valuable discussion.[22] In fact, of course, it is precisely one task of sociological inquiry to discover under what conditions a particular type of social determinant may or may not be operative and to modify theory appropriately. The fact that some nonliterate bands do not have social classes, for instance, and that, therefore, 'susceptibility to this influence may not be universal,' hardly warrants discarding the concept of social class. On the contrary, such empirical findings lead to further conceptual and theoretical development. Failure to use the generation concept because its empirical demonstration is difficult may be detrimental to the analysis of political behavior. It is especially important from a theoretical standpoint to analyze the effects of generations in societies characterized by comparatively greater social instability and internal conflict than the advanced industrial societies of the West in which the few empirical studies utilizing the concept (whether implicitly or explicitly) have been done. This is important not only because of the necessary comparative perspective on generational politics such studies could provide, but also because generational politics seem to be most associated with differences in social stability during the periods in which the different generations came of age (cf. Lipset 1960, p. 267; Centers 1949, p. 168; Hamilton 1967, ch. vi). Thus our findings, based as they are on interviews with workers now living through a social revolution in a country whose history has been marked by social and political instability, are of especial theoretical interest.

Second, these conclusions bear indirectly on the issue of the relevance of 'history' to sociological analysis and theory. The very concept of political generation implies the hypothesis that social processes, relationships, norms, and values sometimes may be inexplicable without reference to the events of the past and that analyses which are limited to consideration only of contemporary relationships may be deficient in significant ways.

Third, to the extent to which the concept attempts to link up behavior and character with *non*-institutionalized but historically significant forms of social interaction, our findings also impinge on social psychological theory. Such decisively relevant experiences as may be included under the rubric of 'historically significant events' (major political issues, concrete internal struggles, general social conditions) may or may not themselves have significant consequences for the social structure and, therefore, for the character, norms, and values of the men and women formed within it. But these very events may have independent psychological effects on their participants, aside from their institutional consequences. 'If you wish to understand persons – their development and their relations with significant others – you must be prepared,' as Anselm Strauss has put it, 'to view them as embedded in historical context. Psychological theory and psychiatric theory, at least of the American variety, underplay this context; and those sociologists and anthropologists who are interested in personal identity tend to treat historical matters more as stage setting, or backdrops, than as crucial to the study of persons.'[23] That the historical context in which they came to manhood played a significant role in the formation of the political identities of succeeding generations of Cuban workers – their political allegiances and norms and their response to the revolution – has, of course, been precisely the point of this study.

Notes

1 Seymour Martin Lipset, for instance, recently noted again that, 'unfortunately, there has been no attempt to study systematically the effect of generation experiences with modern survey research techniques' (1960, p. 265). The statement also appeared much earlier in Lipset et al. (1954).

2 See, however, Eisenstadt (1956) and Inkeles and Bauer, (1961).

3 This concept is essentially identical with the concept of 'cohort' used in demographic analysis; see Ryder (1959).

4 Casuso 1961, p. 64. This work emphasizes the generational politics of Cuba (see especially pp. 77ff.).

5 Exact information has been difficult if not impossible to obtain about the ages even of the major revolutionary leaders, let alone of typical rebel cadre members. Fidel Castro's biographies are not consistent; Spanish sources usually place his birth date at August 13, 1927, English sources at August 13, 1926. See Rodriguez Morejon (1959) and such American sources as Dubois (1959) and Taber (1961). Nonetheless, from talking to individuals who 'should know' in a variety of positions in Cuba, including *comandantes*, administrative personnel, and union officials, aside from the workers interviewed in our study who had fought in the hills, a consensus emerged that the typical age of the rebel youth was about 18–25 years old in 1952, when Batista came to power. Relatively reliable ages of some of the more important leaders in 1962, when we did our research in Cuba, were as follows: Fidel Castro, 35; Ernesto 'Che' Guevara, 34; Raul Castro, 30; Armando Hart, 31; Osmany Cienfuegos, 32; Augusto Martínez Sánchez, 36. Camilo Cienfuegos, one of Fidel's top *comandantes* during the guerrilla war, who died in a plane crash in 1959, was about 30 when he died; Enrique Oltuski, a leader of the urban *resistencia*, was 31 in 1962; Faustino Pérez, coordinator of the abortive 1958 general strike, and head of the urban *resistencia*, 31; Vilma Espín, Raul's wife and an active leader of the *resistencia*, known romantically as 'Deborah' during the war, was 28; Haydée Santamaria, another rebel heroine, 32.

6 'The most barbaric methods of torture, not excluding castration, were daily incidents in the police stations, where *the groans of a whole generation of youths* were heard as they were tortured for information, or for having aided the revolutionary movement' (Casuso 1961, p. 134, italics added). Miss Casuso resigned her position as Cuban ambassador to the United Nations in 1960 and sought asylum in the United States. Similar descriptions of the Batista regime's arbitrary violence against young people during the guerrilla war appear in all the accounts of this period, such as those by Dubois (1959); Taber (1961); and Brennan (1959).

7 For a more detailed account of these events, see Zeitlin (1964) and the references therein.

8 The Ministry of Industries facilitated the completion of this study by providing me with credentials to the administration of the plants I wanted to visit. There was no interference with the wording or content of any questions, nor was there any prearranged schedule for my arrival at the plants, nor, it was evident, had the administrators or union heads been informed of my impending arrival. On several occasions, administrators or personnel chiefs phoned Havana to check my credentials and my insistence that I had permission (which was apparently unbelievable to administrators trying to raise production levels) to take 10 workers from their work for as long as the interviews required.

9 Of the 210 workers selected for the sample, eight refused to be interviewed, were not replaced by others, and are not included in our tables. As a precaution, the eight were included in parallel runs defined as 'hostile' to the revolution, and every significant relationship was either the same or strengthened.

10 Professor Dudley Seers, the well-known British economist, who was also doing research in Cuba at that time, has referred to some preliminary findings of my study as follows: '[Zeitlin's] findings are not inconsistent with the general impression we all [Seers and his coauthors] formed during our stay in Cuba, where we traveled the length of the island and conversed with hundreds of people. (In general, there was clearly little hesitation on their part about speaking their minds.)' (1964, p. 394, n. 70; 31). For my own reports on Cuba at this time see Zeitlin (1962a, 1962b, 1962c).

11 This question was borrowed from the study then in progress by Gabriel Almond and Sidney Verba (1963) and my use of it is hereby gratefully acknowledged.

12 Mention of the revolution itself, of the 'socialist government,' of specific economic and social reforms of the revolutionary government, of increased work security since the revolution, etc., were counted as 'favorable.' All other responses, whether more or less 'neutral' or 'clearly hostile,' were classified simply as 'not clearly favorable.'

23 For example, 'the people,' 'the humble,' 'hardworking,' 'good,' 'sincere,' 'moral,' 'honest,' 'defenders of the poor and humble,' 'the working class.' Responses such as 'socialists' or 'revolutionaries' which did not clearly commit the worker were not counted as favorable; neither were such equivocal replies as 'Cubans,' 'Fidel,' or 'Communists,' nor hostile ones such as 'Russians,' 'Soviets,' 'shameless,' or 'traitors.'

14 Answers to these questions were distributed as follows: (c) 'no,' 136; 'yes,' 44; 'no opinion,' 22; (d) 'more influence,' 170; 'the same,' 17; 'less,' 8; 'no opinion,' 7, (e) 'yes,' 110; 'no,' 92.

15 Item analysis of answers to the five questions indicates that the questions form an acceptable Guttman scale, 88 percent of the workers giving answers exactly (67 percent) or consistently (21 percent) in conformity with a Guttman model. The coefficient of reproducibility equals 0.95.

16 See Munro 1950, p. 501, (1936), Casuso (1961, pp. 68ff.), Smith (1959, pp. 148–56), and Zeitlin (1964, pp. 30–46), and the references therein.

17 Robert Merton conceptualizes reference individuals as follows: 'Emulation of a peer, a parent, or a public figure may be restricted to limited segments of their behavior and values and this can be usefully described as adoption of a role model. Or, emulation may be extended to a wider array of behavior and values of these persons who can then be described as reference individuals' (1959, p. 303).

18 This question was also borrowed from the Almond-Verba (1963) study and is acknowledged gratefully.

19 According to this crude measure, 28 percent of the workers in our sample classified themselves as prerevolutionary friends or supporters of the Communists. This is in accordance with the estimate that, after the Communists were officially purged from the labor movement, they still had 'a strong underground influence in some unions, and some authorities estimate that perhaps 25 per cent of all Cuban workers are secretly sympathetic to them' (International Bank for Reconstruction and Development 1951, p. 365).

20 See Zeitlin (1964, pp. 83–104) and the references therein.

21 Berger 1960. Cf. also: 'In the comparison of different age groups in the *aggregate*, or the same age groups at different historical periods in the *aggregate*, any differences that appear to be generational may simply be *artifacts* of the different social composition of the groups. . . . In principle, this can be solved by the introduction of certain controls or matchings, but it may often be neglected in practice' (Hyman 1959, p. 130).

22 Hyman 1959, p. 124. Hyman repeatedly refers to the concept of generation as 'doctrine.'

23 Strauss (1959, p. 164). See also Gerth and Mills (1953, p. xix).

References

Almond, Gabriel, and Sidney Verba. 1963. *Civic Culture*. Princeton, N.J.: Princeton University Press.

Berger, Bennet. 1960. 'How Long is a Generation.' *British Journal of Sociology* 11 (March): 10–23.

Brennan, Ray. 1959. *Castro, Cuba, and Justice*. New York: Doubleday.

Castro, Fidel. 1959. *Guía del Pensamiento Político Económico de Fidel*. Havana: Diario Libre.

Casuso, Teresa. 1961. *Cuba and Castro*. New York: Random House.

Centers, Richard. 1949. *The Psychology of Social Classes*. Princeton, N.J.: Princeton University Press.

Dubois, Jules. 1959. *Fidel Castro: Rebel Liberator or Dictator*. Chicago, Ill.: Bobbs-Merrill.

Eisenstadt, S.N. 1956. *From Generation to Generation*. Glencoe, Ill.: Free Press.

Gerth, Hans, and C. Wright Mills. 1953. *Character and Social Structure*. New York: Harcourt, Brace & World.

Hamilton, Richard. 1967. *Affluence and the French Worker: The Fourth Republic Experience*. Princeton, N.J.: Princeton University Press.

Heberle, Rudolf. 1951. *Social Movements*. New York: Appleton-Century-Crofts.

Hyman, Herbert. 1959. *Political Socialization*. Glencoe, Ill.: Free Press.

Inkeles, Alex, and Raymond Bauer. 1961. *The Soviet Citizen.* Cambridge, Mass.: Harvard University Press.

International Bank for Reconstruction and Development. 1951. *Report on Cuba.* Baltimore: Johns Hopkins University Press.

Lipset, Seymour Martin. 1960. *Political Man.* Garden City, N.Y.: Doubleday.

—— Paul F. Lazarsfeld, Allen Barton, and Juan Linz. 1954. 'The Psychology of Voting.' Pp. 1124–70 in *Handbook of Social Psychology*, Vol. II, edited by G. Lindsey. Cambridge, Mass.: Addison-Wesley.

Mannheim, Karl. 1952. 'The Problem of Generations.' In *Essays on the Sociology of Knowledge*, edited by Paul Kecksckemeti. New York: Oxford University Press.

Merton, Robert. 1959. *Social Theory and Social Structure.* Glencoe, Ill.: Free Press.

Munro, Dana Gardner. 1950. *The Latin American Republics: A History.* 2nd edn. New York: Appleton-Century-Crofts.

Pedrero, Enrique Gonzalez. 1959. 'Manifiesto-programa del Movimiento 26 de Julio.' Appendix to *La Revolución Cubana.* Mexico City: Universidad Nacional Autonoma de Mexico.

Rodríguez Morejón, Gerardo. 1959. *Fidel Castro: Biografia.* Havana: P. Fernandez.

Ryder, Norman. 1959. 'The Cohort as a Concept in the Study of Social Change.' Unpublished paper delivered at the Annual Meeting of the American Sociological Association, August.

Seers, Dudley, ed. 1964. *Cuba: The Economic and Social Revolution.* Chapel Hill, N.C.: University of North Carolina Press.

Smith, Robert F. 1959. *The United States and Cuba: Business and Diplomacy, 1917–1960.* New York: Bookman.

Strauss, Anselm. 1959. *Mirrors and Masks: The Search for Identity.* Glencoe, Ill.: Free Press.

Taber, Robert. 1961. *M-26: Biography of a Revolution.* New York: Lyle Stuart.

Thompson, Charles A. 1936. 'The Cuban Revolution: Reform and Reaction.' *Foreign Policy Reports* 11 (January 1): 261–71.

Zeitlin, Maurice. 1962a. 'Whose Revolution?' *Liberation*, May: 7–11, 24.

—— 1962b. 'Labor in Cuba.' *The Nation*, October 20: 238–42.

—— 1962c. 'Castro and Cuba's Communists.' *The Nation*, November 3: 284–7.

—— 1964. 'Working Class Politics in Cuba: A Study in Political Sociology.' Ph.D dissertation, University of California, Berkeley.

—— 1966. 'Economic Insecurity and the Political Attitudes of Cuban Workers.' *American Sociological Review* 31: 35–51.

9

Miners and agrarian radicalism

Generally, empirical analyses of class and politics focus on the relative chances for given types of political behavior in different classes, but neglect *the interaction of these classes and the political consequences of such interaction.* Moreover, even when reference *is* made to the possible political relevance of such interaction, the focus has been on how the privileged classes moderate the politics of the unprivileged (cf. Lipset 1960, especially pp. 231ff.). But the possibility that the working class might influence the political behavior of the middle classes has scarcely been entertained; nor has the possible impact of the workers on the development of political consciousness in other exploited classes been explored. The latter is precisely what we focus on in this study: the impact of organized workers in Chile on the development of political consciousness in the peasantry.

In Chile, agricultural relations have gradually become modernized, and traditional social controls have loosened considerably. In the central valley, where Chile's agricultural population is centered, the modernization favored by the Chilean propertied classes may be directly responsible for the growth of rural radicalism. As one writer has put it: 'The principal impact of technological advance and farm rationalization has been to undermine the secure if impoverished position of the agricultural laborers which has been an important feature of the traditional system of employment. Wage rates are barely keeping up with consumer price increases and [these rates] may have fallen recently. Thus while the attempts to increase output and productivity have not been very successful, these attempts have led to changes which adversely affect the landless laborer. These changes in Chilean agriculture may lead to demands for a more radical transformation in the future' (Sternberg 1962, p. 132–3). This breakdown of the traditional rural social structure, the growth of a 'rural proletariat,' and emergence of demands for radical reforms in the agrarian structure may allow other relatively oppressed groups who have similar demands and *are* highly organized to provide leadership for the peasantry as it enters the political struggle in Chile. The most highly organized and politically conscious working-class centers in Chile are in the mining municipalities – centers from which the miners' political influence may be diffused into the surrounding countryside.

Organized Working Class Politics in Chile

In Chile, both the organized labor movement and the emergence of insurgent political parties began in the northern areas of Tarapaca and Antofagasta, where 40 percent of the labor force was already employed in the nitrate mines as early as 1885. Soon after the middle of the last century, large-scale social conflict rivaling similar outbreaks in Europe were occurring with increasing frequency and intensity.[1] The northern nitrate city of Iquique and the southern coal mining area of Lota were frequently the scenes of struggles of civil war proportions in which hundreds if not thousands of workers were killed. The first general strike in 1890 originated in Iquique and spread throughout the country. Despite the violent reaction of the public authorities, the first labor organizations began to emerge – based predominantly in the nitrate mines of the north.[2] The Chilean Workers' Federation (FOCH) was founded in 1908 by conservatives as a mutual aid society. By 1917 it had become a militant industrial trade union; two years later it called for the abolition of capitalism. Between 1911 and 1920 there were 293 strikes involving 150,000 workers. In 1919 the FOCH became affiliated with the Red Trade Union Federation. The FOCH, the largest national union, contained an estimated 136,000 members, of which 10,000 were coal miners and 40,000 nitrate-miners; miners accounted for almost 37 percent of all union members. Of all industries, only in mining were a majority of the workers organized. In 1906, working-class Socialist leader Emilio Recabarren was elected to Congress from a mining area – but was not allowed to take office.

The Socialist Party that grew out of the establishment of the so–called 'Socialist Republic' (June 4–16, 1932) had its most cohesive working-class political base among the copper-miners.[3] Although the Socialist Party condemned both the Second and Third Internationals, it claimed adherence to Marxism and the establishment of a government of organized workers as its goal. Later, the Communists also secured their major base in the mining areas. In the municipal elections of 1947, the last relatively free election before the banning of the Communist Party in 1948 (which lasted a decade), the Communists received 71 percent of the votes in the coal mining zone, 63 percent in the nitrate zone and 55 percent in the copper mining zone; in contrast, they received only 18 percent of the total vote nationwide. The 11 major mining municipalities accounted for 20 percent of the total votes received by the Communists (Coke 1952, pp. 81–2).

The miners' history of class conflict and organized political activity established them as the most active revolutionary force in Chilean society. Their political radicalism is in line with the radicalism of miners in many parts of the world,[4] perhaps nurtured by the miners' 'occupational community.' Because they usually live and work in the same mining towns, the high degree of interaction among the miners results in very close-knit social organization. Concentrated together, and in relative physical and social isolation from the influences of the dominant social classes in the society, this nurtures the emergences of a shared class outlook based on the recognition of their common interests. The question we deal with here is the impact, if any, that these highly organized, politically radical miners have on the traditionally conservative rural poor.

Rural Labor Force

Sharp divisions have existed between the urban and rural sectors of the Chilean labor force. A fundamental factor in the stability, continuity, and power of the propertied classes was the social condition and attitudes of the rural labor force. The system of rural labor established in colonial times continued down through the twentieth century, little changed by the Revolution for Independence or by a century and a quarter of parliamentary and presidential democracy.

Formally free, the rural labor force was bound to the land by the fact that neighboring landowners would refuse to hire a tenant who had left a *hacienda* because he was discontented with his lot. The economic status of the *inquilino* (tenant worker) was the same throughout the nineteenth and most of the twentieth century: a few pennies a day in wages, a one- or two-room house, a ration of food for each day he worked, and a tiny plot of land. Usually he was required to supply labor for some 240 days a year (McBride 1936, pp. 148–55). Debt servitude was widespread and opportunity for the *inquilino* to advance from that status and become an economically independent farmer was nonexistent. The social and religious life of the *inquilino* was restricted by the landowners (*hacendados*) who preferred that their employees had minimal contact with outsiders. The landowners organized the fiesta, the amusements, and the 'civil jurisdiction' within the hacienda (*fundo*). In the middle 1930s these *fundos* approximated the 'ideal type' of an authoritarian system of social control and rigid social stratification.

Within the larger society, some voluntary associations defending working-class interests were able to establish themselves, but the rural poor lived in conditions in which the apparatus of violence and force was regulated by the landed, alternative sources of information were prohibited, and voluntary associations were forbidden. Middle-class parliamentary parties such as the *Radicales* did not advocate a program of socioeconomic reform of the traditional landed system. They were unable to mobilize the peasantry and lower-class rural populace against the landowners' rule. In turn, this forced the middle-class parties to forgo a meaningful and dynamic program for industrial and democratic development, and allowed the Socialists and Communists, and then the Christian Democrats, to become spokesmen for the rural poor and agrarian reform.

In his control of the *inquilino*, the landowner held an effective counterweight to any political program of social and economic development that negatively affected his interests. The alliance of foreign investors, large landowners, and those urban entrepreneurs integrated with them rested on the landowners' control of the *inquilino*; this was the condition *sine qua non* of their continuing political hegemony.

Apart from the *inquilino*, an 'outsider' segment of the rural labor force is not attached to the *fundo*, and consequently is less directly under the dominance of the landowners. These 'free laborers' have constituted about one-third of the rural work force; three decades ago they were already said to 'have the reputation of provoking many difficulties in the relation between the *inquilino* and the farm owner' (McBride 1936, p. 164). The free laborers were reputed to be frequently more independent in their outlook and more likely to object to any excesses committed by the landowners against the workers. With the gradual mechanization of agriculture and the increased payment in wages in recent years, many of the rural population have become dependent on wages for their existence.

Miners and Peasants: the Diffusion Process

Only with industrial development, and especially mining, did the agricultural labor force in Chile begin to have even a hint of political consciousness, impelled largely by their contact with industrial workers. The landowners' strategy had been to isolate the *inquilinos* from the urban working class, prohibiting their independent organization. By restricting their experience to the *fundo* itself, the *patron* had inhibited the development of the *inquilinos'* political awareness. With the rapid growth of the urban working class in the period after World War I, strikes spread to the rural districts for the first time in the history of the country. Uprisings took place on a number of *fundos*. The miners took the leadership in this early attempt at rural labor organization. In 1919, an abortive attempt was made to organize the *inquilinos* into a nationwide federation in the Cometa region in the Aconcagua Valley, 'the intention being to federate the *inquilinos* with an organization of miners' (*El Agricultor* , May 1920, p. 113, cited in McBride 1936, p. 166). Again in the 1930s a broad militant movement of peasant unionization developed, supported by sectors of the urban working class; it was violently repressed by the state and politically defused by the electoral strategy that the leftist parties adopted during the Popular Front (Vitale 1962, p. 88 *et passim*).

In recent years the closed system of the large *fundos* has begun to change under the impact of the growth of capitalist social relations in the countryside and, more important, as political organization, trade unions, and outside communications networks have been able to undermine the information monopoly of the large landowners.

In the 1958 presidential election, elements of the peasantry shifted their traditional allegiance away from the Right. The Socialist–Communist coalition, Frente de Acción Popular (FRAP), and the Christian Democratic Party are competing for the allegiance of this important and newly emerging social force; they have formed their own peasant 'unions' and advocate programs for agrarian reform. In both the 1958 and the 1964 presidential elections, FRAP campaigned actively throughout the countryside. With old political alignments shifting and the balance of social forces changing, the political direction the peasantry will take is seen by all major political parties as a major factor in determining the future of Chilean society. That the miners can play a decisive role in determining the direction the peasantry takes will become clear from our findings.

Our analysis is based on the voting returns of the presidential elections of 1958 and 1964, with primary emphasis on the 195 agricultural municipalities. An ecological analysis of these election results is meaningful; distortions of the results through vote tampering and coercion are believed to have been minimal. In these elections, competing political programs that included the socialist alternative were presented to the Chilean peasantry at a critical moment of its emergence as a national political force. Thus, we focus here on the political impact of the organized mining centers on the peasantry, and on the political differences among its basic segments.

Findings

Agricultural municipalities are defined here as those in which 50 percent or more of the economically active population are engaged in agriculture.[5] Mining municipalities are those in which at least 500 individuals *or* 50 percent or more of the economically active population are employed in the mining sector. Each of the 296 municipalities in the country was located on a map (in Mattelart 1966) and each municipality that directly adjoins any mining municipality was defined as a 'satellite.' A 'satellite' can adjoin several mining municipalities; some satellites adjoined as many as four of them.

The vote for Salvadore Allende, presidential candidate of the Socialist–Communist coalition (FRAP) is taken as an index of radical political behavior. We define a 'high' vote for Allende in 1958 as 30 percent (the national average) or more in the municipality, and a 'low' vote as 20 percent or less; in 1964, a 'high' vote is 40 percent (the national average) or more in the municipality, and 'low' is 25 percent or less.[6]

The mining municipalities, we suggest, are not only centers of political radicalism, but also centers from which that radicalism is diffused into surrounding nonmining areas. These mining 'satellites,' subject to the political influence of the miners in adjoining

Table 9.1 *Percent 'high' vote for Allende among males in municipalities classified by prevalence of agriculture and mining, 1958 and 1964*

Prevalence of mining	Prevalence of agriculture								
	Nonagricultural municipalities			Agricultural municipalities			Entire country		
	1958	1964	(N)	1958	1964	(N)	1958	1964	(N)
Neither 'satellites' nor mining municipalities	45	67	(58)	31	51	(162)	35	55	(220)
Mining 'Satellites'	73	93	(15)	60	80	(30)	69	82	(45)
Mining municipalities	93	93	(28)	a	a	(3)	93	93	(31)

[a] All three mining agricultural municipalities gave Allende a 'high' vote in both elections, 1958 and 1964.

municipalities, should therefore be more likely than 'nonmining, nonsatellite' municipalities to support the Left. This is precisely what we find in both agricultural and nonagricultural municipalities, and in both 1958 and 1964, whether we look at the 'high' or 'low' end of the vote (tables 9.1 and 9.2). The mining municipalities are overwhelmingly pro-Allende, followed by the 'satellites,' the vast majority of which give Allende a 'high' vote; the nonsatellite, nonmining areas, as expected, are least likely to give Allende a 'high' vote. (Indeed, a further breakdown of 'satellites' according to the number of mining municipalities they adjoin also yields a direct relationship between proximity to mining centers and political radicalism. There are too few cases to examine the relationship among nonagricultural municipalities, however. Among agricultural municipalities, 58 percent of the 'satellites' of one mining municipality ($N = 19$) gave Allende a 'high' vote in 1958, and 82 percent of the 'satellites' of two to four mining municipalities ($N = 11$) gave him a 'high' vote. In 1964, the respective figures are 74 percent and 91 percent. In the entire country, in 1958, of the first 'satellite' group ($N = 25$), Allende got a 'high' vote in 64 percent of the municipalities,

Table 9.2   *Percent 'low' vote for Allende among males in municipalities classified by prevalence of agriculture and mining, 1958 and 1964*

	Prevalence of agriculture								
	Nonagricultural municipalities			Agricultural municipalities			Entire country		
Prevalence of mining	1958	1964	(N)	1958	1964	(N)	1958	1964	(N)
Neither 'satellites' nor mining municipalities	21	10	(58)	49	20	(162)	41	17	(220)
Mining 'Satellites'	7	0	(15)	20	3	(30)	16	2	(45)
Mining municipalities	4	0	(28)	–	–	(3)	3	0	(31)

and of the second group, 75 percent. The respective figures for 1964 in these groups are 76 percent and 90 percent.)

In addition to this demonstration of the political impact of the mining centers on surrounding nonmining areas, the following should be noted. (a) The agricultural municipalities, whatever their proximity to mining centers, have proportionately fewer 'high' Allende municipalities among them than the nonagricultural ones. Despite FRAP's appreciable growth in strength in the agricultural areas, the nonagricultural, industrial and urban municipalities still provide the major electoral base of the Left. (b) Yet the strength of the Left grew throughout the agricultural municipalities from 1958 to 1964. This indicates that the *Frapistas* are penetrating and broadening their support in the peasantry as a whole, and not merely in particular peasant 'segments' or strata. (c) It is beyond the scope of this study, but it should be pointed out that the miners' political influence apparently radiates out to other workers, perhaps even others in the *clase popular* made up of a variety of poor from pedlars to artisans and manual laborers. As a cohesive, organized, politically conscious community, the miners' political influence is critical not only in the peasantry but also among other lower strata. The existence of a major mining population whose political influence reaches other exploited strata may explain why class-based and class-conscious politics have emerged so much more clearly in Chile than in other countries in Latin America which, while having large strata of urban and rural poor, lack cohesive working-class centers.[7]

The Miners' Political Consciousness

The high degree of radical political consciousness in Chile's mining areas is indicated by the results of labor union elections held shortly after government troops killed seven and wounded 38 miners during the occupation of striking copper mining areas in April, 1966. *El Mercurio*, Chile's leading newspaper, editorialized after this bloody attack on the miners, on the eve of the union elections: 'The election of union officers that will take place in El Salvador, Potreillos, and Barquito will be realized in an atmosphere of liberty adequate for the workers to express their preferences without the shadow of government pressure over the voters or candidates. These acts are of considerable importance because they will demonstrate what the spontaneous will of the workers really is when they do not feel menaced or intimidated by agitators. . . . Now the workers can take advantage of the new climate in the mines in order to form union committees that serve their interests rather than subordinating themselves to partisan politics' (*El Mercurio*, April 15, 1966, p. 3). The 'spontaneous will' of the workers resulted in an overwhelming victory for the FRAP candidates, even though elections were government supervised.[8] The point is that the way the miners voted in the presidential elections represents real support for the Left – a high level of political consciousness that can be and is effectively transmitted to the peasantry.

In Chile, the organized mining workers' 'isolated' communities have a high level of participation in activities, controversies, and organizations – features that are essential to a democratic society. The reason may be, as Lipset suggests of workers living in an occupational community, that the 'frequent interaction of union members in all spheres of life . . . [makes] for a high level of interest in the affairs of their unions, which translates itself into high participation in local organization and a greater potential for democracy and membership influence' (1960, p. 408).

More important, these same miners consciously seek to influence the politics of others. In February 1966, for instance, *El Siglo*, the Communist daily, reported that 'The two hundred delegates attending the Eighth National Congress of the Miners Federation ... has adopted a resolution that, throughout the country, it will lend the most active class solidarity to the workers in the countryside in their struggles in defense of their rights and for the conquest of a true Agrarian Reform. A few days ago the powerful unions [nitrate miners] of Maria Elena, Pedro de Valdivia and Mantos Blancos in the province of Antofagasta adopted a similar resolution' (*El Siglo*, February 20, 1966, p. 10). The politicization of the peasantry by the miners is thus the result both of a 'natural process' and of conscious effort.

The Left, conscious of the diffusion of radical ideas through informal communication between the working class and the peasantry, intervenes to maximize their advantages from this situation, accentuating and deepening the process of the diffusion of radical ideas. The importance that the Left attributes to this interaction between class-conscious workers and the peasantry is shown by the remarks of Luis Corvalán, Communist Party General Secretary:

> The political and cultural ties between city and the countryside, between the proletariat and the *campesinos*, have developed in many ways. The children of *campesinos* who go to work in industry learn many things which they soon teach to their relatives and friends who have remained on the *fundo* or in the village and with whom they maintain contacts. Thousands of *inquilinos* . . . and small holders have become laborers in the construction of hydro-electric plants, roads, reservoirs and canals, or have been incorporated into the infant industries of sugar or lumber and live alongside many members of the proletariat who come from the cities. Furthermore, the crises and the repressive measures employed against the urban working class have caused many of the workers in the mines and factories to return to the country. *Throughout Chile, on the fundos and in the villages, we have seen many laborers, including some who were union leaders in the nitrate, coal, and copper [industries].* It follows that the political work of the popular parties and especially of ourselves as Communists, should also figure among the major factors that have influenced and are influencing the creation of a new social consciousness in the countryside.[9]

As urbanization and industrialization impinge on the peasantry and cause migrations of the labor force, so also is the political awareness of those individuals who have roots in both cultures heightened. These individuals bring the new ideas of struggle and of class solidarity to their friends and relatives still living in the rural areas and employed in agriculture. To the extent that the Left political parties are effective in organizing and politicizing these newly recruited industrial workers, they have an effective carrier of radicalism into the countryside.

The Diffusion of 'Political Culture' and the Structure of the Agricultural Labor Force

Elsewhere, we have analyzed the relationship between the structure of the agrarian labor force – the internal differentiation of the rural population – and the FRAP presidential vote, and found an inverse relationship between the proportion of proprietors in a municipality's agricultural labor force and the likelihood that it gave Allende a 'high' vote (Petras and Zeitlin 1968). The bigger the proportion of agricultural proprietors in a municipality the less likely it was to give Allende a 'high' vote. Similarly, the bigger the proportion of wage laborers in a municipality's agricultural labor force, the more likely it was to give Allende a 'high' vote. These findings suggest strongly that the rural proletariat, as distinguished from the small holding peasantry, is FRAP's major rural political base.

The question now is what impact the organized working-class political centers, the mining municipalities and their satellites, have on the determination of voting in the countryside. We find that the political differences based on differentiation within the peasantry tend to disappear in the mining and satellite municipalities. In the nonmining, nonsatellite municipalities, however, the original relationship between peasant proprietorship and the vote for Allende holds. Also, whatever the structure of the agricultural labor force (or intraclass differentiation of the peasantry), the mining satellites are more likely to give Allende a 'high' vote than the nonmining, nonsatellite municipalities (table 9.3). The theoretical point is clear: the mining communities and adjoining areas develop a distinctive political culture, radical and socialist in content, that tends to eliminate the importance of intraclass differences among the peasants, and to unite them across these lines.

The fact is that the Chilean Left not only specifically directs its working class activists in the trade unions to unite with peasants in support of their demands but also emphasizes the role they can

Table 9.3 *Percent 'high' vote for Allende among males in agricultural municipalities classified by prevalence of mining and proprietors, 1964*

Prevalence of mining	Percent proprietors							
	70 plus	(N)	50–69	(N)	30–49	(N)	Under 30	(N)
Neither 'satellite' nor mining municipality	29	(35)	46	(24)	51	(37)	80	(54)
Mining 'satellites'	83	(6)	100	(3)	87	(8)	90	(10)
Mining municipalities	100	(1)	100	(1)		(0)	100	(1)

play in uniting different peasant segments: *El Siglo*, the Chilean Communist daily, writes: 'All the workers in all the unions should unite with the peasants, wherever the unions are near agricultural properties in which the peasants are initiating struggles in defense of their interests. The miners' unions must be there to help the organization of the peasant unions. All our fellow miners must be there to bring all their moral and material support to the peasants who are struggling for possession of the land' (February 20, 1966, p. 10). The Communist Party general secretary urges that 'the forms of organization should be in accord with the wishes of the *campesinos* themselves; but we Communists believe that the best form of organization is that of the independent union, with headquarters in the village, in which are grouped the workers from various *fundos* and *all of the modest sectors of the rural population from the wage-hand to the small proprietor*, including the sharecropper, the poor *campesino*, etc.' (Corvalan 1965, p. 141). Communist organizing strategy, the formation of independent organizations comprising all the rural 'modest sectors . . . from the wage-hand to the small proprietor,' adds a conscious element to further the general process of social interaction and diffusion of political consciousness that unites agrarian laborers and small proprietors in the 'satellite' areas adjoining the mining centers.

Conclusions

The miners' organizational skills and political competence, the proximity of the mines to the countryside, the sharing of an exploited position, and conscious political choice, enable the miners to politicize and radicalize the rural population. The sense of citizenship and the necessity of having their own leaders that develops in the mining communities, where the miners themselves, rather than 'other strata and agencies,' run their affairs, also expresses itself in the political leadership and influence that their communities exert in neighboring rural areas. Further, the miners can supply legal, political, and economic resources to aid the peasants concretely, and thus demonstrate to them the power of organization and of struggle in defense of their common interests against landowners. Where the miners have a strong political organization, peasant proprietors and agricultural wage laborers are equally susceptible to radicalism. Political men, like the miners, who make an effort to organize or influence relatively isolated and atomized peasant proprietors spread over the countryside, can provide a link between them. The miners' leadership and ideology provide the peasants with a form of communication and sharing of experience that is necessary for them to recognize and be able to act upon their common interests.

Notes

1 Over one-third of all the strikes and popular demonstrations occurring in the period between 1851 and 1878 involved miners, according to Hernán Ramírez Necochea (no date, pp. 133–4).
2 One of the worst massacres in labor history occurred in Chile at that time, when 10,000 nitrate miners marching in Iquique were fired upon with machine-guns, and 2,000 of them died (Jobet 1955, p. 138).
3 Following the Ibanez military regime, in the midst of a general economic crisis, the 'Socialist Republic' consisted of a series of four military *juntas* beginning on June 14 and ending on June 30, 1932. The officers had no social program and their only achievement was the establishment of the Socialist Party under the leadership of one of them, Col. Marmaduke Grove.
4 Lipset 1960, pp. 242–6. See also Kerr and Siegel (1954, pp. 200–1).
5 The data were compiled from several sources: *Censo Nacional Agricola – Ganadero* 1955; *Censo de Población* 1960; Mattelart 1966.
6 We have used 'high' and 'low' ends of the voting spectrum as an *index*

of radicalism because we are concerned with municipalities as social units, and relative radicalism as an *attribute* of the municipality. Thus, a municipality with a 'high' FRAP vote is a 'radical' municipality. This procedure differs from simply taking the mean or median FRAP vote in the municipalities and therefore focusing on simple *quantitative* differences, whatever the actual vote. Neither procedure is intrinsically 'correct.' One or the other is more useful depending on the focus of the analysis; when looking for the determinants of political radicalism, in ecological analysis, we think our procedure is more useful.

7 The Agricultural Census makes it possible to gauge the political impact of the miners on given agricultural strata but a comparable census for the nonagricultural areas of Chile does not exist. The regular Census does not include occupational breakdowns on the municipal level, so it was necessary to employ other even more indirect indicators of class structure. See Zeitlin and Petras (1969).

8 The FRAP candidates obtained 16,227 votes, the Radical Party 3,287, and the Christian Democrats 3,263. The FRAP elected seven of the 10 new union officers, replacing three Christian Democrats. *Ultima Hora*, April 19, 1966, p. 2.

9 Corvalan 1965, p. 139, italics added. Our translation of the original differs slightly from the version in Smith's book.

References

Censo de Población. 1960. Santiago Dirección de Estadística y Censos de la República de Chile.

Censo Nacional Agricola – Ganadero, vols. I–VI. 1955. Santiago: Servicio Nacional de Estadisticas y Censos, República de Chile.

Coke, Ricardo Cruz. 1952. *Geografía Electoral de Chile*. Santiago: Editorial del Pacífico.

Corvalan, Luis. 1965. 'The Communists' Tactics Relative to Agrarian Reform in Chile.' In *Agrarian Reform in Latin America*, edited by T. Lynn Smith. New York: Knopf.

Jobet, Julio Cesar. 1955. *Ensayo Critico del Desarrollo Económico-social de Chile*. Santiago: Editorial Universitaria.

Kerr, Clark, and Abraham Siegel. 1954. 'The Interindustry Propensity to Strike – An International Comparison.' In *Industrial Conflict*, edited by Arthur Kornhauser, Robert Dubin, and Arthur Ross. New York: McGraw-Hill.

Lipset, Seymour Martin. 1960. *Political Man*. Garden City, New York: Doubleday.

Mattelart, Armand. 1966. *Atlas Social de las Comunas de Chile*. Santiago: Editorial del Pacífico.

McBride, George. 1936. *Chile: Land and Society*. New York: American Geographical Society.

Necochea, Hernán Ramírez. No date. *Historia de Movimiento Obrero en Chile: Antecedentes Siglo XIX*. Santiago: Editorial Austral.

Petras, James, and Maurice Zeitlin. 1968. 'Agrarian Radicalism in Chile.' *British Journal of Sociology* 19 (September): 254–70.

Sternberg, Marvin. 1962. 'Chilean Land Tenure and Land Reforms.' Unpublished Ph.D. dissertation, University of California, Berkeley.

Vitale, Luis. 1962. *Historia de Movimiento Obrero*. Santiago: Editorial POR.

Zeitlin, Maurice, and James Petras. 1969. 'Los Mineros y el Radicalismo de la Clase Obrera en Chile.' *Revista Latinoamericana de Sociología* 5 (March): 121–6.

Part III

Revolution and Reform

10

Cuba – revolution without a blueprint

The world-historical significance of the Cuban revolution is that for the first time in the western hemisphere a revolution has been put through in the name of socialism. It is the first socialist revolution led by independent radicals throughout its most decisive phases. Even when they were to identify with the international Communist movement, and to fuse with the old Communists, they retained the clear initiative within the revolutionary leadership, and gained for Cuba a singular place among Communist states. The Cuban revolution has gone further, and has more profoundly and rapidly transformed the prerevolutionary social structure than has any other 'socialist' revolution anywhere. Most of the fundamental transformation of the political economy – of property relations and of the class structure – occurred within a couple of years of the revolutionaries' consolidation of power; and with the March 1968 nationalization of some 55,000 small businesses, primarily in food retailing and services, virtually the entire economy is now in the public sector: in agriculture, 70 percent of the arable land is in the public sector, leaving only farms of less than 67 hectares (160 acres) to be worked by their owners.

What explains the rapidity and thoroughness of the Cuban revolution, compared not only with other national and social revolutions in our time, but with other 'socialist' revolutions as well? – and, perhaps inseparable from this, why did it become a 'socialist revolution,' unlike, for instance, the social revolutions in Mexico and Bolivia?

The Cuban, Mexican, and Bolivian revolutions have certain similarities which are neither superficial nor unimportant. In each, there was a fundamental agrarian transformation that abolished the existing land tenure system and destroyed the economic base of the ruling strata in the countryside. In each, the old military apparatus was smashed and replaced with armed detachments (or militias) of peasants and workers. In each, strategic sectors of the national economy that were foreign owned were nationalized. In Bolivia, the tin mines were occupied and run by the armed miners themselves. In Mexico, though late in the revolutionary process, the Cardenas regime nationalized the oil industry.

These three revolutions, therefore, are unquestionably set apart from other so-called revolutions in Latin America. Nevertheless, the similarity between the Cuban revolution and the revolutions in Mexico and Bolivia is far less important than the major difference: scarcely any aspect of the prerevolutionary social structure in Cuba has remained intact, primarily because of the expropriation of the former owning classes, the virtual elimination of private property in the system of production and distribution, and the establishment of a centrally planned, publicly owned economy.

What were the features of the prerevolutionary social structure in Cuba that determined the type of social structure created by the revolution? Somewhat differently: what were the constraints and the options that were given to the leaders of the Cuban revolution by the prerevolutionary social structure? What did they have to put up with, what was the social material they had to work with in order to make this revolution – in contrast, for instance, to those who led the revolutions and came to power in Russia, China, and Yugoslavia, or in Bolivia or Mexico? In the book which I wrote with Robert Scheer several years ago (*Cuba: Tragedy in Our Hemisphere*, Grove, 1963; Penguin, 1964), we took the prerevolutionary social structure as given and focused on the interaction between the United States and Cuba and in what way the interchange between them radicalized the revolution. Of course, the two are really inseparable, and it is likely that the main pattern of that interchange indelibly reflected the prerevolutionary social structure. I want now to take that interchange as given, in order to search out the relevance of the prerevolutionary social structure itself.

My leading hypothesis is: Cuba's is the first socialist revolution to take place in a capitalist country – a country in which the owning class was capitalist and the direct producers were wage workers. The argument may be stated in the following schematic working hypotheses.

Cuba's owning class was capitalist – a peculiar type of capitalist class but a capitalist class nonetheless. There were no significant feudal or seignorial elements remaining in the 'upper' economic strata. The major elements of the dominant strata were in exporting (mainly of sugar and other primary products) and in its financing, importing (mainly luxury goods), tourism, and small-scale manufacture of consumer goods for the home market, and were the agents, and representatives, of investors in US-owned manufacturing firms using equipment and materials imported from the United States. These elements tended to overlap and intertwine, and to be integrated by concrete economic interests and social and familial bonds. In short they formed the capitalist class. The agrarian component of this class was export market oriented and employed wage labor on a large scale in the sugar mills and cane fields. As a result, the revolution did not have to be 'anti-feudal.'

Of the classes, the working class was the largest, the most cohesive, and the most politically conscious. It was an organized national class that spread throughout the country, and had a durable revolutionary and socialist political culture set in motion by the anarcho-syndicalists and continued under the Communists. This cannot be said of any other country in which revolutions in our time – whether anticolonial, nationalist, or Communist – have been put through. It cannot be said of prerevolutionary Russia certainly, where the Petrograd workers were an insignificant minority (in numbers) of the total population, though decisive in the revolution. Nor certainly can it be said of prerevolutionary China, nor of Mexico, Bolivia, Algeria, nor of Vietnam. This may come as something of a conceptual shock, since the image of prerevolutionary Cuba held by many, whether friends or foes of the revolution, is that of a peasant society. Nor was it, in an important sense, an 'underdeveloped' country. From the standpoint of an analysis of the economic system and class structure of prerevolutionary Cuba, I believe it is much more fruitful to view it as a relatively unevenly developed or misdeveloped capitalist country of a special colonial type.

In the agrarian sector, there was no subsistence peasantry, nor the nonwage tenant labor characteristic of the *hacienda* or manorial economy. The vast majority of the economically active population employed in agriculture were wage workers. Improved working conditions and higher wages – working-class interests – rather than 'land hunger' were their essential demands and aspirations, unlike the situation in other countries where revolutions calling themselves 'socialist' have occurred. Moreover, what there was of a nonwage working population in Cuba's countryside was a small proprietor stratum – the *colonos* – who were integrated into the market economy and dependent on the large, economically strategic sugar 'centrals' (production centers including mills, workers' housing, and transportation) for credit, milling, and marketing; in the case of tobacco and coffee cultivation, there were also small proprietors and/or tenants whose overall economic significance was marginal. The agrarian sector was based on large-scale capitalist enterprises which employed both industrial and agricultural wage workers.

What strengthened the hand of the ruling class in other social revolutions in this century was a mass social base, largely in the countryside, which they could mobilize as allies to defend their own interests. A counterrevolutionary movement in these countries was possible because the rulers still had legitimacy in and social control of the rural population. It was no historical accident that a bloody civil war was required in revolutionary Russia to put down the counterrevolution, that three decades of armed warfare preceded the triumph of the Chinese Communists, or that the Mexican revolutionaries had to violently confront and overcome the combined might of the Catholic Church and *hacendados* – the large landowners. The Cuban revolutionaries (and this is not to detract from their own extraordinary abilities) did not have to confront a similar situation. The landed upper stratum had been virtually expropriated by the development of capitalism much before the revolution.

Of course, Cuban capitalism was absentee owned, foreign controlled, and quasi-colonial. This meant that not only did the ruling strata not have roots in the countryside but that, indeed, they had no significant independent base of economic power in the country as a whole. The so-called Cuban capitalist class was dependent on American capitalism – politically, militarily, economically. Because of this dependency, they also lacked social legitimacy. The justification of their rule stood nakedly revealed as their control of the means of violence. They stayed in power because they had a military regime (and behind it the power of the US government) to protect them, not because anyone believed that they *deserved* power or that they had the *right* to rule. They were illegitimate in the eyes of virtually the entire population because they had shown their incapacity to rule effectively.

Contrast this for a moment with the situation of the ruling strata in Chile, since it is the only other country in the western hemisphere in which a mass-based Marxian socialist movement has had relative durability – and is rooted predominantly in the working class. Despite this, Chile's ruling strata have considerable legitimacy. A coalition of owning strata which is both landed and industrial has been able to demonstrate its capacity to rule over a period of a century without either foreign control or the intervention of the military as an autonomous social force. In the countryside, the *hacendados* ruled a peasantry involved in tenant labor, living on the great *fundos* and exploited through seignorial and paternalistic relations. Only from the mid-1950s on has agrarian agitation and organization begun to shake this stability. This is in contrast to the instability and massive struggles that characterized the Cuban past, and in which the struggles were directed against a class that was scarcely considered (and perhaps scarcely considered itself) Cuban.

This contrast in the capacity of these classes to rule is also shown by the fact that Chilean political stability and parliamentary democracy have been inseparable. In Cuba, the forms of political democracy associated with capitalism had so to speak exhausted themselves. The brief postwar interregnum of political democracy was considered to be a sham and not substantially more relevant to the needs of Cuba as a nation and to the interests of its people than military rule. Parties and politicians associated with Cuba's 'Congress' were all but universally held in contempt. Parliamentary democracy as the legitimate mode of representative government and the bounds within which major conflicts ought to be resolved and government policy determined had lost legitimacy, if indeed it ever existed; a major ideological obstacle to revolutionary change had therefore been eroded well before the revolutionaries took power.

Eroded also had been whatever ideological dominion over the great majority of workers and 'peasants' the Catholic Church may once have possessed. The Cuban upper strata, therefore, lacked the advantage of a significant ally that ruling classes confronted by revolutionary movements have usually had – an ally whose means of social control and moral suasion supported the existing social order and clothed revolutionary movements in the guise of mammon. That is not to say that the Church hierarchy did not oppose the social revolution. But because the communicants of the Church were drawn largely from the upper and upper-middle urban strata, and little from the countryside or peasantry, its weight in the struggle was not decisive. (It was neither a large landowner nor did it have church centers, schools, monasteries, or nunneries scattered throughout the country – these scarcely existed.) Moreover, it was one of the peculiar benefits (or consequences) of direct US occupation in the founding years of the Republic that Church and State were separated, and the American presence was a secularizing and rationalizing influence.

Large-scale enterprise in the countryside and the intermingling of industrial and agricultural workers in the sugar centrals permeated the country largely with capitalist, rationalistic, secular, antitraditional values and norms of conduct. In this sense, the country was *prepared* for development – the only thing lacking being the revolution itself which took control over the economy and the means of violence from capitalists, both foreign and domestic, and put it in the hands of a sovereign Cuban state.

Whereas the ruling strata lacked legitimacy and had no independent ideology that was expressive of their own peculiar interests and that they could impose on society at large there was in the working class of Cuba a socialist political culture (of anarchosyndicalist and Communist elements) born in an insurrectionary past, which had already existed for no less than three decades (and far longer in segments such as the tobacco workers). The outlook of the typical worker toward the system was impregnated by socialist ideas; what is most important, the vision of a future without capitalism was most firmly and widely held by the most decisive sectors of the working class. This is what Max Weber would have called a 'simple historical fact' of such significance that without taking it into account one cannot understand the socialist revolution. If it was not the vision of the majority of workers in town and country, the dominant vision among them was, nonetheless, anticapitalist, antiimperialist, and socialist. Even the essentially reformist and middle-class leadership of the *Autentico* (and later *Ortodoxo*) party which had considerable influence among workers since the aborted revolution of the 1930s, and which was the only opposition of consequence to the Communists in the working class, clothed its actions and program in a quasi-socialist rhetoric. Its influence among workers, however, was not of the same order as Communist influence and was debilitated by the widespread corruption of the *Autentico* leadership. Most working-class struggles, whatever the leadership and however narrow the economic demands, tended to take on the political slogans of antiimperialism and anticapitalism; it was their one consistent theme. The immediate ends of the struggle and the broader political aims – however tenuously – were linked. Thus, the historically significant impact on the workers' consciousness.

Communist Influence Among Workers

The *Report on Cuba* of the International Bank for Reconstruction and Development concluded that in the years of the most clandestine activity of the Communists about one-fourth of all workers (in 1950) 'were secretly sympathetic to them'; I found, when I interviewed a national sample of workers in 1962, that some 29 percent claimed to have been partisans of the Communists before the revolution. Most important, the ideas held by workers who were non-Communist, even anti-Communist, also tended to be suffused by socialist content. As the *Report* also pointed out, 'nearly all the popular education of working people on how an economic system works and what might be done to improve it came first from the anarcho-syndicalists, and most recently – and most effectively – from the Communists.' It was, I believe, as naturally a part of the Cuban workers' conceptions of the system, their interests, and of the creation of a world in which their exploitation would be abolished, as bread-and-butter unionism is 'natural' to workers in the United States. Both resulted from given historical conditions in which the role of leadership (durable and institutional) was crucial. From the standpoint of the development of the socialist revolution, the importance of this simple historical fact cannot be exaggerated. Despite the vacillations, zigzags, and opportunism of the Communists, one thing occurred: the infusion in the workers of a vision that transcended the Communist leadership itself. The workers could, in fact, abandon the Communists for Fidel to seek the fulfillment of the vision the Communists once represented. When the Revolutionary Government was established, it had a mass working-class base that likely was beyond its leaders in its vision of the society to be created by the revolution. This is in striking contrast to the situation in other countries in which the revolutionary leaders were far beyond their own mass base. The fact of a socialist political culture in the working class – a nationally based, cohesive working class – combined with the force of nationalism and antiimperialism, created a potent revolutionary force waiting to be tapped by the revolutionary leaders once they took power.

Cuba, moreover, was in certain important respects a developed country. I say in important respects and emphasize at the same time the very uneven development of the country. Advanced industrial technology and primitive agricultural implements coexisted in interdependence within the same system. On the one hand, as James O'Connor has shown in the *Origins of Socialism in Cuba*, economic institutions generally appearing in advanced capitalist countries were fundamental in Cuba's prerevolutionary market structure. Production and distribution tended to be controlled by a few firms and producers' associations, and output, wages, prices, and earnings were determined within the framework of such market controls. Thus, Cuba had a vast reservoir of untapped, underutilized, and misutilized resources that the revolutionary government could utilize by reordering and planning the objectives of production and distribution. A relatively developed infrastructure, obviously colonial in nature and possessing its attendant problems but nonetheless of great significance, already was established in Cuba before the revolution. In terms of its ability both to communicate with the nation as a whole and to provide it with immediate, visible, and concrete benefits from the revolution, the revolutionaries enjoyed great advantages compared with the leaders of other social revolutions in our time. The Revolutionary Government could do what other revolutions' leaders could not do: they could put through an immediate and significant redistribution of the national income and improve the conditions of the masses within, so to speak, the first days of taking power. The share of the national income received by wage workers was increased by roughly one-third, according to conservative estimates (such as those by Felipe Pazos, former President of the National Bank of Cuba, in exile). This provided a cement between the regime and the masses in the early phases of the revolution which other revolutionary governments could not create in this way.

The sugar-central, wage-labor, agrarian complex also made it possible to create relatively rapidly and easily a socialist agrarian sector – virtually by shifting the locus of control within it and reorganizing and reordering the objectives of production. This, again, is very much in contrast to the prerevolutionary agrarian structure inherited by other revolutionaries. Most important, the labor movement in the countryside already included wage laborers within the central labor organization; industrial and agricultural workers associated naturally in the countryside and created bonds of social solidarity. Thus, the classical revolutionary slogan of the alliance and unity of workers and peasants was already, in a very important sense, a durable social fact before the revolutionaries came to power. The factories in the field, the sugar centrals containing the sugar mills and associated lands, provided a situation in which agricultural workers living and working on the central's lands came into more or less regular contact with industrial workers. Also, the agricultural worker himself, or his brother, or friends, may have worked at one time as a cane-cutter and another in the sugar mills, providing the industrial and agricultural worker with a fund of common experiences and perceptions. Poor proprietors also often worked in similar situations.

These centrals were, in addition, not only centers of industrial production and a basis for the creation of natural social bonds between 'peasants' and workers, but also centers of political agitation and education. The most important prerevolutionary political base of the Communists was here: 41 percent of the sugar-central workers but only 30 percent of urban workers who had those occupations before the revolution said in our interviews with them in 1962 that they were prerevolutionary supporters of the Communists. Therefore, for all these reasons, the very same acts which the Revolutionary Government would have to take from the standpoint of economic rationality, i.e. to spur development, were also acts that helped secure its mass social and political base.

Think for a moment of what confronted the Soviet Communists – what, from their standpoint, they found necessary to do to destroy the old agrarian structure and replace it with a modern one. The New Economic Plan, distribution of the land and then its forcible expropriation from the very same peasants upon whom the regime rested – none of this was necessary in Cuba (nor the vast chaos and destruction of civil war). On the contrary, almost the very act of taking over and nationalizing the sugar centrals cemented the already extant bonds between workers and peasants; their working conditions and living conditions were immediately and positively transformed. The immediate and long-range interests of both were identical; each needed the other in past struggles and each was affected similarly by the fluctuations in the economy. With the revolution, these common interests became even more intimately associated. Contrast this with the Mexican revolution, where the 'red battalions' of Carranza's workers helped to put down peasant rebellion, or with peasants and tin miners played off against each other in Bolivia in order to maintain the *status quo*. Contrast this with the massive repression of the peasantry under Stalin, and it indicates the profound importance of the prerevolutionary social structure in determining the pace and direction of the revolution in Cuba.

The Cuban revolutionaries – whatever their extraordinary abilities, especially Fidel's – came to power in a society whose prerevolutionary social structure endowed them with vast advantages compared with the leaders of other major social revolutions in this century. Neither the capacity of the revolutionary leaders nor their actions and reaction to the United States (nor the presence of the Soviet Union as a potential ally) can be separated from the *reality* (the 'real world') of the revolutionary process. I think, however, that it can be shown also that the rapidity and thoroughness (as well as the humane and libertarian aspects which I have not discussed here) of the Cuban revolution, and its movement into socialism, to a great extent were the result of the prerevolutionary social structure. Once a leadership came to power in Cuba that was really committed to a national solution to her problems – once revolutionaries committed to economic development and an independent national existence took power, and would brook no interference (indeed, a highly problematic but crucial occurrence provided by Fidel, Che, and their comrades), the revolution's course was profoundly influenced by the prerevolutionary social structure. Therefore, Fidel led a socialist revolution almost without knowing it and the Communists were virtually dragged into socialism by the *fidelistas* because 'history' made this possible.

11

Chilean revolution: the bullet or the ballot

Asked by a reporter what he thought the recent election of Marxist Salvador Allende as the nation's president meant, a Chilean peasant replied: 'Now it's our turn.'

That puts the issue nicely. Does the fact that Chile now has a freely elected president who won 'without soft-pedalling the Marxist revolutionary program he hopes to carry out' (*New York Times*) really mean that at last it's the 'turn' of the peasants and workers? The answer is not so simple as one might at first expect.

For the past several decades, Chile has been the only country in South America in which a large and politically significant organized working class has been led by Marxian socialists.

Allende ran as the coalition candidate of the mass-based Communist and left-Socialist parties, the old Radical Party (whose only ideology is opportunism) and the independent Catholic revolutionaries (MAPU). He pledged to put Chile 'on the road to socialism' by taking over the major domestic and US corporations, the banks and insurance companies, and large agrarian estates, and by instituting democratic planning in the interests of the nation as a whole. Thus, the question: Can the Chileans put through a socialist revolution via the historically unprecedented route of constitutional amendment, presidential leadership, and parliamentary legislation, while the parties, the mass media, and the unified organizations of the propertied classes still vie freely in the political arena, and the old army (46,000 strong) and crack police force, the *carabineros* (24,000), remain intact and untouched?

On the face of it the question seems extraordinarily silly, if not absurd, especially in a period in which the US government has repeatedly intervened in the internal affairs of other countries to resist movements for national independence and social reform. Whether radical or reform governments were elected democratically or not has never mattered in the past, either to the local dominant class or the US government. Time after time – in Iran, in Brazil, in British Guyana and elsewhere – Washington and its dominant-class allies abroad have opposed, undermined, and subverted popularly based constitutional governments. In 1954, the CIA overthrew the constitutional reform government of Jacobo Arbenz in Guatemala and sponsored a dictatorship that returned expropriated properties to the United Fruit Company, repealed social reforms, gave oil concessions to American companies, smashed labor unions, and killed hundreds – perhaps thousands – of workers and peasants.

In Greece in 1967, when it looked like the Center Union Party led by former Premier George Papandreou, an ardent anti-Communist, would win the coming May elections handily, on a platform promising radical change, a military coup supported by a combination of Greek and foreign investors aborted the elections. (The Greek colonels pulled their coup by putting into operation a NATO contingency plan to be used in the event that 'Communists' tried to seize power in Greece.) The colonels and their propertied allies destroyed parliamentary democracy as soon as it looked like their 'structure of privileges' might, in the words of Andreas Papandreou, son of the ex-premier, be 'dismantled or undermined in any fashion or to any degree.' Their dictatorship amounts, as the younger Papandreou said, to no less than 'a covert occupation of Greece by the Pentagon.'

The Stakes in Chile

In Chile the stakes are extraordinary: the immense interests of her own dominant class and of major US and other foreign (mainly British) corporations with investments there. US direct investment alone is conservatively estimated at close to a billion dollars. Over a hundred corporations or agencies of US private interests operate in Chile. US corporations have major investments in electric power and the telephone system, but well over half of the known US investment is concentrated in nitrate, iron, and copper mining. Many so-called 'Chilean' corporations are structurally integrated with US corporations in 'invisible' ways. The Chilean Cotton Manufacturing Company, for example, Chile's fourteenth largest firm, is ostensibly under the control of Chile's Yarur family. In fact, 45 percent of its stock is US owned. More to the point, this 'Yarur' corporation in turn owns 49 percent of Caupolican Textiles (Chile's twenty-fourth largest firm), which, on the surface, appears to be without substantial foreign ownership. The well-known 'Chilean' commercial firm, Hucke Brothers (Chile's forty-fourth largest corporation), still has Hucke family members on the board and in the management. In fact, it is *owned* by W. R. Grace and Company through Grace's other Chilean subsidiaries. And these are not isolated instances.

Aside from its implications for direct business investments in Chile, the establishment of another socialist government in the Americas is of prime political significance. Neighboring Peruvian and Bolivian 'nationalist' military regimes which have put through some radical reforms and imposed new limits on foreign capital are certainly not immune to the influence of a more radical model on their borders. Nor can the rightist military regime and dominant class of Argentina, with which Chile shares a 2,700-mile border, ignore what happens there.

The question is, given these obvious implications of an Allende victory at the polls, how was it permitted to occur? The ballots were counted, Allende came out with the largest plurality (39,000 votes), and the Congress, assembled as an electoral college, with overwhelming support from the Christian Democrats in the House and Senate, elected Allende President. Not only was he elected: he took office and has proceeded these past few months step by step with measures promised in the socialist program he ran on.

Save the Country

Allende was not inaugurated without opposition, of course. In the weeks following his election, there was heightened parliamentary maneuvering, and the ruling-class media called on the Senate and House (since no candidate had won a majority) to exercise their constitutional right to select, not Allende, but the candidate with the second number of votes – Jorge Allesandri, a former President and the representative of the propertied classes. Women draped in black mourning shawls stood outside the walls of the Moneda, the presidential office building, calling on President Frei to 'save the country while there is still time.' Two unsuccessful assassination attempts were made against Allende; then, less than two weeks before Allende's inauguration, General René Schneider, Commander-in-Chief of the Armed Forces, who had announced that the Army would remain loyal to the Constitution, was killed by armed assassins as he was leaving his home. The intention apparently had been to kidnap the general, as part of a coordinated *putsch*, and to issue communiques in the general's name (and those of other actual top military conspirators) calling on the armed forces to 'save the country from communism.' The plan went awry because the general resisted, drew his revolver, fired once, and was killed.[1]

More importantly, the Left was not idly waiting on the good graces of the Army and the Center and Right parliamentarians to install Allende in office. In constant public meetings throughout the country, the 8,000 Allende committees of Unidad Popular kept the people alert and prepared against a possible attempt to rob the Left of its electoral victory. Tightly organized and well-trained 'shock forces' of the Left were assembled in strategic areas of Santiago and other major cities, ready to take whatever action might be necessary to 'guarantee the popular victory' at the polls. And in mass rallies of tens of thousands of supporters, Allende warned that any attempt to cripple the economy or prevent him from taking office would be met by a general strike. 'The country,' he said, 'will stop as a first step. Workers will occupy their factories, peasants will occupy the land, and civil servants their offices.'

In the months preceding the election, workers, peasants, and urban poor had taken increasingly militant grass-roots action. Revolutionary socialists both in and out of the electoral coalition had led land seizures and occupations of vacant urban sites. Allende, in fact, seemed a rather moderate alternative to the armed peasants and urban poor who patrolled to protect the sites they had occupied, many of them accompanied by armed members of the dissident Movement of the Revolutionary Left (MIR), which advocated armed revolution. Financing of food and clothing for those active in the seizures as well as for the purchase of arms reportedly came from bank robberies carried out by *Miristas*. The Left also had a highly efficient intelligence organization of its own which paralleled the government's operations and assured Allende that he would not have to rely on the good faith of the outgoing government alone.

People's Intelligence

Though its information about plots against the government and Allende was ignored before the murder of General Schneider, it was as the result of cooperation between the government and the Left's intelligence operation that the majority of the participants in the coup plot and actual killing of General Schneider were rounded up within days of his murder. (The list of the plotters and assassins reads, as a Chilean friend wrote me, like entries in a Chilean 'Who's Who.') When Schneider was murdered, President Frei immediately appointed José Toha, Allende's security chief (now Minister of the Interior), as Acting Undersecretary of the Interior and deputy director of the federal police investigating the assassination.

This event, while it need not be exaggerated, is sufficiently important to be emphasized. Where else could one expect to find the government intelligence service and the Army acting with such dispatch to find right-wing assassins who were trying to prevent the accession to office of a Marxist President – and to do so in cooperation with the Left's intelligence organization?

Undoubtedly, there is a certain amount of fluff and mystification about the 'incorruptibility' of the *carabineros*, Chile's national police, and the political 'neutrality' of the (largely US trained) armed forces. As a latent threat and ever-present potentially repressive force monopolizing the means of violence, they have helped to maintain the existing order. Under Christian Democratic President Eduardo Frei's 'revolution in liberty,' the use of the armed forces against striking workers accused of 'sedition' and 'rebellion against constituted authority' was no less frequent, and the consequences more dire, than under recent conservative regimes. And plastic-masked specially trained mobile riot-police units were used regularly, as a *Los Angeles Times* reporter put it, 'to smash street demonstrations by strikers and anti-government groups' as well as to dislodge squatters from the land.

Nor has the army stayed out of overt intervention in the 'political process' entirely. Last year, there was an attempted coup against Allende (later passed off as a 'strike for higher pay') led by dissident army officers, and one leader of that abortive revolt has since been implicated in the plot which ended in Schneider's assassination. Mass mobilization by the Left and a general strike, plus a split in the army, stopped the *putsch* in its tracks. (The Left's organizational skills and its sense of humor and showmanship came out well in the general strike: hundreds of Communist-led garbage men converged on the Moneda and surrounded it with their heavily laden garbage trucks to ward off any possible move against the President!)

Political Order: Chile versus Cuba

In general, however, Chile has been a genuine parliamentary democracy in which the role of the police and armed forces and the use of force and violence in maintaining the system have been on a par with that in such 'advanced' capitalist democracies as Britain and the United States. The contrast with Cuba is instructive. There, the ruling strata were directly dependent on American imperialism – politically, militarily, economically – and lacked social legitimacy. The basis of their rule was nakedly revealed as their control of the means of violence. They stayed in power because they had a military regime (and behind it the power of the US government) to protect them, not because anyone believed that they *deserved* power or that they had the *right* to rule. They were illegitimate in the eyes of virtually the entire population.

In Chile, however, the higher circles have enjoyed considerable legitimacy. A coalition of landlords and capitalists has been able to rule for over a century with neither foreign control nor the intervention of the military as an *autonomous* social force. Their resilience is illustrated by the hand-in-glove relationship between Chilean political stability and parliamentary democracy. Contrast Cuba, where the forms of political democracy were long considered an empty shell. Cuba's brief postwar interregnum of civilian government was seen as a sham, little more relevant to their needs or the interests of the nation than military dictatorship had been. Congressional parties and politicians were all but universally held in contempt. But in Chile, as in our own country, although people have a healthy cynicism about 'politics and politicians,' respect for parliamentary democracy also runs deep. Communists and socialists have run their press, held their rallies, and participated freely in elections for the past three decades. Indeed, they played a very significant role in the so-called Popular Front government of the 1930s. When the Communist Party was outlawed in 1941, it simply continued activities under another name (the Proletarian Party) with little government interference. In fact, under the presidency of Gabriel Gonzalez Videla, in 1946, three Communists served for five months as ministers in the Cabinet. With the advent of the Cold War, the Communist Party again was outlawed in 1948 (by the Law for the Defense of Democracy), but the Party continued to have members in parliament.

I do not want to minimize the repression to which leftists have been subjected in Chile or nourish illusions about the uniqueness of its dominant class. Rather, the point is to highlight the contradictory nature and genuine reality of Chile's 'bourgeois' democracy. As Volodia Teitelboim, a leading member of the Chilean Communist Party's Central Committee, commented recently: 'The Cuban and Chilean experiences are very different. They had a military dictatorship for years. We have had a century and a half of almost uninterrupted parliamentary government.' He should have added that Chile also has witnessed almost a century of uninterrupted class struggle.

The Rise of the Left

Since the middle of the last century, Chile has been the scene of frequent large-scale strikes and popular demonstrations. By the 1930s, the organized working class already had become a major political force, led by both socialists and Communists. Chile is the only western capitalist country (since the recent demise of Pietro Nenni's Socialist Party in Italy) with a durable, well-organized Marxian Socialist Party to the left of the Communists; and it also has its own mass base in the working class and organized labor.

The socialist movement in Chile began to become a serious contender for power in the 1950s, as its popular base among the workers broadened. Between 1952 and 1956, the working-class movement became increasingly unified: in organized labor, a single organization (CUT) uniting the unions was formed, and in the political arena a broad electoral bloc emerged, combining the Socialists and Communists and several splinter parties in a coalition called the Popular Action Front (FRAP). From FRAP's formation in 1956, the electoral strength of the socialist movement has risen rapidly. In the presidential election of 1958, Allende got 29 percent of the vote; in 1964, he got 39 percent.

The rise of the Christian Democratic Party paralleled the rise of the Marxian parties. In the space of a few decades it transformed itself from just one more splinter party of the Right with corporatist ideas into a governing reform party emphasizing the need for economic development. While its dominant wing, led by Frei, emphasized reforms within the framework of capitalism, its more radical and militant activists talked about building a 'communitarian society' through 'antiimperialism' and a 'noncapitalist path of development.' Radomiro Tomic, the Christian Democrat candidate in the 1970 presidential election, reflected that tendency far more than he did the centrist one. Tomic ran, as the *New York Times* put it, almost as if he were an opposition candidate and 'tried at times to outflank Dr. Allende on the left.' But to blame Tomic personally, as the *Times* did, for being the 'architect of disaster' in the elections, and for the victory of the Unidad Popular, is to miss the essence of recent Chilean history.

The expectation of a revolution has been in the wind for a decade or more in Chile. When Allende lost (by a narrow margin) in 1958, hundreds of thousands of workers surged into the streets spontaneously, believing they had been robbed in the ballot count; many on the Left were prepared to strike for power, while others were demanding that Allende, not Alessandri, be selected president by Congress (a constitutionally permissible and historically supportable course). Outgoing President Carlos Ibañez called upon the head of CUT, a Christian Socialist, to offer the Left the reins of government and throw his authority in their favor. Heated secret debates ended with the decision of the Communists and Socialists to call for observance of the legal results of the election and to cool off revolutionary fervor.

Six years later, in 1964, Frei was elected on a program explicitly designed as an alternative to the socialist movement. He spoke in a populist and nationalist, even revolutionary, idiom, and called for a 'revolution in liberty.' The Christian Democratic program emphasized the need to 'recover' Chile's resources, especially copper, from foreign control. With its rhetoric of 'mass participation' in reconstructing Chilean society, and its emphasis on the 'dignity' of the poor and the need for vast reforms, Christian Democracy is an additional sharp index of the erosion of the owning class's ideological hegemony that has been taking place in Chile at an accelerating pace in the past 20 years. Few leading Chilean intellectuals now defend 'capitalism' as a humane or just system, and the overwhelming majority of workers are class-conscious, militant supporters of the Marxian Left.

Thrust of the Peasantry

In the past 10 years the peasantry has emerged as a potentially powerful left political force. Under the Christian Democratic government, agitation about agrarian reform was at a perpetual peak. And the number of peasants involved in strikes (protected somewhat by the umbrella of left-wing Christian Democrats who have since allied themselves politically with the Allende coalition) *trebled* in the first year (1964–5) after Frei took office, while the Frei administration went ahead, though slowly and reluctantly, with expropriation (with compensation) of several large estates. Frei had promised new land for 100,000 families, but settled only 30,000 during his term in office (while spending $100 million to compensate former landowners).

But by making the talk of agrarian reform respectable, Christian Democrats gave the Left a major opportunity to speak to hundreds of thousands of peasants in remote and isolated *haciendas* and rural communities which had been practically impenetrable to Socialists and Communists before. The Left has gained strength among all types of peasants in the past years, among both agricultural wage laborers and small proprietors (but particularly among the former).

The political radicalization of the peasantry has continued against a backdrop of small but cumulative changes in the countryside – including electrification, improved transportation, mechanized production – which have undermined the hold of the old system of social control by the large landowners. These changes, coupled with growing political agitation, created a situation in which the socialist movement was not only broadening its already major base among workers in the mines, mills, and factories, but was also gaining tens of thousands of new adherents among the peasants as well. With the growth in the cities of a new movement among the previously unorganized slum dwellers – the so-called movement of the 'Homeless' – this means that scarcely any exploited stratum remains untouched by the Left and by socialist ideas.

Initiatives by younger socialists, many of them in MIR and others in the Christian left Movement of United Popular Action (MAPU), have kept these old Socialist and Communist parties alert and actively organizing, unable to rest with their present base even if they wished to do so. In the months preceding the elections, urban land seizures and peasant occupations seemed to be occurring in a rapid crescendo, and a *New York Times* reporter quoted 'a conservative Chilean civil servant' whose fears and estimate of the situation undoubtedly reflected those of the privileged in general: 'It makes little difference,' he said, 'whether or not Allende wins this election. Without quick and drastic action, the Marxists will win their real battle anyway.'

What's Good for Business

What, then, is to happen to the capitalist economy in the meantime? The Allende government has left no doubt of its intentions to nationalize major companies, banks and insurance companies, and major foreign investments. Does it then expect businessmen to continue to function as if business conditions were normal – as if the ownership and control of their enterprises and profits were not endangered? Will businessmen continue to reinvest at their normal rate in the expansion of their enterprises and the production of goods and services, without the security of a 'proper investment climate,' without being able to make reasonable calculations concerning the profitability of these investments, without knowing if they will, indeed, find themselves without a business tomorrow? The answer seems quite clear in principle, and much of the empirical experience of the government so far seems to confirm it: the 'economy' cannot operate as long as big businessmen believe their country is headed by genuine socialists whose policies threaten the very existence of the capitalist system.

Allende's election, as the *New York Times* put it, 'changed the business climate overnight. . . . The initial response of the business community was near panic, followed by a massive flight of liquid capital. Stock market prices dropped dramatically, as did asking prices for property and businesses. Many with money to save left the country after bidding up the dollar from the official rate of 14 escudos to more than four times that figure. Although many subsequently returned here after securing funds abroad, the business mood at year end was extremely cautious, to say the least.'

Some of the largest enterprises have begun to lay off workers, and the already staggering rate of unemployment inherited by the socialist government (upwards of a fifth of the work force in metropolitan Santiago) has risen further, as the interrelated activities of suppliers, producers and consumers of goods have extended the slowdown throughout the economy. Private construction, for example, both of office buildings and of housing, reportedly has come almost to a standstill. Aside from the immediate unemployment of the workers in the construction industry, this has meant that metal, lumber, cement, glass, and other industries which depend on the construction industry as a principal market also are likely to be affected drastically, as are their workers, in chain reaction. A brass company, for instance, had its sales drop 70 percent in the two months after Allende's election. So the manager shut down the plant 'to avoid insolvency.' 'What was I supposed to do?' he asked. 'I wasn't about to let useless workers get paid from company reserves.' The Allende government took over the management of the firm in late November under a 1945 labor law giving the government authority to 'intervene' when necessary to protect the interests of the employees of a company. It has since 'intervened' in several other large firms, including a major bank and Chile's largest textile plant. And it has taken measures to prevent further mass layoffs.

Just such policies, however, are destined to further erode 'business confidence' and create a 'climate of uncertainty' among the major investors whose decisions have national economic consequences. The Allende government could find itself held responsible for an economic crisis without being in a position to act decisively, as long as it adheres to the commitment to act solely within the existing legal framework. It could find itself managing a deteriorating economy which it is not in a position to control, because the government must await parliamentary pleasure for legislation allowing the expropriation of the enterprises and the creation of a planning organism capable of genuine coordination of production in the national interest. On the other hand, 'whatever efforts it may make to recover lost confidence . . . will not succeed,' as a leading business journal in Chile (*Portada*, October 1970) itself points out, 'because to do so would automatically indicate that [the government] had decided to abandon its program.'

Large enterprises are especially able to frustrate government 'intervenors' and – whether intentionally or not – create economic havoc. On the one hand, these firms control the bulk of the production and sales in their respective industries, many of them being effective monopolies; on the other, interlocking directorates and common large shareowners, as well as reciprocal holdings of the firms in each other, bind them together into a centralized political economic structure. Nor should US capital's penetration of these firms be forgotten here. Government 'intervention' in the management of such individual firms alone cannot provide a mechanism capable of coping with such an integrated system. Short of expropriation, genuine public control of the economy is not possible.

Chilean New Deal?

We may assume that the socialists in Chile's government are well aware of the nature of the alternatives they face, but neither their words nor their deeds so far give a clear picture of how they expect to resolve this dilemma. Nor, of course, do they hold all the options. On the one hand, the government has clearly stated its intention to nationalize, *within the coming year*, the domestic and foreign banks, the large mining companies owned by Kennecott and Anaconda, and 'some large monopolies in production and distribution'; and it continues to reiterate on all occasions its fundamental aim to begin to create a 'socialist and pluralist society.'

On the other hand, the government claims to foresee a considerable period during which the economy will continue to have a major private sector, although the state will be 'the prevailing' sector. Moreover, the socialists have to put into effect a short-run program within the present capitalist framework to stimulate employment and production. Thus far, the government has decreed a price freeze for all industrial and consumer goods: bank inspectors are exercising control over private bank credit; substantial wage increases have gone to public and private employees, and efforts are under way to begin an emergency construction program financed by additional taxes on corporations. Meanwhile, powerful capitalist representatives have had frequent meetings with Allende at which they have reportedly pledged their cooperation if 'Allende would outline an economic program they could live with.' Sergio Jarpa, president of the conservative National Party, has announced, 'We're not prejudiced about what the new government is going to do. If it's good for the country we will go along even though it has a socialist label.' And one of Chile's big businessmen is quoted as making the extraordinary statement that 'We lost the election and we are going to have socialism in Chile. Dr. Allende asked for our cooperation. . .'

While the government's immediate plans unquestionably would

take certain basic sectors under state ownership and control, they would nevertheless not necessarily put Chile 'on the road to socialism' nor fundamentally alter her economic structure. Since the Popular Front government of the 1930s established the Government Development Corporation (CORFO) in 1939, the state has played a major role in investment, especially in machinery and equipment. CORFO has controlled, on the average over the years, about a fifth of gross domestic investment. State-owned and mixed enterprises (with both the government and big private investors owning the bulk of the stock) have been established in areas deemed necessary for economic development which private capital would not enter because of the uncertainty of profitable returns. Once successful, however, the mixed enterprises have been gradually turned over to private owners. Mixed enterprises that still operate (such as the Pacific Steel Company) typically have exclusive management contracts with foreign corporations, and the policies of these enterprises have tended to be guided by profit considerations for the largest Chilean corporations and the needs of the private sector as a whole.

In other words, the socialist government could actually put through major reforms, which the capitalists themselves would never have sponsored, that might release forces for the expansion, rather than the contraction, of capitalism in Chile – much as the New Deal policies of the 1930s in the United States and the post-World War II nationalizations in Britain under the Labor government were resisted by big business, though these very policies helped to maintain capitalism in these countries.

The Chilean situation is different in that the Chilean socialist movement is well to the left of the British and more committed to a real socialist program. But, because they have chosen the path of parliamentary socialism, they will have to compromise and negotiate critical measures along the way, and this will hinder their ability to respond to situations decisively and radically.

Moderate Communists

If the government succeeds in its short-run efforts to stimulate the economy and regain 'business confidence,' the immediate crisis – and therefore confrontation with big business and its allies – could be avoided. In the process, the aroused energies of the masses and organized cadres and their readiness for action could be dissipated as the country settles once again into 'normalcy.' So far the government's responses to spontaneous occupations of large landed estates by agricultural laborers and to workers' strikes and urban land seizures have been contradictory, and this may in part reflect actual policy differences within the coalition government and between ministers. In general, however, the Left seems to be urging the cadre to take it easy, cooling out independent worker and peasant initiatives and attempting to stabilize the economy while it consolidates its position. Yet it is worth recalling that this is precisely what the Cuban revolutionary government did under Castro's leadership in the early months, and such surface appearances tell us little, if anything, about the plans of the Chilean socialist leadership.

Of course, whatever its plans, it does not hold all the cards, and the situation could change rapidly and profoundly if the dominant class and its foreign allies should themselves choose to have a showdown – or unintentionally provoke one. Then, as Allende has made clear, the socialist leaders would be compelled to take action they may not have desired or even anticipated: 'A government must weigh what obstacles it will encounter,' Allende has said. 'Perhaps if obstacles are artificially created, if there is a conspiracy by ultrareactionary sectors, if the current attempt to provoke economic chaos is accentuated, we'll be forced to take our steps more quickly and decisively – that is, the process could be radicalized, not because we want it to be, but because we have no other choice.'

Withal, bargaining and compromise – if not stalemate – are firmly rooted Chilean national traditions, while the socialist government also has internal problems because it rests on a diverse coalition. Of special significance is the fact that the Socialist Party is itself highly pluralistic, containing a diversity of ideological currents (though it is heavily weighted on the side of the Marxian and pro-Fidelista left).

A critical factor in the Left coalition is the tightly organized and disciplined Communist Party. If its past is any indication, the Communist Party is likely to attempt at every turn to moderate government policies, and will be the cornerstone of compromise and hesitation rather than revolutionary audacity and initiative. It has long been one of the most Stalinist parties in the world, conforming almost reflexively to every shift in Soviet policies and programs. In the past decade, the Soviets – and therefore the Chilean

Communists – have put their emphasis on 'peaceful coexistence' and on the establishment of cordial trade and diplomatic relations with the United States and the countries of Latin America.

Even the Cuban experience did not shake Chile's Communist Party out of its previous parliamentary rhythms, and Fidel and Chilean Communist leaders have had several public polemical debates about the revolutionary path to power in Latin America. Apparently this is known even in Washington: Evans and Novak, 'sadly confident' that the end is near for freedom in Chile, report '... the hope by top U.S. policymakers that the well-organized Communist Party, which is to the right of Allende's Socialist Party in the ruling coalition, may itself be a moderating influence. Perhaps, prodded by Moscow, the Communists might block flagrantly revolutionary moves in either foreign or domestic policy.'

The Acid Test

More important, perhaps, in understanding the potential of the socialist leadership is the fact that it has been shaped largely by its experience in the labor movement – which necessarily has involved battles for immediate reforms – and, to a profound and immeasurable extent, its participation in electoral politics. 'Most of us in the Communist Party,' as Central Committee Member Teitelboim put it recently, 'have worked in the parliamentary system for 30 years.' The same is true of the socialists. Therein, of course, lies a special sort of dialectic: for while it raises the prospect (which, if it occurs, will have tremendous significance for the development of the international socialist movement) of a socialist government ruling through a genuine parliamentary democracy, it also means that the *revolutionary* capacity of the Chilean socialist movement has yet to be tested. This is not to detract from the political and organizational abilities of the communists and socialists – and it would be arrogant and incorrect to do so, considering their already *unprecedented* feat of creating a popular base so broad as to bring them into government by the electoral path.

What it does mean, though, is that because they have not been tempered by years of dangerous clandestine political activity, nor by guerrilla warfare, they may underestimate the struggle ahead. Never having experienced colonial rule and oppression, never having needed to organize under conditions of dictatorship nor to resist an occupying foreign power, the Chilean Left's leaders may unconsciously delude themselves about what it will take to 'defeat definitively the dominant class in Chile,' as the Communist Minister of Finance (a former manual worker and trade-union organizer) stated the government's goal recently. Carried away by their own rhetoric, to quote Allende's inauguration speech, that 'Chileans can be proud of having always managed to give preference to the peaceful political course rather than to violence,' they may prepare themselves poorly to do battle if and when that dominant class (together with its domestic and foreign allies) forsakes 'the peaceful political course' in order to save the old order. Again, it would be silly to say that Chile's Socialists are not aware of this possibility on an intellectual level. The question is what meaning their intellectual understanding has for their practical political and organizational work now.

They seem to have fallen rather quickly back into the pattern of activity shaped by their parliamentary experience, and are now deeply involved in preparing for the coming municipal elections in April – which they speak of as their 'next major battleground.' Luis Corvalán, secretary general of the Communist Party, and himself a senator, declares: 'We must transform these elections into a great national political battle against the enemies of change, in favor of the program of the Unidad Popular and in support of the government presided over by comrade Salvador Allende.'

In this connection, the recent self-criticism of Andreas Papandreou, leader of the Left in Greece's anti-Communist Center Union Party which the colonels' coup prevented from taking power, is especially relevant. His self-criticism – in his *Democracy at Gunpoint* (Garden City, N.Y.: Doubleday, 1970, pp. 346–7) – is all the more compelling, because his Party promised, not the 'construction of socialism' in Greece, but the salvation, through deep-going social reforms, of capitalism.

> Our willingness to negotiate, to temporize, to postpone action was mistaken by the forces of the Establishment as weakness, as avoidance of the confrontation and its consequences. And by the time the confrontation had come, we had lost the momentum that the great electoral victory had bestowed upon us. . . . The junta struck and the country was set back at least fifty years. . . .
> Had we given serious attention to the establishment of a clandestine, resistance-oriented organization, had we formed nuclei throughout the country, had we given clear instructions for action in response

to a coup, had we distributed radio transmitters and mimeograph machines, and had we rented apartments under cover to protect the leadership of the organization, then possibly we could have frustrated the coup within the first few hours. And while it is true that I organized the Democratic Leagues and gave them this type of assignment, it must be admitted candidly that neither I nor my immediate circle chose to concentrate our energies in this direction. This was due in part to the peculiar fact that no one had emotionally accepted the possibility of a coup, although all signs of an impending coup were there. The forthcoming elections absorbed the thoughts and activities of all party members, and captured the attention of the population.[2]

Notes

1 General Schneider's assassination resulted from the CIA's efforts, under orders from then President Richard M. Nixon, 'to play a direct role,' as the Church Committee reported in 1975, 'in organizing a military coup d'etat in Chile to prevent Allende's accession to the Presidency.' The Committee's report was 'punctiliously factual,' as Thomas Powers observes in *The Man Who Kept the Secrets*, and careful not to claim that the CIA actually shot Schneider. But, as Powers says, 'if the CIA did not actually shoot General Schneider, it is probably fair to say that he would not have been shot without the CIA.'

2 A military coup on September 11, 1973 overthrew the socialist government; Allende and more than 20,000 civilians died resisting the armed forces, and the river Mapocho ran red with their blood for months afterwards. As this April 1971 article on the first several months of Allende's presidency makes clear, it was not merely the United States that opposed and sought the overthrow of his government. The coup and its horrific aftermath were the culmination of intensifying class struggle within Chile over the nation's destiny. Chile's own arrogant and proud landed and capitalist families not only successfully mobilized the mass support of small business and other middle-class elements against Allende's working-class-based government, but also did their best to promote a coup. Nonetheless, the coup was also the result of US intervention in Chile's affairs. The CIA's covert action exacerbated dissension and created economic turmoil and political chaos, without which the hitherto staunchly constitutionalist military could not have been induced to end Chilean democracy. As former CIA director William Colby himself concludes, 'Certainly, having launched such an attempt [in 1970, to foment a coup], CIA was responsible to some degree for the final outcome. . .' Thomas Karamessines, CIA deputy director for clandestine operations from 1970 through early 1973, also testified in congressional hearings on Chile in 1975 that Nixon and Kissinger had ordered the CIA

to 'stay alert, and to do what we could to contribute to the eventual achievement of the objectives and purposes of Track II' (as the original CIA attempt to promote a coup in 1970 was code-named). He added: 'I am sure that the seeds that were laid in that effort in 1970 had their impact in 1973. I do not have any question of that in my mind either.' Nixon and Kissinger's 'firm and continuing policy' was, as Karamessines described his 'marching orders,' 'that Allende be overthrown by a coup.'

'We preached to the military to ignore the constitution and overthrow a popularly elected government . . . . [We] did everything in our power to destroy the economy of Chile,' as Morton Halperin, Kissinger's own former assistant and ex-deputy assistant secretary of defense, testified before congress in 1975. 'And then we were told by the Administration that we were not responsible for the coup because the day before the coup the generals who carried it out did not come to us and say, 'should we carry out the coup?'' In reality, Kissinger misled Senate investigators when, in Executive Session, he denied being intimately informed of the coup planning. In his 1986 book on Allende's Chile, Nathaniel Davis, US Ambassador to Chile at the time of the coup, disclosed that Kissinger falsely claims in his memoirs that neither he nor Davis had known of a 'specific plan,' 'time frame,' or 'date' for the coup. On the contrary, according to Davis, they had 'detailed information on the plotters,' and Davis could have, but did not, warn Allende, because it would have been a 'betrayal' of the plotters' trust! Of course Davis also knew that Nixon and Kissinger would not have allowed him to breach that trust and warn the man whose government they wanted smashed.

12

Democratic investment

American capitalism is in an unprecedented crisis, marked not only by the combined assault of stagnation and inflation on the lives of working men and women but by a tendency toward the disintegration of our basic industries. An epidemic of plant closings has hit our country, from Maine to California, leaving wasted communities and wasted lives behind. By cutting the real ('social' and private) wage bill, weakening labor's bargaining power, despoiling the wilderness to cheapen domestic raw material costs, and providing tax cuts for the rich, the Reagan regime's policies could stimulate a short-term 'recovery' through a spurt of profit taking. But they will not stem the forces of inflation, assure real capital formation and productive employment, or resurrect our basic industries, any more than would recycled Keynesian policies of public works and public jobs, demand management (mainly military spending), or other liberal palliatives.

Only deep structural changes can begin to resolve this crisis. But these changes can come from above, as well as from below, in a way that both enhances the prerogatives of capital and dilutes democracy. For not only radicals but capitalists have a vision of the future and can call for fundamental change. Since the inception of the economic crisis in the mid-1970s, several investment bankers and business leaders have begun to urgently advocate what *Business Week* calls 'centralized government economic planning.' Recognizing the depth of their system's crisis, these prominent businessmen want neither *laissez faire* capitalism nor the old liberalism, but a new corporatism: enforced social austerity, labor discipline, and massive public investment in private industry directed by the state. What they want is state planning of the economy, but planning that is by them and for them, inaccessible to elected officials and sheltered from popular demands. If democracy cannot, in Felix

Rohatyn's phrase, 'allocate pain,' the state, under their direction, will.[1]

This is also the main thrust of the major business and Congressional proposals that urge making 'government an ally . . . of business' (US Senate Democratic Task Force on the Economy 1980, p. 1). The authors of the Democratic Task Force's economic report recently announced that they are ready to abandon the 'American tradition [that] holds . . . that state power should be used to counterbalance corporate power,' and to substitute a form of government intervention that, in the Task Force's words, would 'be insulated as much as possible from political pressures' (1980, p. 25), that would be, as Rohatyn urges, 'publicly accountable but . . . run outside of politics.'[2]

Rohatyn advocates a refurbished Reconstruction Finance Corporation (RFC) equipped 'to accomplish the objectives of a comprehensive national economic recovery program,' and to provide, as one of its 'basic functions,' a 'safety net' for 'financially distressed' corporations (Lazard Frères & Co. 1980). Capitalized by federally guaranteed bonds sold on the open market, 'the RFC should,' in his view, '. . . become a permanent part of our economic establishment' and a 'vibrant instrument' for the planning of industrial growth. In essence, the RFC would be a huge state investment banking operation with immense powers to shape the national economy. It would provide public financing, usually through infusions of equity capital rather than credits or loans, where its directors deemed it necessary to modernize ailing infrastructure and old industrial enterprises and make them globally competitive. By such equity investments, the RFC would become 'a part owner or creditor, until such time as it can, in the public interest [sic] divest itself of the enterprise in which it invests and this investment is eligible for normal market channels.'

The RFC's presidentially appointed directors would include 'experienced people from business, finance, and labor.' Despite the provision for labor representation, however, when Rohatyn says that 'before committing itself to invest,' the RFC (like New York's Municipal Assistance Corporation under Rohatyn's direction) would 'extract concessions from various participants,' it is obvious that most of these concessions would be extracted from labor. The 'industries that have a sound case for it' would get the public's money and 'the relevant unions would . . . make wage concessions,' including a freeze on cost-of-living adjustments; they would also have to accept 'changes in work rules that would increase productivity' (speedup, fewer precautions for on-the-job safety and health), a 'reduction in manpower,' and 'shifts in pension costs' to workers.

And what sacrifices and austerity would be asked of the business community or of the huge corporations, which, left to themselves, would 'let our basic industries go down,' as Rohatyn admits, 'one after the other'? What risks of capital and what concessions would *they* have to make? Would the RFC impose a freeze or reduction of managerial compensation (salary, bonuses, stock options, and perquisites), of the banks' interest charges, or of the profits of the principal shareowners? What sacrifices does Rohatyn suggest for 'the lenders, the banks and insurance companies'? Well, 'to convert some loans to preferred stock and to join with the RFC in committing additional capital.' The RFC might also, in exchange for assistance, 'insist on management changes and changes in the board of directors if it deems them appropriate.' So this is what Rohatyn and his fellow financiers and businessmen mean by 'relatively evenly distributed burdens and benefits, . . . regardless of class'!

The presence of a few labor appointees on the RFC's board, accountable not to union members or working men and women but to the president who appointed them, would merely help to legitimate the concessions wrung from the working class, and encourage 'labor peace.'

The RFC and similar agencies would be a new state form of public planning in the private interest, and of socializing the risk and privatizing the profits.[3] Nothing in the proposed RFC's sources and methods of financing, the constitution and composition of its governing board, or its explicit objectives could assure that its planning policies accorded with democratically determined social priorities. Business would possess a direct and publicly legitimated means of state power, intended by the proposed RFC's charter to override the democratic process and ensure the 'allocation of pain' to labor and the rest of us and the benefits of state planning to itself.

Thus, we are at a critical historic turn. Not only Reagan's counterrevolution but the 'fallback alternative' of his business critics, who have had enough of 'the mythical free market,' have 'sharpened the alternative [and] . . . narrowed the choice: democracy or the corporate state' (Wolin 1981). To affect that historic choice, labor and the Left need to propose and demand democratic economic alternatives to corporatism.

This means entering a treacherous but unavoidable political terrain for radical democrats: imagining and fighting for winnable, realistic, 'nonreformist reforms' that matter, and that in practice, to use Sheldon Wolin's words, create 'alternative modes of common life.' It means that any remaining disdain on the Left for practical politics must end, and it requires not only protest and resistance but the translation of democratic theory and political principles into effective action in the electoral arena. It requires moving beyond the politics of redistribution to a politics of production: finding ways to politicize the investment process, now controlled by private capital and a few immense corporations, and put on the political agenda the question of how, by whom, and for what social ends the decisive investment decisions are made.

We know that under capitalism profit is a necessary condition for productive investment, and that productive investment is necessary for continued production, consumption, and employment. But capital flows where profits are expected, regardless of whether the investment is productive, provides employment, or serves the needs of the community. No invisible hand assures that capital is productively allocated or that the public interest is served. On the contrary, it is precisely the misinvestment and disinvestment of highly concentrated private capital that is at the root of the stagnation, inflation, and industrial deterioration that now beset us.[4] Thus, the flow of capital can no longer be left in private hands alone, but must become subject also to democratic modes of determining its deployment.

In theory, with private ownership of the capital stock intact, the increasing socialization of the flow of capital and its democratically determined allocation must go hand in hand with the continuation and expansion of profitable production in private industry. In practice, what is required is a method of accumulation of public capital that impinges on the sole prerogative of capitalists to determine the rate, magnitude, and direction of social investment, but does not reduce (and might even enhance) their global competitiveness. In short, this means a 'historical compromise' that balances the private right to earn profits with the public right to decide democratically how to reinvest a portion of them in the public interest. This opens the way for the citizenry's ever-widening participation in making the most crucial investment decisions – concerning everything from land use and industrial location to the techniques and organization of production – that are now almost entirely the domain of a few giant banks and corporations.

To realize such a transformation means winning political power, and that means taking local politics seriously – for not only the federal government but also city, county, and state governments dispose of vast public resources and affect our lives. What these local governments do – and in the United States they have far more power and can do much more than in most other advanced capitalist countries – is often more transparent, more open to public scrutiny, and more accessible to popular pressure than what the federal government does.

It is at the local government level that a community-based movement for economic democracy can begin to put down roots, win political power, and create exemplary democratic modes of public planning that let residents participate directly in shaping their economic life. Such a movement has begun in California within the Democratic Party and in coalition with organized labor wherever possible; in several cities, sharp political struggles have been fought over questions of economic democracy, tenant rights and rent control, commercial and industrial development, affordable housing, plant closings, energy policy, and democratic public planning. In Santa Cruz, San Francisco, Berkeley, Chico, and Santa Monica, socialists or progressives are now represented in local government or (as in Santa Monica and Santa Cruz) actually have a majority on the City Council. The specific proposal that follows is thus meant for California, and is intended to move political debate about democratic economic alternatives beyond standard liberal formulations.

Translating into action the principle that the more democratic the investment process, the greater the public benefit, means that the citizenry at large and the labor movement in particular has to become involved in the 'selective public steering of capital,' as California's Governor Jerry Brown puts it. To ensure that public investment steering is representative, accountable, and democratic, a radically new governmental form has to be established: an autonomous, democratically constituted agency that would both be the repository of sufficient public capital and be empowered with the comprehensive authority to try, by the deployment of its own capital and credit, to guide the investment process in the public interest. Its overall task would be to attempt to assure rational economic development, to assure socially desirable capital formation and productive, secure, and healthful employment in California.

One institutional form that the democratization of investment might take would be an autonomous public investment reserve system, established by the California legislature, much as the Federal Reserve System was established by Congress. Unlike the Fed, whose governors come from the country's top banks, the California Public Investment Reserve System (PIRS) would be governed by elected representatives. Since, as I propose below, a major source of its capital endowment would come from the pension funds of public employees and unions in the private sector, they should have an appropriate method of democratically electing their representatives to the board of PIRS (pronounces 'purse'). Similarly, a method of election would be necessary to assure that the residents of the areas in which PIRS investments were made, whether in industry or public infrastructure, would be represented; a number of PIRS districts, designed to accord with regional peculiarities as well as to assure relatively equal representation for their residents, would be established. To assure the fullest participation of local residents in these investment decisions, district-wide elected councils could be established that would then elect their representatives to the PIRS board.

The conceptual point, however the principle is implemented, is that the employees whose pensions were vested in PIRS and the residents of the regions involved – cities might also pool their public pension funds in PIRS – would be represented on the PIRS board and board members would be accountable for their policies to an electorate able to scrutinize, debate, and judge them. Not personality, vague generalities, or rhetoric, but specific investment and allocation policies carried out in specific areas and aimed at serving specific constituents and the rational needs of all of the State's residents would be at issue.

Every large corporation operating in California would be required to fully disclose its detailed investment plans to PIRS's board – its plant by plant, product by product, region by region plans for the location, expansion, and contraction of given lines of production, its actual and anticipated rates of reinvestment (and disinvestment) in California, and any plans for mergers, acquisitions, consolidations, or purchases of the assets of other firms that might have an impact on our economy. PIRS would be empowered to obtain all investment and financial data, including information on corporate ownership and control, necessary to assess the social and economic impact of the corporations' investment and disinvestment decisions on the people of California.

PIRS would have sufficient public reserves to influence the industrial location strategies and investment policies of private capital by allocating funds regionally and by releasing them during slumps or selectively allocating or withholding them during booms. It would provide low-interest loans and credits as well as equity capital to firms which reinvested in new plant and equipment and expanded productive, healthful, and job-creating employment or offset economic dislocations and met other *democratically designated* public priorities. These priorities might include the production of social goods such as decent, attractive, affordable housing for workers, community recreation and health maintenance centers, renewable energy systems, and clean and energy-efficient mass transit, etc. PIRS would assist in financing the retooling of stagnant industries and the establishment of new ones on the cutting edge of technical advance (and perhaps the conversion of 'defense industries' as military spending is reduced), in exchange for a public share of the equity and appropriate representation on the boards of the companies involved.

The question is, then, where are the investment funds for PIRS to come from? There are four major sources: first, temporarily idle public funds, which come to an estimated $18 billion in California; second, state and local public employee pension funds, which amount to some $30 billion in California. These funds constitute an extraordinarily large pool of capital over which California's citizens now exercise virtually no control or discretion as to investment priorities. And present investments do not even keep pace with inflation. PERS, the public employees' fund, recently earned only 7 percent on its assets; STRS, the teachers' fund, only 7.5 percent.[5] This is certainly a source of public funds to be better, and more prudently, invested for public purposes.

A third source, private union pension funds, amounts to $228 billion nationally, of which only $92 billion are jointly administered by labor and management; the bulk is invested entirely at the discretion of employers (Eaton 1980) – and is often invested in antilabor, union-free, strike-breaking industries as well as in the economies of low-wage, repressive, Third World countries. A thorough study, reported in *Business Week* (September 17, 1979), found 'that union-negotiated pension funds – that is, the deferred wages of workers – are helping to support some staunchly nonunion companies.' Looking at Labor Department information on 142 union pension fund investments in 99 major companies in 1976, the Corporate Data Exchange found that these pension funds are invested in 50 nonunion companies, 40 companies that are frequent violators of federal health and safety or equal opportunity laws, and 30 companies that are major investors in South Africa (*Pension Investments; A Social Audit* 1979).

In California, an estimated $30 billion is held in private pension funds (*Public Investment Policy of Edmund G. Brown, Jr.* 1980; see also Governor's Public Investment Task Force 1981). For such funds to become available to the working people of California to decide for themselves how their hard-earned savings are to be invested, it will require a concerted effort of the labor movement as well as of the individual unions to regain control of what is rightfully theirs. These monies were never intended to become a new source of profits for private business. They should be invested – under government guarantees to protect principal and a rate of return – in consultation with the men and women from whose earnings these pension funds have been accumulated. The labor movement will have to seek both political means and effective bargaining methods to regain control of this huge pool of money so that it can be democratically invested under the direction of PIRS.

The fourth main – and most rightful – source of public capital will come from what otherwise might be misinvested and disinvested private capital. This might be called a down-payment on the future of California. If a company wants to invest in California, if it wants to invest in a community, then it will have to take into account in its costs that a specified percentage of its net investment – say 10 percent – would have to be placed at the outset in trust for the people of California, deposited in PIRS, as well as a 10 percent share of the firm's annual 'value added' calculated from its total wage bill. These 'security deposits' taken by the residents of California would be subject to deferred taxation. They might be permanently deferred, depending on whether or not such companies proved to be good citizens. In fact, funds might very well be returned to the same companies if PIRS so decided. The point is that a democratically elected board of governors, representative of organized labor and of the community of Californians, would be deciding, in accordance

with the PIRS charter, what to do with a share of the profits earned
in the state and would be able to assure socially desirable
reinvestment.[6] These profits, now in the form of PIRS funds, would
be selectively released to applicant companies if they showed that
they were engaged in productive and job-creating investments.
These funds, in other words, would be selectively steered and
redistributed within the business community itself to those companies whose records indicated that their activities benefited California.

This is a fundamental point about how the PIRS steering process
would work. The firms that did not take their profits out of the
state, the firms that reinvested in California, would be rewarded by
the allocation of public capital, coming not from the taxpayer
but from the profits (security deposits) of firms that had been
irresponsible.

Small manufacturers, in particular, would probably be the disproportionate beneficiaries of these public funds for several reasons:
first, they are the most likely to be cost efficient, productive, and
innovative technically; second, per dollar invested, they create far
more jobs than the giants; and third, they are precisely the firms
that find it hardest to get equity investments from the major
institutional investors and financing from the big banks. (see Adams
1977; US Small Business Administration 1977; Birch 1979). Assisting
the small and middle-sized manufacturers would be in the public
interest, as well as in the interest of the specific communities in
which they are located.

The crucial problem that PIRS would address is, who pays the
costs of malinvestment, misinvestment, and disinvestment by private
industry? We want to make sure that it will be the private sector
that pays the costs of private misinvestment rather than the working
people and the communities that are devastated by it. This means,
in technical language, that the 'externalities' would be 'discounted,'
and rather than the corporations externalizing costs and privatizing
profits the costs of irresponsible corporate conduct would be borne
by the corporations themselves.

This would be a form of compulsory savings, not for workers but
for business. Large corporations operating in California would have
to save and reinvest a share of their profits there. Otherwise they
might engage in esoteric investments and send their capital abroad,
as they have been doing at an increasing rate. Pooled under the
control of PIRS, these savings would be selectively reinvested to
guarantee that firms engaging in activities detrimental to the people

and the communities of California paid the costs, whereas firms reinvesting in the state would be rewarded.

What problems might PIRS face?

Obviously, as long as the flow of capital and trade are unrestricted across state lines, the compulsory deposition of a share of corporate savings might induce some of the largest companies not to put new investments here or even induce them to leave; this is a real risk, and a reality we would have to be ready to confront politically. But let us remember that right now the citizens of California have nothing whatsoever to say about the corporations' disinvestment; if they decide to shut down and run away, as the auto, steel, rubber, meat-packing, detergent, and other industrial giants have been doing, no law now prevents it. The only question is whether we might be making things worse for ourselves by penalizing corporate malinvestment and rewarding productive investment. I doubt it, for several reasons.

First, the corporations would not want to antagonize a population – and market – as large as ours and risk consumer boycotts and a host of other profit-draining public relations problems here.

Second, why would the companies relocate for the price of a security deposit? The influence of tax abatements for land and equipment and other subsidies and favors to big business has been overrated. Their real effect upon location decisions is probably negligible. Rather more important are the characteristics of the given market, labor force, and infrastructure (see Pierce 1980). How many companies would allow their competitors to preempt California's market and resources by refusing to comply with the state's laws?

Third, it must be emphasized that many companies would benefit from deferred taxation on their forced savings, while the available pool of public capital for which they would be eligible to facilitate their productive reinvestment in California would be far in excess of their individual contributions to it. At the same time, small and middle-sized manufacturers who might either be exempt from the compulsory deposition or pay a smaller percentage than the large companies (under a 'progressive' or graduated security deposit system) would have access to equity capital for which they are now starved by institutional investors. Thus, they should welcome this form of public investment and the improved opportunity it would give them to compete with the corporate giants for California's – and other – markets. In turn, knowing this would make the giants a bit more wary of abandoning California; for they would not just be moving their operations away, but would be losing their markets to new competitors based in the state.

Fourth, right now the state of California's public employee pension funds are among the very largest stockholders in many of the nations' leading banks and corporations.[7] If the trustees of these public employee pension funds began to assess where to invest in terms of potential social impact, and shifted their stockholdings from companies whose business conduct and investment policies went counter to designated social purposes, then all companies relying on the stock market for equity financing would find it in their interest to pay attention to them. If the public employee pension funds exercised their voting rights over their stockholdings in various corporations and obtained appropriate representation in corporate management, this would surely favor the corporations' compliance with California's PIRS security deposit requirements and investment guidelines. And if this were also true of the pension funds of labor unions of workers in California's private sector, then these constraints on capital flight from California would be compelling.

Fifth, the aim is for organized labor to win control of its own pension funds nationally. In the aggregate, these union pension funds were a crucial source of equity financing for the largest blue chip firms in recent years when the stock market was unattractive to private investors.[8] A coordinated union pension fund investment strategy would provide immense support for the democratic public steering of capital. It would provide a strong incentive to the corporations to continue to invest in California and in other states that follow its lead in establishing new democratic governmental forms of public investment for the public benefit.

Notes

1 Among the leading businessmen reported in the press as favoring these (or similar) views on the crisis and the need for 'planning' are Felix Rohatyn of Lazard Frères; William McChesney Martin, ex–head of the Federal Reserve; Gustave Levy of Goldman, Sachs; Henry Ford II; Robert V. Roosa of Brown Brothers Harriman; Irwin Sweeny Miller; Alfred Hayes, ex–head of the Federal Reserve Board in New York; George Ball of Lehman Brothers; Henry Kaufman of Salomon Brothers; and Ray Garrett, former chairman of the Securities and Exchange Commission.

2 The quotations from Rohatyn are from various articles in which his

sketch of a new Reconstruction Finance Corporation appears: 1979, 1980, 1981a, 1981b, 1981c. Useful articles about his views in the business press appear in *Business Week*, January 27, 1975, and *Fortune*, October 1975. A *Newsweek* cover story on him appeared on May 4, 1981. Also see the informative article by Alfred Watkins (1981). A formal presentation of the case for 'a new economic recovery corporation' is made in an unsigned 'Memorandum Concerning an Agency to Assist a National Economic Recovery Program' (Lazard Freres & Co. 1980). An editorial in *Business Week*, October 26, 1981, formally urged the Reagan administration to create a new entity such as the Reconstruction Finance Corporation.

3 But contrast, for instance, the proposals of the International Association of Machinists (IAM) and United Automobile Workers (UAW). Both call for the establishment of a National Development Bank (NDB) to help finance investment in distressed areas and industries by targeting the current range of federal business subsidies and tax credits. The IAM's 'Rebuilding America Act' specifies, in the words of IAM president William W. Winispinger, that the NDB's board would be 'appointed by the President, with the advice and consent of the Senate and House Ways and Means Committee,' from among trade unionists and consumer and environmental groups; connected to the NDB would be 'regional or even state and local development banks . . . to serve specialized areas and sectors of the economy. Any such sub-bank would have democratically elected representatives serving on the board of directors' (1981, pp. 14–15). The UAW emphasizes that such an NDB must be part of 'a coordinated program of democratic national planning, with built-in guarantees and accountability.' See *Solidarity* (1981).

4 On the sources of the present economic crisis, see Zeitlin (1981).

5 'Temporarily idle funds' are funds 'invested or deposited by public agencies'; these 'short-term taxpayer funds . . . are roughly analogous to personal checking accounts and accounts of less than one year of maturity' (Governor's Public Investment Task Force 1981, p. 41). Estimates of public and private pension funds and their earnings are reported in Governor Brown's July 30, 1980, speech, 'Public Investment Policy.'

6 The PIRS charter would specify a range of policy objectives, and might also include statutory provisions to ensure that PIRS investments accorded with civil rights, equal-opportunity, and worker-protection laws.

7 For instance, California's Public Employees Retirement System (PERS) is among the top five shareholders in Bank of America, Chase Manhattan, and Crocker National. The University of California fund is one of the top six holders in such giants as Southern Pacific, General Telephone and Electronics, Commonwealth Edison, ARCO, and Pacific Gas and Electric. PERS is the sixth largest institutional investor, the fourth largest bondholder, and the twenty-second ranking equity holder in the United States. California funds appear 48 times among the top 25 stockholders

of 93 of the largest US corporations. These figures are based on my brief analysis of data found in the US Senate Committee on Governmental Affairs (1980).

8 According to Jason Epstein (1977), during the period between 1964 and 1974, when the Dow Jones was static and rates of return were lower than the rate of inflation, pension funds were used 'to prop up the market while much of the smart money got out more or less intact.'

References

Adams, Walter. 1977. 'Competition, Monopoly, and Planning.' In *American Society, Inc.*, edited by Maurice Zeitlin. Chicago, Ill.: Rand McNally.

Birch, David L. 1979. *The Job Generation Process*. Cambridge, Mass.: MIT Program on Neighborhood and Regional Change.

Eaton, William. 1980. 'AFL–CIO Urges Pension Fund Aid to Sick Industries.' *Los Angeles Times*, August 22, 1, 16.

Epstein, Jason. 1977. 'Capitalism and Socialism: Declining Returns.' *New York Review of Books*, February 17: 35–9.

Governor's Public Investment Task Force. 1981. *Interim Report*. March. Los Angeles, Calif.

Lazard Frères & Co. 1980. 'Memorandum Concerning an Agency to Assist a National Economic Recovery Program.' September 23. New York: Lazard Frères & Co.

Pension Investments; A Social Audit. 1979. New York: Corporate Data Exchange.

Pierce, Neal R. 1980. 'Taking City Hall to the Cleaners: Corporations' Demands for Tax Favors is Pure Bribery.' *Los Angeles Times*, November 9, part 7: 5.

Public Investment Policy of Edmund G. Brown, Jr. 1980. Sacramento, Calif.: Office of State Printing.

Rohatyn, Felix. 1979. 'Public–Private Partnerships to Stave Off Disaster.' *Harvard Business Review*, November–December: 6–8.

—— 1980. 'The Coming Emergency and What Can Be Done About It.' *New York Review of Books*, December 4: 20–4, 26.

—— 1981a. 'Reconstructing America.' *New York Review of Books*, March 5: 16, 18–20.

—— 1981b. 'A Matter of Psychology.' *New York Review of Books*, April 16: 14, 16.

—— 1981c. 'America in the 1980s.' *The Economist*, September 19: 31–8.

Solidarity. 1981. 'Welcome to the "Enterprise Zone."' September: 12–13.

US Senate, Committee on Governmental Affairs. 1980. *Structure of Corporate Concentration: Institutional Shareholders and Interlocking Directorates Among Major U.S. Corporations*, vol. 1. Washington, D.C.: Government Printing Office.

US Senate, Democratic Task Force on the Economy. 1980. 'Report of the Subcommittee on Industrial Policy and Productivity.' Mimeograph. Washington, D.C.

US Small Business Administration. 1977. *Report of the SBA Task Force on Venture and Equity Capital for Small Business.* Washington, D.C.: Government Printing Office.

Watkins, Alfred. 1981. 'Felix Rohatyn's Biggest Deal.' *Working Papers*, September–October: 44–51.

Winpisinger, William W. 1981. 'Reindustrialization: Some Proposals and Comments.' Remarks at the American Trust Reindustrialization Conference, Cleveland, Ohio, November 2.

Wolin, Sheldon S. 1981. 'Editorial.' *Democracy* 1 (3) (July): 5–6.

Zeitlin, Maurice. 1981. 'How We Got Here, and How to Get Out.' *Voice* (United Cement, Lime and Gypsum Workers International Union), January: 14–19.

Index

labor force, trends, in USA, 182,
184; *see also* class segments
Larner, Robert J., 11–12, 14, 16, 17,
19, 23, 25, 48n., 49n., 51n., 62,
80, 88, 104, 105n.
Lawson-Johnston, Peter, 50n.
Lenin, Vladimir I., 134n.
Levy, Gustav, 303n.
Lewis, John L., 210
Lintner, John, 28
Lipset, Seymour M., 53n., 242n.,
255
Lundberg, Ferdinand, 13, 46, 48n.,
52n., 53n.
Lutterman, Kenneth G., 178n.
Luxemburg, Rosa, 48n., 106n.
Lynd, Robert, 52n.

McDermott, John, 188
McNaughton, Donald S., 143
Maceo, Antonio, 236
Machado, Gerardo, 227, 228, 233,
236n.
Mage, Shane H., 107n.
Malozemoff, Plato, 119, 121
managerial theory, 3, 9, 10, 25,
74–6, 142–3, 156–60; *see also*
ownership, corporate, and
control,
Mannheim, Karl, 221
manual labor, 142, 189–90, 214n.;
see also working class
manufacturing, in USA, and
'democratic investment,' 301–3;
see also 'key' industries
Marti, José, 236n.
Martin, McChesney, William, 303n.
Martínez, Sánchez, Augusto, 243n.
Marx, Karl, 45, 46, 47, 89, 90, 95,
99, 106n., 107n., 113, 114, 134n.,
191, 192, 215n., 216n.
Mayer, Albert J., 166
Means, Gardiner, C., 10, 12–13, 14,
17, 19–20, 23, 27, 28, 37, 46, 48n.,
49n., 62, 63, 64, 74, 75, 111,
133n.
Medoff, James L., 187, 216n.
Mellon, Richard King, 158
Menocal, Mario Garcia, 232

mergers, corporate, 79, 160
Merton, Robert K., 4, 48n., 244n.
Metcalf, Lee, 16, 157, 158
Mills, C. Wright, 109, 122
mining, and agrarian radicalism, in
Chile, 247–60; and class politics,
in Chile, 255; and Communists,
in Chile, 249; and unionization,
in Cuba, 229, 231, 232, in Chile,
248, in USA, 197
Mintz, Beth, 134n., 136n.
Miró Cardona, José, 236n.
monopoly power, 41, 80, 81, 82, 88,
95–6, 105, 213
Monsen, R. Joseph, 68, 69, 81, 104
Moore, Barrington, Jr, 54n.
Morgan, J. P., 13, 66
mortality rates, and class, 165; of
US servicemen, in Korean war,
166, in Vietnam war, 165–80
Mosher, Samuel, 119, 121
Movement of the Revolutionary
Left (MIR), Chile, 278, 283
Mueller, Willard F., 96
Mujal, Eusebio, 228
multinational corporation, 22, 27
Murch, Boynton, 120

Nader, Ralph, 159
National Resources Committee
(NRC), USA, 13, 18, 27, 44
nationalism, in Cuba, 222, 234
nationalization, in Chile, 23; in
Cuba, 229
Nenni, Pietro, 281
New Deal, 147, 150, 287
Nixon, Richard M., 291n., 292n.
nominees, 75

O'Connor, James, 116, 134n., 272
occupational community, 249, 255
occupational distribution, and
class, in USA, 152–5, 156; and
gender, 154–5; and Vietnam war
casualty rates of US servicemen,
165–80
Odorizzi, Charles M., 119, 120, 121